Harvard Historical Monographs, LXIV

*Published under the Direction of the Department
of History from the Income
of the Robert Louis Stroock Fund*

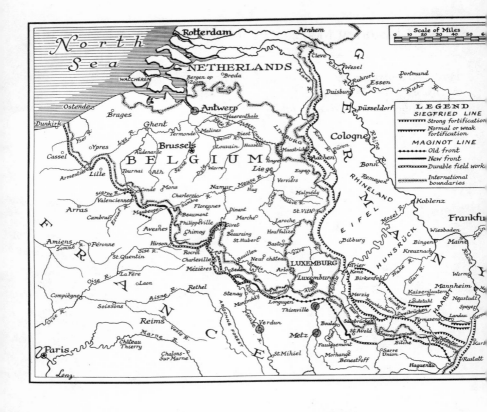

Fortifications systems at the outbreak of the Second World War
Map: Russell Lenz

To the Maginot Line

The Politics of French Military
Preparation in the 1920's

Judith M. Hughes

Harvard University Press
Cambridge, Massachusetts
1971

For Stuart

> Only our love hath no decay;
> This, no tomorrow hath, nor yesterday,
> Running it never runs from us away,
> But truly keepes his first, last, everlasting day.

> John Donne, "The Anniversarie"

Acknowledgments

In view of the fifty-year rule that restricts access to France's archives, and the general reluctance of French authorities to soften the rigors of that rule for the benefit of foreign scholars, I remain unburdened by debts of gratitude to French officialdom. All the more reason to express my appreciation to those who generously aided my work. For overcoming the resistance of the guardians at the Bibliothèque Nationale and thus allowing me to consult the notebooks of her father, I am extremely grateful to Madame Bécourt-Foch. Similarly without the intervention of François Goguel, the Senate Archives would have remained closed to me. Madame la Maréchale de Lattre de Tassigny not only showed me her husband's papers for the period concerned, but in a number of conversations reminisced about the life of a young officer and his family during the 1920's. To Jacques Millerand I owe the greatest debt. For along with his offer of documents and manuscripts belonging to his father, he gave me real friendship. His Sunday afternoon teas, replete with anecdotes about *la petite histoire* of the Third Republic, were indeed highpoints of a year in Paris.

ACKNOWLEDGMENTS

At Harvard, where an earlier version of this book was prepared as my doctoral dissertation, I have long-standing obligations. My first mentor was William L. Langer, who with his wide-ranging knowledge and down-to-earth approach helped me formulate the crucial problems. Beyond this initial guidance, Professor Langer was one of the few people who never thought it odd that a woman should be interested in military history. Stephen A. Schuker, my friend and colleague, has been a constant source of information as well as a steady partner in intellectual duels. For more than seven years we discussed all aspects of French military planning, and more particularly French diplomacy, and he challenged every interpretation I advanced. Though I suspect he will still disagree with some of the positions I have clung to, my efforts to counter his hard-hitting logic have had a telling effect on the structure and argument of the book. I am particularly pleased to acknowledge my gratitude to David S. Landes, who directed the original thesis. In his reading of several versions of the manuscript he relentlessly spotted inconsistencies, inadequate explanations, and infelicities of English usage. A tough taskmaster to a sometimes complaining student and friend, he will, I hope, finally be convinced that I appreciate the care and attention he gave my work.

Above all I want to thank my husband, Stuart, to whom this book is dedicated. He has lived with this subject from the day of our marriage and has satisfied his wife's excessive need for discussing all findings and arguments as well as providing invaluable editorial assistance. Throughout he has combined the calm support of a psychiatrist with boundless patience and affection.

Cambridge, Massachusetts   Judith M. Hughes
January 1971

Contents

Tables

To the Maginot Line

Introduction

In the years preceding the outbreak of the First World War, France appeared to have resumed its role as a power of the first rank. Its alliance with Russia and the subsequent understanding with Great Britain, breaking through the isolation in which the country had remained for nearly twenty years after its defeat by Germany in 1871, confirmed the nation's return to an important place in the councils of Europe. Moreover, one had merely to point out the global extent of the French Empire in order to provide incontrovertible evidence that France had been no laggard in the race for overseas possessions. In 1914, the French might thus lay claim not only to the status of a continental power, but also to the title of a world power, which was just then emerging as the most sought after prize in diplomacy.

Yet such an assessment of France's international position would have been misleading. For the French hardly belonged in the company of the four nations that geopoliticians in various foreign offices were designating as the probable world powers of the future. In fact when Germany launched its own drive for a place in the sun, it scarcely considered its western neighbor as serious competition. Rather, its leaders, hoping to save their country from being confined to the role of a mere continental power, saw Russia, the United States, and, of course, Great Britain as Germany's chief rivals. Despite Russia's backwardness, its sheer expanse combined with its vast untapped resources led to common agreement that the tsarist empire would undoubtedly become a colossus with which to reckon. The United States was similarly viewed in European capitals, where diplomats were not slow to appreciate America's enormous industrial growth and entry into the politics of the imperialist era. While the status of both these giants was still only a future probability, Great Britain, reinforcing with its naval superiority its maintenance of the world's largest and most prestigious empire, seemed secure in its special domain. Compared with these four, the situation of France was anomalous indeed: the proud possessor of the second largest colonial empire, the nation had neither the economic nor the military resources that alone could legitimate or assure world power status.

Still more, France's prewar position as a continental power was not without ambiguity. During the period of their diplomatic isolation after 1871, the French had remained at the mercy of their former enemy. Quite simply, France alone could in no way have challenged Germany's might, and without allies the French voice had been muted in European affairs. Just as the Austro-German alliance had since the late 1870's kept the Habsburg monarchy from being completely eclipsed in continental diplomacy, so with the turn of the century the Triple Entente of France, Russia, and Great Britain had assured the French a role in international politics while guaranteeing the nation's very existence. From dependence upon German sufferance, the French had shifted to reliance upon their own allies. Bondage of some sort seemed to be the unavoidable price France had to pay for its continental status. That such was necessary, indeed essential, for the country's survival, suggests how fragile was the French position as a power of the first rank.

After four years of war France's international position was scarcely changed. Despite the fact that it had been a French commander, Marshal Ferdinand Foch, who had led the allied armies to victory and who had signed the armistice with Germany in November 1918, despite the presence of French forces on German territory in temporary occupation of the Rhineland, despite the certainty that Alsace and Lorraine would be returned to France, the nation's diplomats were in no position to alter their country's condition of thinly veiled servitude. Although the British prime minister, David Lloyd George, and the president of the United States, Woodrow Wilson, traveled to Paris in January 1919 to negotiate the terms of a final peace settlement, the location of the conference itself in no way implied that the French had been granted a new freedom of action in international affairs. Rather, the journey of the two allied leaders was simply a mark of respect for France's dead, a symbolic witness to the immense suffering that nation had endured.

France had survived, through an unparalleled exertion of national and human energy, nearly four years of stalemate and attrition, while the most productive part of the country had been under enemy occupation. That survival was the nature of the struggle had been commonly understood. For three of those four years all political factions had stood united; though ministries might change, the Union Sacrée, in which even Socialists participated, had remained intact. And when in 1917, the year that President Raymond Poincaré was to call in retrospect "l'année trouble," the torment became unbearable, when political and military collapse seemed close at hand, the nation's nerves had been steeled once again for further sacrifice by the men who together ranked as the architects of victory, Foch and Poincaré, and along with them, Philippe Pétain, commander of the French armies, and Georges Clemenceau, the last and most successful of the country's wartime prime ministers. These were the chiefs who for a moment seemed to shape their country's destiny. Their time was brief, and even as Wilson and Lloyd George were disembarking on French soil, it was already passing.

What follows is the story of how, once the war was over and won, France's political and military leaders tried, and failed, to safeguard their nation's security. Handicapped by, yet sharing, their countrymen's profound desire to avoid another war, they devised policies and enacted legislation that helped make real their own worst fears—renewed hostilities on a single front with a rearmed Germany. Though the catastrophe did not occur until 1940, the country's military policy had become firmly fixed a decade earlier, when the decision was definitively taken to fortify northeastern France and to construct the works that came to be known as the Maginot Line. Having secured their only common border with the Reich, France's leaders were unlikely to order their young compatriots to advance beyond their own frontier in an attempt to prevent the revival of German military might. What had once loomed up as merely a threatening and precarious future was thus slowly transformed into an ever-present nightmare.

Yet this is not a tale of wrong calculations or missed opportunities. Set in their proper context policies that have been previously labeled mistakes appear less avoidable and the reasoning behind them more coherent and appropriate than has ordinarily been supposed. What follows, then, is an account of how France's leaders tried to cope with insuperable problems—which ultimately involved the question of life or death—while unable to control the eventual outcome. It is a human drama of how men faced or did not face the dilemmas besetting their country, of how they lived with the semiconscious realities of their longing for peace and their powerlessness to assure its permanence. Thus despite (or even because of) the tragic outcome, one's own capacity for sympathy cannot but be enlarged as one gropes to comprehend the ineluctable difficulties of another era and the human frailties of those forced to confront them.

1 | France at the End of the War

The Population Problem

To celebrate the first fourteenth of July in five years that had dawned in peace, and to honor its victorious armies, the French government planned an elaborate military procession for Bastille Day 1919. At eight-thirty in the morning the band of the Twenty-eighth Infantry Regiment started up with the "Soldiers' Chorus" from *Faust*. Immediately following the band came the procession of a thousand *mutilés,* led by three unfortunate creatures stretched out in a carriage and being pushed by a fourth. Then, in rows of eight, those with the worst deformities marched under the Arc de Triomphe and proceeded to the places that had been reserved for them.[1]

Indeed, to enable the mutilés to watch the celebration as comfortably as possible, many of the best seats had been designated as theirs. From the entrance of the Champs-Elysées to the Rond-Point, and then on the Place de l'Etoile itself, special stands had been set up. Victory and peace did not bring with it license to forget those who had died and

1. *La France militaire,* July 15-16, 1919.

those who were still suffering. Whatever complaints the mutilés may have subsequently voiced about neglect and feelings of uselessness, they were never shunted out of sight, relegated to special hospitals, and generally removed from society so that others, more fortunate, might forget what the war had cost. Instead they were given priority in civil service jobs, helped to find employment elsewhere, and had seats reserved for them on all public transportation. The physically handicapped were accepted by the community, serving as a reminder of the frightful experience they had all traversed.[2]

Yet on July 14 the spectators did not need the mutilés to recall to them the ordeal they had suffered. Long before the troops paraded down the Champs-Elysées, the exaltation of mid-November 1918 had largely evaporated. As Frenchmen became aware of the magnitude of the immediate and long-term costs of the war, the mood shifted to one of uncertainty and depression. "While the war was going on," wrote an editorialist in *Le Temps,* "we were sure our losses would be terrible. But we had decided not to count them until afterwards. With the armistice barely signed, it became necessary to make the count, and what a frightful total! Never did the number of our dead seem more horrible than on the day when no more were being killed. The torment having passed, the happiness that we had hoped to find again is forever poisoned by the memory of those who are gone."[3]

Throughout the war, in the interest of preserving morale, the French government had kept the nation uninformed

2. See *Le Temps,* July 8, 1919. For a general discussion of the problems France faced in late 1918, see Henry Contamine, "La France devant la victoire," *Revue d'histoire moderne et contemporaine,* 16 (January-March 1969), 131-141.

3. *Le Temps,* March 8, 1919. See also *Le Temps,* December 29, 1918; *Echo de Paris,* December 8, 1918; January 26, 1919; and André Beaunier, in *Echo de Paris,* October 7, 1919.

about its losses. And even after the conflict ended, the authorities were reluctant to release figures on casualties. Only once did a government spokesman disclose such statistics to the Chamber. In the course of a discussion on pensions, and after considerable prodding, Louis Abrami, under-secretary in the War Ministry, gave the November 1, 1918 figure for dead, missing, and prisoners as 1,831,600. This did not include the navy or statistics for the period immediately prior to the armistice; moreover, with the fighting ended, the listing of prisoners would have to be revised. When pressed further on the matter, Abrami quickly sidestepped the subject and turned to less sensitive topics.[4] For five years thereafter no official figures on war dead were given out by a member of the government.

This reticence did not go unnoticed. In early 1919, Joseph Claussat proposed a resolution calling on the government to make known the number of those killed and missing. He wanted to end the political manipulation of the figures, charging that the numbers varied by a hundred or two hundred thousand depending on whether one was bellicose or pacifist.[5] Inexact statistics were in fact used to support fallacious arguments; General Henri Mordacq, Clemenceau's chief military advisor, in defending the officer corps, cited inaccurate figures which suggested that losses among officers had been substantially—instead of only slightly—higher than among soldiers.[6] To be sure, even with the best will in the world the government would have found it very difficult, if not impossible, to produce exact figures on war losses. Before

4. JOC *Déb.*, December 26, 1918, p. 3598.
5. JOC *Doc.* 1919, annexe no. 5746, pp. 867-868.
6. General Henri Mordacq, *Le ministère Clemenceau*, III (Paris, Plon, 1931), p. 114.

January 1, 1916, there had been no central agency in charge of collecting and verifying these statistics. Although thereafter a fifth bureau of the Army General Staff had been set up to gather and organize this information, it had never been completely successful in sorting out the material for the first year and a half of the war.[7]

When a year had passed and still neither the Chamber nor the government had taken any action on Claussat's resolution, Louis Marin, in his capacity as a member of the Chamber Budget Commission, drawing together the fragments he had previously published and adding further material to them, presented the first and only substantial report on war losses. Since the government persisted in maintaining silence—through fear, Marin surmised, of the impact a knowledge of such losses would have on morale—he had undertaken the painstaking and difficult task of providing the information himself.[8] Subsequently the Chamber Army Commission did report on the war effort, but when the results were issued in 1924, the tables that appeared collated only material on the extent of mobilization; Title II, which was to have been a résumé of losses, was not printed.[9] When Michel Huber, director of the French statistical service, wrote the volume on French population in the early 1930's for the series on the war published by the Carnegie Endowment for International Peace, the only figures on *dead* he could cite were those given by Marin; statistics of *wounded* had been made available in 1924 by the medical section of the War Ministry.[10]

Statistics can usually do little to stir the imagination, but

7. JOC *Doc.* 1920, annexe no. 633, p. 40.
8. *Ibid.,* p. 34.
9. JOC *Doc.* 1924, annexe no. 335, pp. 1275ff.
10. Michel Huber, *La population de la France pendant la guerre* (Paris and New Haven, 1931), p. 409.

even the most lethargic must respond to the magnitude of the French casualties. By the end of the war, military losses, in dead and missing, had reached the figure of 1,397,800, distributed in the following fashion:

Table 1. French military losses as of November 11, 1918 (in thousands, according to the accounting of August 1, 1919).

	Dead	Missing	Total
Europeans	1,010.2	235.3	1,245.5
North African natives	28.2	7.7	35.9
Colonial natives	28.7	6.5	35.2
Foreign Legion	3.7	0.9	4.6
Total: Enlisted Men	1,070.8	250.4	1,321.2
Officers	34.1	2.5	36.6
Total: Army	1,104.9	252.9	1,357.8
Sailors	6.0	4.9	10.9
Naval Officers	0.3	0.2	0.5
Total: Navy	6.3	5.1	11.4
General Total	1,111.2	258.0	1,369.2
Dead between November 11, 1918, and June 1, 1919	28.6	––	28.6
GRAND TOTAL	1,139.8	258.0	1,397.8

Source: Michel Huber, *La population de la France pendant la guerre* (Paris and New Haven: Presses Universitaires de France and Yale University Press, 1931), p. 414.

Losses on this scale could not but have affected all those who survived, in the sense of having had someone close—a friend or a relative—killed or incapacitated. Many were the families who had lost more than one son; to have had three killed, as had General de Castelnau, was not uncommon. The *monuments aux morts* erected in nearly every French community

Table 2. Comparative statistics of war deaths for belligerent nations.

Country	Number in thousands			Percent of dead and missing	
	Active male population	Mobilized	Dead and missing	Active males	Mobilized
Allied Countries:					
France	13,350	7,935	1,400	10.5	17.6
Belgium	2,350	365	41	1.9	11.2
United Kingdom	14,569	5,704	744	5.1	13.0
Australia	1,806	413	59	3.3	14.4
Canada	–	629	52	–	8.2
South Africa	2,108	136	7	0.3	5.2
United States	32,320	4,272	68	0.2	1.6
Italy	12,133	5,615	750	6.2	13.4
Russia	–	15,070	1,700	–	11.3
Rumania	2,276	1,000	250	11.0	25.0
Serbia	–	1,008	365	–	36.2
Portugal	1,888	100	4	0.2	4.0
Enemy Countries:					
Germany	20,428	13,250	2,000	9.8	15.1
Austria-Hungary	16,235	9,000	1,543	9.5	17.1
Bulgaria	1,378	400	33	2.4	8.2

Source: Huber, *Population de la France*, p. 449.

Table 3. French losses according to age.

Classes	Mobilized	Dead and missing	Percent
1887 and earlier	58,400	1,800	3.2
1888	90,000	2,700	3.0
1889	156,000	5,250	3.3
1890	160,000	5,900	3.7
1891	169,000	6,950	4.1
1892	214,000	9,700	4.5
1893	213,000	13,400	6.3
1894	224,000	14,650	6.5
1895	226,000	15,600	6.9
1896	240,000	17,800	7.4
1897	242,000	20,950	8.5
1898	240,000	25,600	10.7
1899	244,000	29,650	12.2
1900	237,000	38,700	16.3
1901	251,000	44,350	17.7
1902	255,000	47,750	18.7
1903	254,000	48,850	19.2
1904	256,000	50,600	19.8
1905	262,000	51,200	19.5
1906	256,000	49,850	19.5
1907	263,000	54,750	20.8
1908	266,000	59,350	22.3
1909	273,000	63,000	23.1
1910	265,000	63,900	24.1
1911	282,000	68,000	24.1
1912	279,000	77,200	27.1
1913	290,000	77,950	26.9
1914	292,000	85,200	29.2
1915	279,000	77,700	27.8
1916	293,000	54,050	18.4
1917	297,000	38,950	13.1
1918	257,000	20,600	8.0
1919	229,000	3,400	1.5
1920	––	200	––
Total	7,812,400	1,243,500	16.0

Source: Huber, *Population de la France,* p. 422.

attest better than any table to the geographical spread of the decimation.[11] Their dense columns of names appear wildly out of proportion with the size of the village or town in question. The war dead, in fact, totaled just over 10 percent of the active male population, a proportion higher than in any other belligerent nation except Serbia and Rumania.

The war, in addition, had claimed its special victims: among the men mobilized, more than one quarter of those who by 1920 would have been between the ages of twenty-five and thirty failed to return. The death statistics show a dramatic rise, reaching a climax with the young soldiers conscripted into the army just on the eve of the war. More than 29 percent of that ill-fated class perished in the holocaust.

Table 3 does not include casualties among officers. Although their rate of loss was in fact slightly higher than that of the soldiers, the statistics issued did not break down these losses according to age groups. It was clear, however, that the bulk of officer deaths had been in the lower ranks, among the younger men who, if they had lived, might have been regimental commanders at the outbreak of the Second World War. Of 17,000 graduates of Saint-Cyr who participated in the war, 6,000 were killed; while among the classes entering the military academy just before the war and during the war itself, and who were sent off to the battlefield without having completed their training, less than half returned.[12]

These figures give some indication of the scale of losses among the French elites, though a number of correctives

11. For a table of regional distribution of war losses, labeled as to be consulted "sous toutes réserves," see *ibid.,* p. 426.

12. The precise figures seem uncertain. The *Echo de Paris* (April 4, 1919; July 8, 1919) gives two different totals. In both cases the mortality rate of the youngest classes of Saint-Cyriens is given as more than 50 percent.

Branch of Service	OFFICERS			Number mobilized up to Nov. 11, 1918	Percent of losses among mobilized
	Dead	Missing	Total		
Infantry	27,020	2,240	29,260	100,600	29
Cavalry	820	45	865	8,400	10.3
Artillery	3,070	70	3,140	34,200	9.2
Engineers	670	20	690	7,400	9.3
Aviation	1,035	110	1,145	5,300	21.6
Air observation	33	1	34	600	5.7
Supply	105	–	105	2,400	4.4
Automobile service	66	–	66	3,400	1.9
Others	1,222	12	1,234	31,300	4.1
TOTAL	34,100	2,500	36,600	193,600	18.9
ENLISTED MEN					
Infantry	917,400	240,600	1,158,000	4,957,000	22.6
Cavalry	18,800	2,600	21,400	280,500	7.9
Artillery	79,800	3,000	82,800	1,373,000	6
Engineers	25,300	2,300	27,600	432,500	6.4
Aviation	3,430	170	3,600	102,500	3.5
Air observation	550	10	560	21,000	2.7
Supply	7,280	210	7,490	210,000	3.6
Automobile service	3,460	40	3,500	203,000	1.7
Others	14,880	1,370	16,250	533,500	3
TOTAL	1,070,900	250,300	1,321,200	8,213,000	16.1

Source: JOC *Doc.* 1920, annexe no. 633, p. 66.

15

should be added. While a graduate of Saint-Cyr would qualify according to everyone's definition as a member of the French elite, it would be less clear whether this was true of the officer corps as a whole. By 1919, 105,000 out of 195,000 officers had risen from the ranks, 33,000 were career army officers, and the remaining 57,000 were reserve officers.[13] The most interesting figure—unfortunately lacking—would be the mortality rate among the reserve officers; for these were the men, well-educated and usually with a solid social background, who would most likely have returned to positions of leadership within the society.

We cannot, in fact, give an accurate account of the war's impact on the top echelons of French society. Though attempts were made to break down casualties into professional categories, the groupings were crude and the method of determining an individual's profession rough; the usual contention that agricultural workers suffered the most is, nonetheless, borne out.[14] There is only scattered evidence to support the frequent claim that the intellectual classes were particularly hard hit.[15] But in such a specific (and crucial) case as that of the Ecole Normale Supérieure, the assertion is unquestionably accurate.

Statistics on war dead give only part of the picture of the war's cost. There were those who returned mutilated or invalided, some of whom took part in the festivities on July 14, 1919, and who could not help but be a continuing psychological and financial burden. By January 1, 1928, the number

13. Huber, *Population de la France*, p. 417.

14. M. de Ville-Chabrolle, "Les mutilés et réformés de la guerre 1914-1918 en France," *Bulletin de la statistique générale de la France*, 11 (July 1922), 417.

15. In his *Histoire de la Troisième République*, V: *Les années d'illusion 1918-1931* (Paris, 1960), p. 15, Jacques Chastenet states that 23 percent of those mobilized belonging to the liberal professions were killed. Since the citation given to support this figure is inaccurate, it is unclear how Chastenet arrived at it.

Table 5. Casualties at the Ecole Normale Supérieure.

Entering Class of	Mobilized	Killed	Wounded
1908, 1909, 1910	79	39	3
1911, 1912, 1913	161	81	64
1914	80	20	18
1916, 1917	26	3	–
	346	143	85

Source: Huber, *Population de la France*, p. 425.

Table 6. Distribution of war-incurred disability.

	Number	Percent
More than 50% disability	228,500	22
25-50% disability	306,500	29
Less than 25% disability	505,000	48

Source: Huber, *Population de la France*, p. 442.

who had received, and were still receiving, pensions was 1,040,000.[16]

Although men rated less than 50 percent disabled might be fitted into most occupations, having, for example, merely one stiff leg or the loss of hearing in one ear, those considered 85 percent disabled found it difficult to provide for themselves. With at least one limb amputated, such veterans were given a pension equivalent to a minimum subsistence wage, while proportionally smaller payments were made to the others. Here, at least, the youngest men had not suffered the most. The age distribution of the disabled was very different from that of the dead; incomplete statistics suggested

16. Huber, *Population de la France*, p. 440.

that the highest toll was among those who were between thirty-five and forty years old in 1920.[17]

The waves of shock produced by the war losses went beyond the 1,040,000 disabled, the 630,000 widows, and the 719,000 orphans; the structure of the French population had been shaken.[18] The 1,400,000 dead constituted only part of the population loss; during the period 1911-1921 there had been among civilians an excess of deaths over births of 1,250,000 as well as a sharp decline in the number of marriages.

Though concern over depopulation had been a frequent theme before the war, the discussions that started after 1919 had a markedly more anxious and urgent tone.[19] "The length of the war has produced a crisis of the family," wrote an anguished investigator from Bordeaux. In that city there had been an almost 50 percent decrease in the number of marriages from 1915 to 1917, and for the same period the number of civilian deaths had been twice that of births. The report had its amusing aspect—one of the few in a generally bleak discussion. It suggested that American soldiers be persuaded to stay in France, marry French girls who might otherwise be forced to remain single owing to the lack of eligible Frenchmen, and raise large families.[20]

17. *Ibid.,* p. 445.
18. *Ibid.,* pp. 447-448.
19. For example, *Echo de Paris,* January 2, 1919; July 10, 1919; July 23, 1919.
20. AN, F[7] 12936: Le commissaire spécial à M. le Directeur de la Sûreté Générale, Bordeaux, November 25, 1918. In fact large numbers of girls in one particular age group were not left single. Of the men from the particularly hard-hit age group who survived the war, a higher proportion than normal contracted marriages, while the males from the rest of the population chose their mates over a wider age span than had been customary. See Louis Henry, "Perturbations de la nuptialité résultant de la guerre 1914-1918," *Population,* 21 (March-April 1966), 273-333.

approximate figures for 1914-1918).

	Population							No. per 10,000 of total population			
Year	Total	Civilian	Marriages	Live births	Civilian deaths	Excess of births over deaths among civilians	Military deaths	Marriages	Live Births	Deaths: Civil and military	Annual civilian deaths per 10,000 civilians
1911 (Mar.-Dec.)[a]	39,605		251	616	611	+ 5		152	186	185	
1912	39,710		312	750	692	+ 58		157	189	174	
1913	39,790		299	746	702	+ 44		150	187	176	
1914 1st half	39,800		148	370	390	− 20		149	186	196	
1914 2nd half	39,500	35,800	47	340	350	− 10	350	48	172	354	195
1914	39,800	36,200	195	710	740	− 30	350	98	178	274	204
1915	38,800	34,200	82	450	720	−270	310	41	116	265	210
1916	38,200	33,900	120	360	670	−310	260	63	94	243	198
1917	37,600	33,500	175	390	680	−290	140	93	104	218	203
1918	36,900	33,000	195	450	830	−380	240	106	122	290	251
1919	37,000		529	475	710	−235		286	128	192	192
1920	37,300		597	793	646	+147		320	213	174	174
1921 (Jan.-Feb.)[b]	37,500		75	133	112	+ 21					

Source: Huber, *Population de la France*, p. 453.
[a] Census of March 5, 1911.
[b] Census of March 6, 1921.

Others were less willing to use persuasion to battle depopulation; repression triumphed in the hasty passage of anti-abortion and anti-birth control legislation in 1920. Proposals had been made since 1891 to deal with the increasing number of abortions and to combat France's declining birthrate; but it was not until after the war that the assault on other forms of birth control became equally prominent. Harsh penalties of fines and prison terms were enacted for aiding an abortion, and even for providing birth control information—measures that were still in effect in France until the mid-1970's.[21]

Those concerned with depopulation not only viewed reproduction as a patriotic duty, but on occasion claimed that birth control propaganda was subsidized by the Germans, and that anyone who sympathized with spreading such information was a willing tool of the nation's enemy.[22] To contemporary ears accustomed to considering conception and birth private matters, such rhetoric may sound excessive. To the French of this period, however, it seemed quite clear that the solution of major national difficulties hinged on raising the birthrate; a typical pamphlet linked problems of finance, currency, cost of living, as well as security, to the question of depopulation. Such diverse figures as Denys Cochin, Robert Pinot, and Ernest Lavisse—representing the Right, industry, and liberal *universitaires*—affixed their signatures to this document.[23]

The practical military implications of France's postwar demographic structure were clear and frightening; the con-

21. JOC *Doc.* 1919, annexe no. 6679, pp. 2347-2348; JOC *Déb.*, July 23, 1920, pp. 3068-3074.
22. JOC *Déb.*, July 23, 1920, p. 3068; cf. Conseil Supérieur de la Natalité, *Voeux concernant le projet de loi sur le recrutement de l'armée* (Paris, n.d.).
23. AN, 94 AP 374: Brochure of l'Alliance Nationale pour l'Accroissement de la Population Française, Albert Thomas Papers.

tingents to be called from 1935 to 1939—the so-called *années creuses*—would have only half the usual number of conscripts. And this pattern might be repeated from generation to generation. To people accustomed to measuring French military strength by comparing French and German birthrates, these statistics rendered acute an already existing source of anxiety. Even with the addition of Alsace and Lorraine, the French population was smaller in 1921 than it had been in 1911; to make up for the war dead and the excess of civilian deaths would take thirty-five years, on the assumption that there would be 60,000 more births than deaths per year.[24] "The Treaty means nothing," said Clemenceau, "if France does not agree to have many children ... for if France renounces large families, we will have taken all the cannon from Germany for nothing. Do whatever you wish— France will then be lost."[25]

Relief from Military Burdens

France might rejoice like a man who has "escaped death after a catastrophe or a horrible illness;" but no one would ever wish for such an experience again. War per se had lost its value; even for the victor it was a *"mauvaise affaire."* The

24. The population totaled 39,605,000 in 1911 as compared to 39,210,000 in 1921. Huber, *Population de la France,* pp. 456, 892. Comparative German figures show that the fall in the number of births in the Reich during the war years was less drastic and less prolonged than in France. Moreover, before the war Germany's population had been increasing rapidly, and after the war demographic recovery came very fast: in 1919, there was already an excess of births over deaths of 282,120. See Rudolf Meerwarth, "Die Entwicklung der Bevölkerung in Deutschland während der Kriegs- und Nachkriegszeit," in *Die Einwirkung des Krieges auf Bevölkerungsbewegung, Einkommen und Lebenshaltung in Deutschland* (Stuttgart and New Haven, 1932), p. 52.

25. Quoted by Shelby Cullom Davis, *The French War Machine* (London, Allen and Unwin, 1937), p. 31.

notion that periods of war and peace followed each other somewhat like the seasons had become intolerable; war could no longer be accepted as a fact of life.[26] Such expressions of weariness, coupled with an almost instinctive desire to put away the tools of war, were only natural. Above all the country wanted to relax after the strain and challenge of a great national effort. This overwhelming fatigue and desire for demobilization, both military and psychological, was the dominant mood. All thoughts turned to re-establishing, or finding again, the comforts and security of a peaceful, orderly existence. No one, in early 1919, envisaged as the result of the recent and costly victory a peace so fragile and tenuous as to offer France nothing more than a troubled and uneasy future.

The prime concern of all was security narrowly understood—not a desire for hegemony or a position of dominance in Europe. And demobilization as it proceeded in 1919 did not impair France's safety. The armistice had left French troops in occupation of the Rhineland, and the strength and stability of those forces were assured. Louis Deschamps, the under-secretary for demobilization, informed the members of the Senate Army Commission that the Rhine army, to be composed of nine infantry and two cavalry divisions drawn from the youngest classes, would not be eligible for demobilization. Behind these troops a reserve would be formed by the corps in the frontier regions, again constituted by men from these same classes. Moreover, at the critical moment France had the necessary, if limited, forces to impose the treaty. In June 1919 General Charles Mangin's Tenth Army,

26. *Le Temps,* February 28, 1919; André Beaunier, in *Echo de Paris,* July 22, 1919; and *Le Temps,* December 5, 1918.

whose headquarters were at Mainz, had been reinforced and brought up to fourteen divisions in order to spearhead an advance, if a German refusal to sign the treaty should make one necessary. Strengthening these forces had been a relatively simple matter; demobilization had stopped with the class of 1906, and the necessary manpower had been on tap. Such a maneuver might become more difficult after mid-October 1919, when all classes except those of 1918 and 1919 would be sent home.[27]

Having been assured by Deschamps that the Rhine army was secure, the Senate Army Commission let drop its inquiry into the helter-skelter way in which demobilization was proceeding.[28] For it was a *barrier* that the senators wanted, and more particularly a bulwark that would provide for France's security while reducing to a minimum the need for large armed forces on the country's eastern frontier. And although France might currently be safe behind its troops stationed in the Rhineland, the future was more problematic. How to insure the future, what arrangement would best provide for France's safety: these were the questions that lay at the heart of the debates over the Rhineland occupation.[29]

In early 1919, Clemenceau and Foch together had outlined the provisions they wanted to incorporate in the peace treaty with Germany. Their terms, while calling for the Rhine as Germany's western frontier and Allied occupation of bridge-

27. Senate Army Commission, Procès-verbal, May 28, 1919; July 3, 1919.
28. *Ibid.,* May 28, 1919. See also *La France militaire,* February 14-15, 1919.
29. I differ with the emphasis of Jere Clemens King, *Foch versus Clemenceau* (Cambridge, Mass., 1960). The diplomatic issues in the Rhineland controversy are amply discussed in David Lloyd George, *The Truth about the Peace Treaties,* 2 vols. (London, 1938); Georges Clemenceau, *Grandeur and Misery of Victory,* trans. F. M. Atkinson (New York, 1930); and André Tardieu, *La paix* (Paris, 1921).

heads across the river, had been vague on the potentially divisive point of the future of the Left Bank.[30] By officially maintaining that territorial annexation was not France's aim, Clemenceau had encouraged men of diverse political views to follow the government's standard; both those who wanted the Left Bank to remain politically attached to Germany, but under some form of international military control, and those who advocated the establishment of an independent state under thinly disguised French domination (which was Clemenceau's own position)[31] could rally to his support.

In April 1919, when Clemenceau, unable to overcome Wilson's and Lloyd George's vetoes of permanent occupation, accepted a compromise—a fifteen year occupation plus an Anglo-American guarantee—he displeased a wider segment of opinion than merely the diehard nationalists. For most Frenchmen agreed with Clemenceau's initial position that the Rhine should be the permanent military frontier of Germany. This was made abundantly clear at the start of the Chamber discussions on the treaty. Albert Thomas, a moderate Socialist and former minister of munitions, followed the darling of the nationalists, Maurice Barrès, to the tribune and asked, as Barrès had done, why France was abandoning the permanent occupation of the Rhineland and thereby forfeiting its best guarantee against future invasion.[32] In similar vein, the Center-Right leader Louis Barthou commented in his report for the Chamber commission studying the peace terms that the great majority had been in favor of the Rhine being fixed as

30. Mordacq, *Le ministère Clemenceau*, III, 79-80.
31. A. Ribot, ed., *Journal d'Alexandre Ribot et correspondances inédites* (Paris, 1936), pp. 259-260, 273.
32. JOC *Déb.*, August 29, 1919, pp. 4069ff.; see *Echo de Paris*, August 30, 1919, for surprise at the agreement between Thomas and Barrès.

Germany's frontier, though they now felt constrained to vote for the treaty.[33]

While the continuing debate both within and outside the Chamber could have no diplomatic impact, it did highlight the eagerness to reduce military effort to a minimum. For Foch the first concern remained to provide France with the frontier that could be defended with the least difficulty. The Rhine, he claimed, fitted this requirement and would be three times easier to safeguard than France's political frontier. And although André Tardieu, the government spokesman for the treaty and one of the chief architects of the document itself, stressed the possibility of reoccupation and had added that France's acquiescence in Allied demands would give it an unshakeable claim to their support,[34] it was precisely this point that aroused the greatest skepticism. Sixteen or seventeen years later, President Poincaré maintained, his country's moral superiority might not be so apparent. German propaganda could, without difficulty, distort the facts and represent France as the aggressor. Moreover, a French military advance might not find the territory unoccupied; German forces could easily seize the Rhineland before France had a chance to act.[35] In sum the Rhine frontier seemed indispensable, and, as Foch noted, it could serve "for the smallest number of troops as a solid and lasting barrier under whose shelter alone our industry and our agriculture" could "be reconstituted.[36]

Without unlimited control over the Rhineland it was un-

33. "Le Rapport de M. Louis Barthou," *Le Temps,* August 8, 1919.

34. JOC *Déb.,* September 2, 1919, p. 4093. It was in this speech that Tardieu made his most detailed parliamentary defense of the treaty.

35. Poincaré to Lloyd George, April 28, 1919, published in *Le Temps,* April 12, 1921.

36. Foch Cahiers, Dossier E, April 13, 1919.

clear to many how the treaty itself would be enforced. "Will we, say in 1925, be ready to start a war because our bill hasn't been paid?" commented Pertinax, the chief foreign policy analyst for the conservative *Echo de Paris*. Only by permanently occupying the Rhineland, he claimed, could France avoid the agonizing choice, each time Germany failed to fulfill its commitments, between crossing the frontier and appearing as the disturber of the peace, and doing nothing and thereby exposing its weakness.[37] Only so long as France held the bridgeheads across the Rhine, would it be in a position to advance whenever that should prove necessary—and thereby insure, that, to a certain extent, the treaty would be self-executing. "In a word," Foch remarked in his notebooks, "the Rhineland is a lever that we have in our hand and with which we can call the tune."[38]

It is not surprising, then, that Tardieu should have found himself hard pressed to overcome the dismay that greeted the news that the Rhineland would be occupied for only a limited period of time. The crux of his defense was that the Allies' consent to participate in the occupation had been conditional upon limiting its duration. Addressing the Chamber, he pointed out that Allied cooperation and guarantees made it certain that his country would not be alone, militarily or diplomatically, in enforcing the peace settlement. "France cannot always put her soldiers in the front line," noted *Le Temps*—which in this case was careful to follow the official position. "People say," the article continued, in the form of a syllogism, "that the occupation of the Rhine would serve as security for the joint claims of the Allies. But if claims are

37. *Echo de Paris*, April 7, 1919; see also Pertinax's articles in the *Echo de Paris*, April 1, 1919, and April 21, 1919.
38. Foch Cahiers, Dossier E, April 28, 1919.

joint, why should we be the only ones to hold on to the security? If we should be the only ones to hold on to it, how would we proceed to enforce these claims, if and when Germany should stop paying?"[39]

Yet rather than underline French hesitancy about acting unilaterally, as *Le Temps* had done, Tardieu emphasized the military burdens that would fall on France if it undertook to occupy the German territories alone: indeed, permanent occupation, which was tantamount to annexing a dangerously hostile population, would be a potentially bottomless pit of responsibilities and entanglement. In addition to these extraordinary burdens, France would have to maintain the cadres for general mobilization and training of conscripts. Thus it would be difficult, "if not impossible, to effect the reform of the military laws that our economic and social needs so obviously demand."[40]

Now the discussion had reached bedrock. Foch and Tardieu each maintained that *his* prescription would permit France to ease its military burdens: the one argued for a frontier that would enable the country, if necessary, to defend itself and enforce the treaty in semi-automatic fashion; the other thought that France could induce its Allies to do at least half the fighting. Better still, each contended that the adoption of the alternative policy would require France to remain on something resembling a permanent war footing.

In employing this last argument both sides could hope for popularity with the general public. For on no question in

39. *Le Temps,* April 3, 1919. For the relations between the government and the press, see Pierre Miquel, " 'Le Journal des Débats' et la paix de Versailles," *Revue historique,* 232 (October-December 1964), 379-415.

40. JOC *Déb.,* September 2, 1919, p. 4091.

1919 was there such widespread consensus—military burdens would have to be eased; France could ill afford to waste precious manpower by extended military service. *La France militaire,* a daily newspaper concerned solely with army matters, went as far as saying that many would question whether the price paid for victory had been worth it if the length of military service and general military expenditure could not be reduced below the level of the immediate prewar years.[41]

Yet what was most striking about the initial discussion of military legislation was the general acceptance, which varied little from Right to Left, of the principle of a one-year term of service. While it was only natural that after so much blood-letting there should have been pressure to use the nation's resources for more productive activities, it was more surprising that public figures should have stated so specifically that such a reduction in the length of service was the goal of reform of the military establishment. Clemenceau and his advisor, General Mordacq, in their first discussion of major military problems, came immediately to the conclusion that two-year service was politically unacceptable and that the principle of one year was inescapable. "We might perhaps be obliged to pass through intermediate stages, but in any case, these stages could not last very long."[42] Pétain, in the course of inspecting an army installation, announced that one-year military service would very likely be adopted; at the same time he instructed his staff to begin the background studies for such a proposal.[43] Lt. Col. Jean Fabry, the editor-in-chief

41. *La France militaire,* April 5, 1919; June 7, 1919; June 8-9, 1919; August 10-11, 1919. See also General Malleterre in *Le Temps,* August 6, 1919, p. 3.

42. Mordacq, *Le ministère Clemenceau,* III, 44-45.

43. *La France militaire,* September 25, 1919; and *Echo de Paris,* February 20, 1922. See also Lt. Col. de Thomasson, "Un grand officier d'Etat-Major, le Général Buat," *Revue des deux mondes,* 7e période, 20 (March 1, 1924), 207.

of *L'Intransigeant,* who as deputy from Paris after 1919 quickly became a leading conservative spokesman on military affairs, advocated a complete overhauling of the military organization, with twelve-month service as the basis of the peacetime army.[44]

The behavior of Senator Paul Doumer, a politician of the Center-Right and future president of the Republic, was similarly illuminating. In April, at the time of the Rhineland controversy, Doumer had proposed in the Senate that the government insert into the treaty all the guarantees which the military command deemed necessary. This resolution, however, was not accepted and a compromise motion, less threatening to civilian authority, was passed.[45] In October Doumer published a detailed plan for military reorganization which launched discussion of this issue among those parliamentarians and publicists who were interested in army matters.[46] His proposal was justly criticized as a rehash of the pre-1914 organization, altering that system only in so far as was essential to permit the realization of one-year military service; Doumer had, moreover, calculated the required number of troops in an arbitrary fashion and had thus been able to claim that one-year service would fulfill this specification.[47] Doumer's motives were basically no different from those of Albert Thomas, who with Pierre Renaudel drew up the official Socialist project, which with a few more feats of sleight of hand claimed that eight-month service was feasible.[48]

44. *L'Intransigeant,* December 17, 1919.

45. Ribot, *Journal,* pp. 269-270.

46. Paul Doumer, "Note sur la réorganisation de l'armée française," *Revue politique et parlementaire,* 101 (October 1919), 63-92.

47. Lt. Col. Emile Mayer, "Observations sur le rapport de M. Doumer," *Revue politique et parlementaire,* 101 (October 1919), 92-98; and Doumer, "Note," p. 75.

48. JOC *Doc.* 1920, annexe no. 277, p. 179; see also Henry Paté's proposal calling for one-year military service, JOC *Doc.* 1919, annexe no. 7021, p. 2946.

Though some of these public figures subsequently decided that it was necessary to retract their initial support for one-year military service, or, at least, to argue for deferring it, the idea had become implanted in the public consciousness and it was impossible to dislodge it. *La France militaire* warned its readers that one-year service would be only the final step, and that the military organization would have to go through a transition phase that might last as long as the occupation of the Rhineland.[49] But the editors failed to elaborate for their readers what this temporary stage would look like or what sacrifices it would entail. Instead they concentrated on that distant future when the world would be peaceful and Frenchmen would have to bear arms for only a limited time. If the editors of *La France militaire* could be so imprecise, it is not surprising that others, who had political careers at stake, might be unwilling to hold the question of the length of military service in abeyance until France's foreign commitments became clear. The promise was there and the principle implicitly accepted; it would be difficult to postpone its enactment.

The Army and Politics

The army and more especially the officer corps, no less than the rest of society, were eager to resume an orderly peacetime existence. For them the adjustment was obviously more difficult than for the civilian population. Beset with a number of concrete problems, they groped to find their place in postwar France. In particular they found that at the conclusion of hostilities their country had too many officers. This surplus created both a legal tangle, in that the precise

49. *La France militaire*, August 19, 1919.

number of officers provided by the prewar legislation of cadres had been exceeded, and an organizational one, for as France demobilized, there were too few units remaining for the available officers to command.[50] The problem of excess officers not only affected promotion within, and recruitment of, the officer corps, but brought into relief the precarious position of the officers and the way they viewed their own situation.

What worried officers of every rank most was the threat to their *situations acquises*. For all proposals aimed at dealing with the problem of excess officers threatened to undermine the positions they had gained during the war. For example, one way to decongest the lower and middle echelons would have been to reduce to their former status all those officers who held their ranks *à titre temporaire*. These officers had been promoted in the course of the war but had not been given definitive title to their ranks; for with the creation of a vast number of new units, those who were minimally qualified had received positions of command. And to remove officers from ranks that in numerous cases they had held for a number of years would undoubtedly cause a great deal of bitterness.[51]

For many, moreover, their temporary rank was a matter not simply of having moved up the ladder, but of having crossed the divide from the world of noncommissioned officers. Though attempts to safeguard the position of these men

50. Definitive figures are hard to find. On June 1, 1919, there were 71,640 officers, a total that was considered to be 10,272 too many: JOC *Déb.*, July 30, 1919, p. 3792. On May 1, 1919, the Budget Commission reported that there were 81,000 officers, and the commission wanted that number reduced to 31,735 in France and 11,570 in the Rhineland: JOC *Doc.* 1919, annexe no. 6441, p. 2052.
51. *La France militaire*, January 4, 1919; February 12-13, 1919.

figured in discussions of the question of officers à titre temporaire,[52]   such efforts remained platonic. No lobby existed to defend the interests of this category of officers, and some spokesmen, at least, agreed with the government that though these men had performed admirably during the war, they did not have "the qualities requisite for an officer in peacetime"; some were "not equipped to be instructors, which would be their essential function," and "a small number of them would find themselves embarrassed with respect to their family, education, and style of life."[53]   In the end many of these officers were forced to return to their former situation in accordance with a government circular of April 10, 1919, which made it a precondition of their re-enlistment that they resign the temporary ranks they had won during the war. Others—how many it is impossible to know, since the government never issued any statistics—took their chances on the examinations designed to test whether they had the general education considered necessary for an officer and leader of men. Though many commentators professed the desire that the officer corps be recruited on the most democratic basis possible, they did not mean thereby that the essential quotient of "French culture" should be neglected.[54]

Younger officers who held their higher ranks à titre temporaire were initially treated less brutally. Though these were often the most dashing and possibly even talented, to give them definitive title to ranks they were likely to hold for a long time would jeopardize the chances for promotion of men still younger, those graduating from Saint-Cyr after the

52. JOC *Doc.* 1919, annexe no. 7182, p. 3168.
53. *La France militaire,* January 26-27, 1919.
54. *Ibid.,* January 30-31, 1919; April 26, 1919; June 1-2, 1919; August 12, 1919; September 3, 1919.

war. With retention of their wartime ranks doubtful, and with promotion thereafter still more so, men young enough to adapt to civilian careers and not irrevocably committed to the army were encouraged to leave. It was expected that those near the age limits, with retirement so close, would have little incentive to depart.[55] How many brilliant future commanders joined the resulting exodus is impossible to know. Yet it is not too farfetched to suppose that it was on balance the more talented who departed and the mediocrities who remained.

Nor was the situation of top-ranking officers substantially better. Older men who had achieved the ranks of brigadier general and general of division lived with similar uncertainty. While they mostly had definitive title to their ranks, it remained unclear how long they would be allowed to enjoy them before being forced to retire. For the new reduced age limits—sixty-two for corps commanders, sixty for division generals, fifty-eight for brigadiers, and fifty-six for colonels—decreed in late 1917, though not formally voted by parliament, were not revoked. When the government did introduce legislation to codify these age limits, senior officers reacted bitterly. Since there had been an almost complete turnover among general officers during the war,[56] it was only natural that the men concerned should want to retain their status for a few more years. Moreover, coming at a time when the problem of officers with temporary title was still far from solution, the government's proposals appeared a particularly gratuitous slap at older men. Senior officers felt that they were being sacrificed to the avidity of the "young Turks,"

55. *Ibid.,* January 16-17, 1919; January 18, 1919; see also Paul-Marie de la Gorce, *The French Army,* trans. Kenneth Douglas (New York, 1963), p. 282.
56. *La France militaire,* February 2-3, 1919.

whose promotions, they thought, had often been excessively rapid. Their active and vocal supporters, though they understood the government's concern to keep open the possibilities of promotion, wanted it to act by persuasion—through monetary incentives for early retirement—rather than by fiat.[57]

Far from considering themselves an aristocratic caste, officers tended to compare their position with that of civil functionaries, deserving of the same kind of security of status and tenure. Why should officers be obliged to think first of the corporate good, some reasoned, when other groups of state servants thought first of their personal advantage? When civilian state employees were given a pay raise while nothing was done to augment military salaries, they became doubly resentful; for at the same time the rising cost of living was making the material conditions of their life intolerable. At the end of 1919, with retail prices in Paris almost three times as high as in 1914,[58] officers could not possibly maintain the standard of living appropriate to their position. In this regard they responded no differently from other French bourgeois to the insecurity caused by the postwar inflation. In sum, an impressionistic sampling suggests that the officer mentality was a composite of the attitudes of a frightened rentier or civil servant combined with a self-conscious elitism based on educational achievement rather than on birth.[59] This image

57. An 94 AP 371: General Ozil to Albert Thomas, March 1919, Albert Thomas Papers. See also an interview with an anonymous senior officer, *La France militaire,* April 11, 1919; and *La France militaire,* January 8, 1919; March 8, 1919; April 24, 1919.

58. Elinor Lansing Dulles, *The French Franc 1914-1928* (New York, 1929), pp. 511, 519.

59. See *La France militaire,* November 30, 1918; January 30-31, 1919; March 5-6, 1919; March 7, 1919; June 1-2, 1919; July 24, 1919; General Lavigne-Delville, *Inquiétudes militaires: officiers et fonctionnaires* (Paris, 1924); Raoul Girardet, *La société militaire dans la France contemporaine 1815-1939* (Paris, 1953), pp. 318-319.

was widely at variance with the thoroughly unreal and romantic depiction of the officer corps that its defenders were accustomed to offer in literary effusions or in public polemic.

To relieve its distress and to safeguard its status the army was dependent upon parliament and the political process. Yet on the whole range of concrete difficulties afflicting the officer corps, legislative action was hesitant and incomplete. This is not to suggest that the army was entirely neglected. Rather it was that the consideration it received was more rhetorical than real. Although army matters remained on the back of the parliamentary stove, moderate and conservative politicians reacted sharply to any displays of antimilitarism. It was obviously easier for them to defend the honor of the army than to find solutions to concrete problems. And it was equally clear that while the Right shared the feeling of other political groups that financial considerations drastically limited pro-army measures, the military nonetheless looked upon the Right as their natural defenders.

A case that illustrated this complex of attitudes was the question of pay raises—a crucial matter for successful army recruitment as well as for morale. The War Ministry, well aware of both the urgency and the importance of the issue, worked out a proposal to raise monthly pay for all ranks. Though this draft would have brought the general scale into line with that of civil servants of comparable rank, it would not have fully compensated for the rise in the cost of living.[60] The ministry's plans, however, seemed to take into account more adequately than those drafted by General

60. Among the lower ranks pay would have been approximately doubled, whereas on the upper levels it would have been increased by only about 50 percent: *La France militaire*, March 23-24, 1919.

Headquarters, the need for excellence in the officer corps. General Headquarters did not propose to raise pay, but rather to increase various subsidies, especially those relating to family expenses. This project, developed under the aegis of Marshal Pétain, was criticized for confusing subsidies with just pay for honest work—a sure way to populate the army with sluggards who, because they would be receiving generous support for their large families, would have little incentive to excel. General Headquarters was subsequently persuaded to withdraw its proposal in favor of that of the ministry—and thereby to give precedence to individual accomplishment over stimulating population growth.[61]

When the proposal came before the Chamber Budget Commission as part of a supplementary military appropriations bill, it ran into difficulties. Though disclaiming any lack of sympathy with the officers' desire to be paid a living wage, the commission detached the pay proposal from the appropriations bill and substantially changed it. Instead of a direct pay raise, the commission reverted to subsidies, this time putting the emphasis on allowances for the high cost of living. The total pay specified, however, was less than what the ministry had proposed. The *rapporteur* justified this change by remarking that the commission, "under the cover of a crisis that would doubtless be only transitory, . . . did not want to give the brutal and almost exclusive bait of money to what should remain the choice profession of an elite." Moreover, the commission decided to appropriate only enough funds to cover subsidies for a significantly smaller number of officers than in fact existed. Here lay the key to the commission's tactics: an attempt to force the government to put

61. *Ibid.*, February 21-22, 1919; February 26-27, 1919; February 28, 1919; March 1, 1919.

before the Chamber, without too much delay, proposals for military reorganization.[62]

The officer corps reacted to this classic parliamentary maneuver with stupefaction. Yet at the same time, having been persuaded by an ardent supporter of the military, Louis Marin, that the revised scheme presented by the Chamber Budget Commission was all that was feasible, the editors of *La France militaire* temporarily overlooked the commission's hatchet job. Instead they concentrated their rage on comments that a few left-wing deputies had made in the course of the Chamber debate. Couching their remarks in typical antimilitarist rhetoric—that is, praising the soldiers while denigrating the officers—these deputies had proposed that increased subsidies be restricted to those below the rank of major.[63] But this suggestion was so beside the point, as was clear from the Chamber discussion itself, that the enflamed reaction of the editors of *La France militaire* seems disproportionate. The obverse of the coin was the excessive praise heaped upon the Senate, which passed the Chamber proposal unchanged, but with a prefatory resolution expressing gratitude for the valor the army had displayed during the war.[64]

To be sure it was not only verbal assaults against which the Right felt it had to rise to the army's defense. The Black Sea mutinies and the disturbances in other navy depots in the spring of 1919 suggested that proto-Communist insurrection and revolution was a possible danger. Interestingly enough, at the time, the incidents were completely hushed up—small notices about difficulties in Russian waters were not per-

62. JOC *Doc.* 1919, annexe no. 6441, p. 2052.
63. JOC *Déb.*, July 31, 1919, pp. 3820ff.
64. *La France militaire*, August 2, 1919; August 9, 1919; August 10-11, 1919; August 19, 1919.

mitted to appear until a month after the event.[65] It was only considerably later, when all danger had passed, that Communist perfidy in the Black Sea became a favorite polemical whipping boy of the Right. This is not to deny that the extreme Left—which organized itself as the Communist party at the end of 1920—continued to attack the army and military service and even tried to subvert reservists and conscripts; it was too easy and obvious a way to sound revolutionary, at very little cost in terms of program and intellectual effort, for them to forego. Rather it is to suggest that when the danger was real, if only in terms of seriously weakening morale, the Right had the good sense not to magnify it; when it had passed, the Right could comfortably and profitably resume one of its favorite themes, defending the honor of the army.

Though generating a certain amount of heat and giving the impression that army matters were a live issue, Right-Left rhetoric on the subject was often detached from consideration of the fundamental issues of military planning. When such specific matters as the length of military service and army organization came up for parliamentary debate, the tone was subdued and ideological controversy was largely absent. These discussions suggested that rhetorical hostilities could be at least temporarily suspended. Concern about French security could provide a common meeting ground and lead to a partial cessation of polemic, though not to the complete suppression of doctrinal prejudice.

Such debate, and the shaping of French military policy, would be directed by the victors of the November 1919 elec-

65. Mordacq, *Le ministère Clemenceau*, III, 234; Miquel, " 'Journal des Débats,' " pp. 397ff.

tion, the Bloc National. Primarily an electoral alliance, the Bloc National was intended to be a continuation of the wartime Union Sacrée. It largely owed its triumph at the polls to a judicious use of the new electoral law, which reintroduced *scrutin de liste,* plus a complicated form of proportional representation favoring interparty alliances. The successful coalitions varied somewhat from one electoral district to another, but in general the lists covered the political spectrum from the Right (except for the royalists) to the Center, sometimes including, sometimes excluding members of the Radical party. The Right emerged from the election considerably strengthened in the Chamber and was able to provide a firm base for the cabinets that were formed in the following years. While the ministries could rely on the backing of the strongest parliamentary group, the *Entente républicaine démocratique,* composed of members of various conservative political parties and associations, this formation did not set the tone of the ensuing governmental majorities. It was the more moderate though less numerous members of the *Alliance démocratique* (which had changed its name in 1920 to the *Parti républican démocratique et social* and whose members sat in the Chamber with the *Groupe de la Gauche républicaine démocratique* and the *Groupe des Républicains de gauche*) who provided the main stimulus and personnel in subsequent ministries.[66]

All groups belonging to the Bloc National had put themselves forward during the electoral campaign as the defenders of French security, both internal and external. The common rhetorical coin of the campaign was stridently anti-Bolshevik,

66. For the clearest discussion of political parties and parliamentary groups, see Jean Carrère and Georges Bourgin, *Manuel des partis politiques en France* (Paris, 1924), especially part 1.

anti-Socialist, and anti-German. But with regard to the moderate Right, at least, these polemics should not be taken at face value. The anti-Socialist rhetoric they employed in the campaign should not lead one to believe that they were prepared to launch an ideological crusade. Nor should their repeated pronouncements that they would safeguard and execute the Versailles Treaty be taken as an indication that they had a very clear idea of what this might entail. Their acceptance of the eight-hour law voted in April and of the treaty's restrictions on the occupation of the Rhineland suggested rather an inclination to yield to overwhelming pressure.[67]

The style of the *Alliance démocratique* and of those who can be distinguished as the moderate Right was that of practical men of affairs. They were not the exalted young men who had combined nationalism with militarism in the years before the war, just grown a little older. Though they respected Maurice Barrès in a sentimental way as a symbolic figure of French greatness and as an eminently civilized parliamentary colleague,[68] their political roots, unlike his, did not go back to the romantic and histrionic nationalism of Paul Déroulède. Their origins were diverse, but many had begun their political careers as members of the loosely defined *progressiste* tendency, and a number owed their political allegiance and some of their political training to René Waldeck-Rousseau. It was not until labor unrest and new forms of taxation became major political issues that these people took on a more conservative coloration. The vote on three-year military service in 1913 added a final ingredient and sharpening of

67. See René Rémond, *La droite en France de 1815 à nos jours* (Paris, 1954), pp. 196-199; Charles S. Maier, "The Strategies of Bourgeois Defense" (Ph.D. diss.; Harvard University, 1967), chap. 2.

68. For example, Edouard Herriot, *Jadis,* II: *D'une guerre à l'autre 1914-1936* (Paris, 1952), pp. 120-121.

political personality. In fact the coalition which voted that law anticipated the one which emerged victorious in the election of 1919.

These men who had spearheaded the fight to get France militarily prepared before 1914 came out of the holocaust with their self-confidence remarkably little shaken—perhaps with it enhanced. Though appalled at the frightful cost of the war, they did not doubt that they were in some sense the saviors of their country. They had, in the face of increasing demoralization, and even defeatism, kept war production and the political machinery functioning. As a result they felt they had a special claim to interpreting the French national interest; their sense of exclusive possession did not change, though the war was to have a delayed effect on the interpretation they gave it.

For above all, they were elitists with a clear conscience. The result could be the kind of smugness and narrow-mindedness, depicted so perceptively by the novelist Roger Martin du Gard, of an Oscar Thibault; though the elder Thibault's Catholicism was more central to him than was typical of the moderate Right, his self-righteousness and pompous rectitude found its echo in the people under discussion here. This good conscience about their elite position, and about the status quo in general, may, in part, have been the result of the system of their recruitment. Though birth and wealth were often decisive, the debt they owed to these advantages could be obscured or forgotten in surmounting the mandarinate hurdles erected by the French educational system. The culture thereby acquired, which "placed one in the superior echelon of society,"[69] was theoretically open to all,

69. André François-Poncet, *Réflexions d'un républicain moderne* (Paris, Grasset, 1925), p. 127.

and gave those who had successfully reached the heights a particular sense of virtue and merit.

In view of the differences in education and practical experience between the leaders of the moderate Right and those of the Left, the former's claims to pre-eminent expertise and competence may not at first seem unjustified. With a few exceptions such as Léon Blum and Edouard Herriot, who had used the Ecole Normale Supérieure as an avenue of social mobility, the leftist chiefs were significantly less well-educated than the business men baccalaureate-holders of the *Alliance démocratique*. Moreover, the training of the leaders of the Left was more abstract and rhetorical than that received by the conservative graduates of the Ecole Libre des Sciences Politiques. Though French economic education in the 1920's was primitive, to say the least, the Left politicians were able only rarely to avail themselves of what little there was.

But expertise necessarily operated within the limits set by assumptions and priorities. The range of acceptable choice and possible alternatives was often defined by emotional and psychological commitments—some of which would be only dimly perceived by those who regarded themselves as experts and thought that their actions were governed by impartial rationality. Indeed, the politicians who considered themselves primarily responsible—and who were in fact largely responsible—for watching over the interests of the army and seeing military legislation through parliament, suffered under a double handicap. The more excitable and extreme of them tended to take words for actions and to defend military values with passionate rhetoric while neglecting or misunderstanding the army's practical needs. The more moderate and technically expert were so complacent about their own expertise and fitness to govern that they failed to recognize the extent to which they—no less than the Left—were motivated above all by the desire to preserve France from ever again undergoing such a blood-letting as had occurred between 1914 and 1918. This sentiment, not fully conscious, drastically limited the range of choice available to them, even as they remained convinced at the conscious level that they were doing everything possible to insure the defense of their country.

2 | Foch and the Disjunction of Diplomacy and Military Planning

Foch and Pétain

The day that began with the procession of the mutilés—July 14, 1919—witnessed the triumph of France's two greatest military figures. Following shortly after the incapacitated came the three marshals of France; Joseph Joffre, called back from semiretirement, was understandably overshadowed by Ferdinand Foch and Philippe Pétain. The latter two enjoyed that day a glory less ambiguous than any they were ever to know again. Though Foch might already have felt that his was tainted by failure to secure the Rhine as Germany's military frontier, Pétain was to experience a far more dramatic and tragic apotheosis and downfall. Yet both men always appeared to their admirers and detractors as more than life-size; their images, bedecked with the laurels of victory, worked on the imagination until the course of French history seemed to depend on their actions. Indeed, the military history of the 1920's is often implicitly described as a struggle between the two, with Foch the unheeded protagonist who might have been able to save France from disaster.[1]

1. See General André Beaufre, "Liddell Hart and the French Army, 1919-1939," in Michael Howard, ed., *The Theory and Practice of War* (London,

Marked temperamental differences had always separated these two men, enabling them to perform very diverse roles during the war and shaping their reactions to the problems of the decade following. Of the two Pétain had had the more extraordinary wartime experience. He had started the war as a mere colonel on the verge of retirement, after a career that had been honorable but not distinguished—with its one noteworthy moment a stint of teaching at the Ecole Supérieure de Guerre, where he had argued in the face of accepted doctrine that material factors, especially artillery, were of prime importance in warfare. After the outbreak of hostilities he rose quickly in the command hierarchy; his meticulously organized attacks and his care in spending lives indicated that he was well-suited for a war which reduced the role of the leader to that of a machine-tender. In late February 1916, he was placed in charge of the army group protecting Verdun. Again he displayed his talents as an organizer, first assuring the very tenuous supply line and then establishing artillery defenses to counteract the repeated German attacks. It was ironic that Pétain, known to be so sparing in lives, should have made his reputation as the hero of Verdun; for here, in the bloodiest battle of the war, the losses among the defenders were greater than those suffered by the attackers.

In the following year, after the disastrous and costly Nivelle offensive of April, when the troops still reeling from the catastrophe were in a mutinous state, Pétain was made commander of the French armies. By a combination of firmness in dealing with a few ring-leaders and humanity in redressing the grievances of the ordinary soldiers, he restored cohesion and order to the shaken army. He made constant trips to the

1965), pp. 129-143; General P.-E. Tournoux, "Si, l'on avait écouté Foch," *Revue des deux mondes* (September 1, 1959), 84-93.

troubled sectors and, despite his somewhat inhuman calm, communicated his sympathy and concern for the suffering of the men. It was a remarkable display of personal magnetism, which few, if any, other French commanders could have matched. Thereafter Pétain reshaped the army by reorganizing its training for both defense and offense, initiating a new method of defense in depth and replacing men in the attack as much as possible with firepower. But primarily he waited, keeping his units intact until the flow of American reinforcements should tip the balance against Germany. Finally in July 1918 the Allied armies were able to take advantage of the numerous offensive possibilities Pétain had carefully prepared.[2]

Behind Pétain's calm and apparent lack of nerves lay a profound and disabused skepticism. Initially it may have seemed that he could be classed with those, like the future Marshal Fayolle, with whom Pétain was always very close, who were shattered and shocked by the enormous bloodletting of the first few months of fighting. During this time it appeared that the ability or inability to stomach the mass slaughter divided the High Command more sharply than any political or religious differences. But Fayolle finally rallied, and at the end of the war joined in the general—though usually private—criticism of Pétain for lacking faith in the attack, even daring to label him a defeatist.[3] What was taken by Pétain's critics for lack of aggressive spirit was in part an

2. General A. M. E. Laure, *Pétain* (Paris, 1941), pp. 3-243; General Bernard Serrigny, *Trente ans avec Pétain* (Paris, 1959), pp. 1-173; B. H. Liddell Hart, *Reputations* (London, Murray, 1923), pp. 215-233.
3. Marshal Fayolle, *Cahiers secrets de la grande guerre,* Henry Contamine, ed. (Paris, 1964), pp. 60-61, 272; General Charles Mangin, *Lettres de guerre 1914-1918* (Paris, 1950), pp. 33-34, 145, 165, 168, 282; A. Ribot, ed., *Journal d'Alexandre Ribot et correspondances inédites* (Paris, 1936), pp. 256-257.

unwillingness to drive his troops too far or too hard, a sense of the limits to what could be demanded of men—perhaps at times, an underestimation of their capacities. Not having been an adherent of the *offensive à outrance* before 1914, Pétain discovered in the experience of war a confirmation of his belief that only if human sacrifices were minimized by the weight of matériel, could commanders permit themselves to send their men into combat.

It was skepticism of this sort, which acted as a damper on Pétain's energy and forcefulness, that allowed him to make the compromises essential to smoothing relations with political figures. His tendency to be selective and prudent in exerting effort meant that though he could be "immovable before political pressure where it impinged his dominant sense of caution, . . . he yielded to its influence on matters that seemed to him less menacing."[4] He was not the self-righteous sort who could "find quarrel in a straw," nor the melancholy kind who could feel no attraction for more worldly pleasures. In this latter regard, Pétain's life had been profoundly changed by the war; until 1914 he had led the existence of a lonely bachelor. Subsequently his wartime position had made him the pleased object of flattery and admiration from previously unknown men and women.[5] Cautious, down to earth, yet somewhat detached, understanding the need to limit sacrifices, Pétain had been in perfect harmony with the political mood in 1917—in some sense, he was to remain so for the next quarter of a century.

4. Liddell Hart, *Reputations*, p. 228.
5. See Léon Noël, *Témoignage d'un chef: le Général Guillaumat* (Paris, 1949), p. 67. In September 1920, Pétain was married, with Fayolle serving as his only witness: *Echo de Paris,* September 15, 1920. The ceremony was not performed in church, because his wife had been previously married, and though he later supported the church, Pétain had never been a practicing Catholic.

Where Pétain was prudent and stolid, Foch was demanding and excitable. Even in appearance they were the antithesis of one another, "When debating important questions with Pétain, [Foch] gave observers the impression of a gamecock pecking furiously—his arguments had a muscular accompaniment—at a graven image."[6] Foch's utterances, delivered in this staccato manner, were likely to be of a sybilline quality, which fortunately his staff officers were able to interpret, though they might have to puzzle over his meaning for days. While Foch was not noted for the clarity of his thinking, the essential outline of his thought had a sledgehammer consistency. Intensely convinced of his own beliefs—with a passion not unrelated to his fervent Catholicism—he had felt free from any inward questioning.[7]

Indeed, as both teacher and commander, Foch had always preached the same lesson: the prime importance of the moral factor in warfare. While serving as professor and later commandant of the Ecole Supérieure de Guerre, Foch had revised the heretofore accepted thinking on the psychology of war. No longer considered a constant, the solders' fighting spirit became a variable which must be stimulated and kept at peak intensity by the leader. Foch's was no mean contribution to the mood which prevailed among the High Command before 1914, though his emphasis on the need for reconnaissance and security before maneuvering suggested that his followers were more reckless than he. Thus he entered the war with a

6. Liddell Hart, *Reputations*, p. 217.
7. The best biographical studies of Foch are B. H. Liddell Hart, *Foch: The Man of Orleans* (London, 1931), and General Maxime Weygand, *Foch* (Paris, 1947). Foch's own account of his wartime experience can be found in *The Memoirs of Marshal Foch,* trans. Colonel T. Bentley Mott (New York, 1931). Among reminiscences the most evocative is Commandant Charles Bugnet, *En écoutant le Maréchal Foch* (Paris, 1929).

simplified schema imposed on his disorderly thought processes, and while mindful of danger, was prepared to demand and give the utmost in moral exertion.

Foch's wartime career was more checkered than that of Pétain. He started as the commander of the prestigious Twentieth Army Corps, which was scheduled to advance in Lorraine; but when the extent of the German offensive became clear, Foch was forced to relinquish his attack and was shifted to command a newly created army at the battle of the Marne. There his constantly repeated refrain of *"attaquez"* came at precisely the right moment, for it coincided with the German retreat. Foch had considerably less success in the Artois offensive of 1915 and the Somme offensive of 1916, and after this last attack he was removed from command of the Northern Army Group. It was not until Pétain was appointed commander-in-chief of the French armies in May 1917 that Foch returned from the shadows to become chief of the French General Staff. Throughout the remainder of that year only minor actions were undertaken, as the French and British negotiated and haggled over plans both to stem an expected German offensive and to launch their own in 1918.

They were disputing the formation and composition of Allied reserves when the German blow fell. Unprepared for the weight of the German divisions, the British lines began to cave in and a breach between the British and French armies threatened. This danger was only heightened by the dispositions of the two Allied leaders. Haig, the British commander, seemed preoccupied with protecting the channel ports, while Pétain was intent on maintaining the solidity of the French armies, with the ultimate assignment of covering Paris. At this point Foch threw himself into the debate, expressing with fiery eloquence his determination to thwart the danger—

whatever the risks—of a breach between the French and British. After further hurried and anxious conferences, Foch was appointed to coordinate the actions of the two armies around Amiens and subsequently became supreme allied commander. Contemptuous of the organizational and tactical difficulties that had led Pétain to take a pessimistic view, Foch by force of will had saved the Allies from disaster.[8]

In July 1918, at the second battle of the Marne, Foch's philosophy of attack once more found its appropriate moment. Thereafter the Allied offensive rolled along, progressing by "a series of rapid blows at different points, each broken off as soon as its initial impetus waned, each so aimed as to pave the way for the next, and all close enough in time and space to react on each other."[9] While Foch had now found his opportunity, it was a somewhat changed man who conducted this last offensive of the war. The repeated slaughter of French infantry by machine guns and artillery had made him revise his notions about the importance of matériel. Material factors he could no longer treat as of secondary importance, and for the next ten years Foch was to be constantly preoccupied with the need for improving French capacity for war production.

Though Foch's outward mode of life did not undergo such a profound change as Pétain's—throughout the 1920's he continued to lead a pious and sober existence—he nonetheless emerged more shaken than the latter from his wartime experience. His past certainties had been shattered, and even his continued moral strenuousness had an air of unreality about it. With his growing awareness of material and quantitative factors in warfare, Foch was forced to recognize France's

8. Liddell Hart, *Foch,* chap. 16; Foch, Record book-diary, March 26, 1918.
9. Liddell Hart, *Reputations,* p. 179.

essential weakness in manpower and industrial capacity. He lived in a state of constant anxiety, dreading the future his country—deficient in these important respects—would have to face.

Indeed, Foch's behavior during the Rhineland controversy in 1919 can best be understood as a reflection of his profound anxiety. His actions at that time ought to be seen in this context, and not as the behavior of the seditious general that historians have so often presented.[10] Foch himself contributed to the misunderstanding. In 1929, shortly after the marshal's death, in the context of a Rhineland about to be evacuated ahead of schedule, his friend Raymond Recouly published the record of their conversations under the title *Le mémorial de Foch,* and the embers of the earlier controversy were rekindled. Clemenceau, writing furiously during the last months of his life, responded with a harsh and vindictive treatment of the Foch of 1919 in his *Grandeur and Misery of Victory.* But in thus giving vent to his accumulated rancor, Clemenceau forgot that at the time Foch had largely kept such feelings under control. Subsequent historians, writing from the vantage point of 1940 or 1958, when the behavior of certain French army leaders had become suspect, sought the origins of embittered military-civilian relations by going back to the incidents of 1919. But the historian's penchant for distant causes or analogies has led only to a further wrenching of those events from their authentic context.

Common sense suggests a less machiavellian interpretation of Foch's behavior. In view of Clemenceau's systematic and often brutal exclusion of Foch from the diplomatic dis-

10. See Jere King, *Foch versus Clemenceau* (Cambridge, Mass., 1960); Philip Charles Farwell Bankwitz, *Maxime Weygand and Civil-Military Relations in Modern France* (Cambridge, Mass., 1967), pp. 18-21; Paul-Marie de la Gorce, *The French Army,* trans. Kenneth Douglas (New York, 1963), pp. 153-169.

cussions in Paris—it was only through Foch's close friend and chief of the Imperial General Staff, Sir Henry Wilson, that he was able to learn the terms of the treaty[11] —Foch's attempts to exert pressure appear a natural if sometimes untactful response to a humiliating situation. Unless one assumes that military advisors are not to speak until spoken to—a supposition contrary to most human behavior—Foch's interventions before the Council of Four and the French cabinet lose their force as evidence of near treason. As for his consultations with other political figures, notably Poincaré, these were simply the common coin of military-civilian relations. Sir Henry Wilson behaved no differently, though because he enjoyed easy social access to members of Lloyd George's cabinet, his *démarches* could be kept on a more informal basis.[12] There is absolutely no indication in Foch's private notebooks that he ever considered anything more drastic than personal efforts at persuasion; rumors of a possible coup d'état were utter nonsense.

The most serious charge against Foch is that he continued to conspire with General Charles Mangin to aid the Rhenish separatists after Clemenceau had called a halt to such activities. In June 1919, immediately after Dr. Hans Dorten's ill-fated attempt to establish an independent republic, Clemenceau, convinced that this state was not viable, sent Jules Jeanneney, under-secretary for war, to Mangin with a letter and oral instructions telling him to have nothing further to do with the separatists.[13] But it was more than fear of possible

11. Major-General Sir C. E. Callwell, *Field-Marshal Sir Henry Wilson: His Life and Diaries,* II (New York, Scribner's, 1927), pp. 183, 185, 186.

12. *Ibid.,* chaps. 27 and 28.

13. Georges Clemenceau, *Grandeur and Misery of Victory,* trans. F. M. Atkinson (New York, 1930), pp. 216-224; King, *Foch versus Clemenceau,* pp. 97-98, 105-106.

political repercussions that prevented Clemenceau from discharging Mangin and publicly exposing Foch. Throughout early 1919 Clemenceau had told the military leaders to act cautiously and at the same time to keep him informed of what was happening. They had perhaps overstepped his guidelines, but this did not deter Clemenceau, a few weeks after Jeanneney's trip, from encouraging Mangin to begin talks with separatists in Hesse. It was not until October that Clemenceau finally acted on the realization that because the Rhinelanders would not be able to free themselves, it would be fruitless for France to continue helping them under the table.[14]

Though Foch's position and standing had been seriously undercut by Clemenceau's repeated criticism of him to the other Allied leaders, he nonetheless tried for the next five years to implement the treaty. He behaved during that time in quite different manner from what one might expect of a "seditious general." His conscientious attempts to safeguard France with the means provided him suggest an ability to forget past humiliations. Foch's role after the war was more that of a diplomat than of a military commander or organizer. As supreme allied commander until the beginning of 1920, when the armistice convention gave way to the regime of the treaty, he had wielded military and civilian power in the occupied provinces of Germany. After the peace went into effect, Foch's authority over the Rhine provinces was reduced to that of commander of the Allied occupation troops. Moreover, as president of the Comité Militaire Allié de Versailles (CMAV), he had responsibility for the execution of the military clauses of the treaty.[15] The various Interallied

14. AN, 149 AP 21: "Notes, rapports . . . situation politique dans la région rhénane," January 28, 1919-October 16, 1919, General Charles Mangin Papers.

15. The CMAV was composed of one general from each of the Allied countries, with Foch the presiding officer and Weygand the secretary-general.

Control Commissions, installed in the capitals of the defeated nations, were to report to the CMAV, which in turn was subordinate to the Conference of Ambassadors—the pinnacle of continuing postwar allied institutions.[16] Aided by General Maxime Weygand, who had been his chief of staff throughout the war and who at the same time shared his energy and made up for his lack of concern with detail, Foch turned to the difficult task of coordinating allied efforts with France's military needs.

While Foch was thus occupied with France's international involvements, the job of reorganizing the French military establishment fell to Pétain. In fulfilling his functions as vice-president of the Conseil Supérieur de la Guerre—a position he held until 1931—Pétain relied heavily on the two generals who served as French chiefs of staff during that decade. Neither of these men was as close to Pétain as Weygand was to Foch; both had become associated with the commander of the French armies only at the end of the war. General Edmond Buat, who was chief of staff from 1920 until his premature death at the end of 1923, joined Pétain's staff as chief of operations in July 1918. Prior to that time he had alternated between staff and line posts, and, more significantly, had served in 1912 as *sous-chef de cabinet* and in 1915 as *chef de cabinet* for War Minister Millerand. A man of great organizational abilities and impressive technical expertise, his charming manner and distinguished bearing facilitated his relations with political leaders.[17] He was succeeded by General

16. General Maxime Weygand, *Mémoires*, II: *Mirages et réalité* (Paris, Flammarion, 1957), pp. 64-66.

17. Colonel Romain, "Un grand soldat: le Général Buat," *Revue hebdomadaire*, 33, no. 3 (January 19, 1924), 348-358; Lt. Col. de Thomasson, "Un grand officier d'Etat-Major, le Général Buat," *Revue des deux mondes,* 7e période, 20 (March 1, 1924), 197-212. The Belgian ambassador to France commented that "le Général

Marie-Eugène Debeney, who remained as chief of staff from 1924 until 1929. Slightly older than Buat, Debeney had finished the war as the renowned commander of the First French Army, which had played an important role in the final offensive. During the early 1920's, as commandant of the Ecole Supérieure de Guerre and the Centre des Hautes Etudes Militaires, he supervised the intellectual formation of younger officers, imprinting on them the lessons of the last conflict.[18]

Although neither of these two generals could be considered vassals of Pétain, their functions necessarily put them in closer contact with him than with Foch. The latter's glorious international position did not give him a commanding influence within the French military establishment. Yet the country's military policy cannot be viewed simply in terms of Pétain's ten-year dominance and Foch's semi-exclusion. A wider angle of vision is required—one that includes the international and intellectual as well as the domestic political contexts of military planning. Besides the inevitable pressure of internal politics, France's relations with its allies defined both the objectives and the limits within which the army's strategists were obliged to operate.

The International Desiderata for Military Planning

In declaring that France had been saved at the Marne first by Russia and then by the United States, Foch was simply

---

Buat est considéré comme le cerveau de l'armée française": *Documents diplomatiques belges,* I (Brussels, Palais des Académies, 1964), no. 154, p. 370 (henceforth cited as *DDB*).

18. Liber, "Le Général Debeney," *Le correspondant,* 293 (new series, 257) (December 15, 1923), 992-1014.

repeating a commonly accepted truth.[19] But behind this aphoristic description of his country's rescue from defeat during the First World War, lay an awareness of the new conditions limiting French postwar military policy. The protracted character of the conflict of 1914-1918, coupled with France's staggering losses, had underlined the nation's numerical inferiority and the necessity for giving priority to alleviating the manpower shortage. After 1918, Foch and those like him calculated that simply to hold out in another long conflict would require not only sustained support in the East, but an adequate base of operations in the West. France would never again enjoy the freedom of action that it had displayed in 1914 and that even then had rested on the illusion of a brief war.[20]

No matter how a renewed conflict with Germany began, France needed to be prepared for the eventuality of total war; no limited actions could be undertaken unless at the same time the mechanism for an all-out conflict was assured. In fact, the notion of restricted warfare, in so far as it applied to France during this period, must be viewed as part of a continuum; if the French could not call a halt to hostilities, through either military victory or diplomatic negotiations—and if as a consequence their territory were again jeopardized—their military planners had to be ready to throw all their country's resources into the struggle. For their nation never had the options open to its British ally: to exert economic pressure through its naval power, to subsidize allies, and to dispatch small expeditionary forces—in short to

19. Foch Cahiers, Dossier F, August 16, 1921; see also *Le Temps,* June 14, 1919.

20. For a discussion of prewar French mobilization plans, see Samuel R. Williamson, Jr., *The Politics of Grand Strategy: Britain and France Prepare for War, 1904-1914* (Cambridge, Mass., 1969), chaps. 5 and 8.

fight a limited war. Although Britain had deviated from this traditional policy in committing a mass army to the western front during the First World War, there were those who called upon the British to return to their former practices.[21] The French enjoyed no such advantages: with Germany directly on their border, France's military leaders could not avoid planning for a direct confrontation with their country's powerful neighbor.

Even in the early 1920's, they seemed most concerned with the necessity of fully utilizing France's resources. The need for total mobilization had been driven home by the protracted struggle of 1914-1918.[22] It was also true that in view of France's industrial inferiority, such mobilization would not place that country on an equal footing with Germany. One might go farther and suggest that the prospect of all-out war with a potentially more powerful enemy had built into it the assumption that French success was dependent upon Allied support. Certainly French political leaders, regardless of military theorizing across the Channel, counted on British aid in the event of a renewed conflict with Germany, and despite the absence of a formal alliance between the two countries, such assistance was always a crucial element in French thinking.

If by waiting France could be confident that Allied support would be forthcoming, which would tip the balance in its favor, then it could ill afford to risk its army and security in the first moments of war. Indeed, the noted British military writer Liddell Hart attacked the French sharply for having

21. See, for example, B. H. Liddell Hart, *The British Way in Warfare* (London, Faber & Faber, 1932), chap. 1.

22. For an excellent discussion of the impact of the war on French thinking about economic mobilization, see Richard D. Challener, *The French Theory of the Nation in Arms 1866-1939* (New York, 1955), chap. 3.

taken the offensive in 1914, citing with approval the view of the prewar French military critic Colonel Grouard: "The war ought to be, on the French side, defensive politically and militarily: politically, because it is only on this condition that we can count on the intervention of our allies; militarily, because we are forced to it by the relative rate of mobilization of the respective armies, and also by the nature of the ground on the frontier."[23] In sum French army leaders were led by reasoning of this sort to view long-range military problems within a defensive framework.

To assure allied support in the event of a major conflict was thus the principal task confronting France's leaders. The Versailles Treaty had not yet gone into effect, however, before French diplomats began to appreciate how difficult their assignment would be. The decade of the 1920's had scarcely opened when it became painfully apparent that the country's long-range situation was far more precarious than it had been before the war.

In the autumn of 1919, when the Versailles Treaty had been submitted to the Chamber, French parliamentarians had confidently assumed that the promised Anglo-American guarantee would be signed without delay. France's leaders, considering the fulfillment of this pledge tantamount to an alliance, had counted on it to help compensate for the limited duration imposed on the occupation of the Rhineland. Their disappointment was correspondingly intense when the United States Senate refused to ratify the Versailles Treaty or to accept the postwar obligations Wilson had undertaken. Foch, however, viewing America's entry into the First World War as an unanticipated though providential act, adjusted to this

23. Liddell Hart, *The British Way in Warfare*, p. 61.

return to isolation with comparative equanimity. For him, the desertion of Great Britain was the more crushing blow. When France's ally across the Channel refused to carry out its part of the bargain, pointing out that its own promise had been contingent upon American participation, Foch saw his immediate aim—though not his abiding hope—for joint military planning dashed to the ground.[24]

At the same time, the revolutions of 1917 and the consequent loss of Russian support had undercut France's chances for succor in the East. However Foch might abhor communism, the chief source of his hostility to Russia's postwar regime was its disruption of the French alliance system. His initial concern was to achieve a new stability in eastern Europe that could both halt the disorganizing impact of bolshevism and act as a counterweight to Germany. But ultimately it was as reinforcement for France's own precarious security that Foch looked to the East. In a compulsive fashion, born of his profound anxiety about his country's future, he noted repeatedly the number of divisions the new nations of eastern Europe might be able to mobilize in the event of all-out war. He kept juggling the figures until the combined total of their forces and those of France approximated his estimate of German strength.[25]

If this kind of support can be taken as the long-range desideratum of French foreign policy, it suggests an altered perspective on France's relations with eastern Europe. A number of commentators have argued that France had an obligation to safeguard the Versailles settlement in the East; indeed this implied moral imperative underlies much of the

24. See, for example, Foch Cahiers, Dossier E, June 1, 1919, and February 14, 1920.
25. *Ibid.,* Dossier E, March 5, 1920; March 31, 1920; and April 1, 1920; Dossier F, May 26, 1921; June 2, 1921; September 1922.

criticism of French supineness in the 1930's.[26] But that was not the way Foch and other French leaders saw it. To be sure, they recognized a certain mutuality of interest, especially between their country and Poland; as continental states potentially menaced by Germany, Foch considered that the bonds between these two were stronger than those between France and countries that were at a safe distance from Germany. Yet it was self-interest, mutual or not, that determined the attitude of Foch and his colleagues toward commitments to the new nations in the East.

This prudence about involvement in eastern Europe became apparent in the actual instances of French intervention there. Though Foch in 1919 had originally entertained notions of an allied campaign against the Bolsheviks in Russia, by the end of the year he was talking in terms of simply organizing a combination of the border states.[27] It seems doubtful that allied intervention would ever have involved a significant commitment of troops; for at the time when Bolshevik fortunes were at their lowest, in April and May, the Allies limited their aid to advisors and matériel. French conservative opinion, even when most enthusiastic about Admiral Kolchak's chances for success and despite all its verbal violence against the Soviet Union, reflected the same hesitancy about committing French forces.[28] Indeed the shipment of munitions and the sending of military advisors was both the model and the extent of French involvement in eastern Europe,

26. See, for example, Geneviève R. Tabouis, *Ils l'ont appelée Cassandre* (New York, 1942); Pertinax, *Les fossoyeurs,* 2 vols. (New York, 1943); Alexander Werth, *The Twilight of France 1933-1940* (New York, 1942).

27. Callwell, *Sir Henry Wilson,* pp. 177-224; Piotr S. Wandycz, *France and Her Eastern Allies 1919-1924* (Minneapolis, University of Minnesota Press, 1962), p. 139; Foch Cahiers, Dossier E, January 1920.

28. *Le Temps,* March 27, 1919 and March 31, 1919; compare Arno J. Mayer, *Politics and Diplomacy of Peace-Making 1918-1919* (New York, 1967), chap. 23.

repeated in aiding Rumania, Czechoslovakia, and most significantly Poland.

At the Paris Peace Conference the Allies had concentrated their attention on Poland's western frontier. At the same time the conjunction of this nation's rebirth and civil war in Russia opened the question of Poland's eastern boundaries— to be settled, it seemed, by military force. In February 1919 Polish and Russian troops had already come into armed contact. By June the Poles had advanced to Zbrucz, in Lithuania, and by mid-September they were prepared to make peace with the Bolsheviks. While the Allies hesitated before taking a definite stand on the question of Poland's eastern frontiers, Polish forces continued to advance; in December, when the Allies finally agreed upon a boundary line—the famous Curzon line—Polish troops were already a hundred miles farther east. Throughout the winter of 1919-1920 the Poles and the Bolsheviks engaged in tentative peace negotiations. The breakdown of these talks in April coincided with the launching of a new Polish offensive in the Ukraine. Initially the operation seemed to be a success, but by early June the military situation began to change to Poland's disadvantage; throughout July and August the Polish position deteriorated rapidly, and the Red Army penetrated deeply into Poland.

Polish military misfortunes finally roused the Allies to concerted action. Their failure to decide on a common policy prior to the summer of 1920 was due in large measure to disagreements about relations with the Soviet Union. Lloyd George, eager to regularize contacts with the Bolshevik leaders in order to re-establish trade relations, was consistent in his reluctance to defend an enlarged Poland. Throughout 1919 Clemenceau had wavered back and forth, caught between two contradictory desires. On the one hand he seemed to favor only a small Poland in order to protect Russia's interests—for to force any of the counterrevolutionary leaders to accept a diminished Russia would be to damage seriously his cause, and in the eventuality of a White victory, Russia would again become an important French ally. On the other hand, Poland was given the principal place in Clemenceau's scheme to create an eastern barrier against the Soviet Union, and he declared that it "would be a great mistake if we did not maintain Poland to dam up the Russian flood and to provide a check on Germany."[29]

With Poland about to be overrun, these considerations lapsed into irrelevance. The Allies now bravely announced their determination to aid the Poles. Though Lloyd George would "give no assistance to Poland for any purpose hostile to Russia," he did feel "bound under the Covenant of the League of Nations to defend the integrity and independence of Poland within its legitimate ethnographic frontiers," and he declared that the British government would "defend its existence with all the means at their disposal."[30] Clemenceau's successor, Prime Minister Millerand, phrased a similar resolve in terms of geopolitical fears that the Polish barrier between Germany and Russia would collapse.[31] It was only in writing about the incident years later that Millerand felt compelled to describe French action in support of Poland in

29. Quoted by Wandycz, *France and Her Eastern Allies*, p. 131. Chaps. 4 and 5 of this book give the best overall account of the Polish concerns of the Allies through mid-1920. See also Wandycz's subsequent book, *Soviet-Polish Relations, 1917-1921* (Cambridge, Mass., 1969), and Weygand, *Mirages et réalité*, pp. 80ff.

30. British Cabinet Papers, Cab. 23/22: 41/20, appendix 1, July 20, 1920. The references to the Covenant of the League and Poland's "ethnographic frontiers" clearly indicate how carefully Lloyd George was guarding himself against having to give any real assistance.

31. *Documents on British Foreign Policy 1919-1939,* first series, VIII (London, 1958), no. 83, p. 712 (henceforth cited as *DBFP*).

idealistic rhetoric comparable to that employed by Lloyd George; he then claimed that "the fate of western civilization" had been "at stake on the banks of the Vistula."[32] Regardless of the language used, the actual aid offered suggested that there were distinct limits to France's interest in Poland. The first concrete measure that the Allies took was to despatch an Anglo-French mission to Warsaw on July 22. Composed of two diplomats, Jules Jusserand, French ambassador to Washington, and Lord D'Abernon, British ambassador to Berlin, and a British general as well as General Maxime Weygand, the mission was instructed to investigate the military and political situation in Poland, and to advise the Poles in their forthcoming armistice talks with Russia. If these negotiations should break down, as they did, further allied "moral and material" help—all that had ever been envisaged— would be contingent upon the Poles' acceding to the Allies' behests.[33] The evident demoralization of the Polish troops and the suspected duplicity of Marshal Pilsudski, who was both chief of state and commander of the armed forces, made the Allies loath to support what seemed like an unstable enterprise. When Lloyd George and Millerand met at Hythe on August 8 and 9—the situation in Poland having become even more desperate—they were careful to make the conditions for allied help precise. They insisted not only that the Poles give some clear indication of their willingness to resist, but that a commander-in-chief be appointed who would have no other functions and who would act upon allied military advice, even to the point of maintaining a

32. A. Millerand, "Au secours de la Pologne," *Revue de France,* 12, no. 4 (August 15, 1932), 578.
33. Weygand, *Mirages et réalité,* pp. 92-99. See also Foch Cahiers, Dossier E, July 14, 1920; July 24, 1920; August 25, 1920; August 27, 1920.

specified number of divisions and resisting on a prescribed line.[34]

Even if all these conditions should be met, the amount of allied aid would be small indeed. The British government was prepared to contribute "boots, clothes, and saddlery," while the French would supply arms and munitions.[35] In addition France would send officers to help staff the reorganized Polish army, leaving to Great Britain the task of establishing a naval blockade of the Soviet Union and maintaining communication between the Allies and Poland.[36] Before these agreements became effective—but while the British continued to put pressure on the Poles to accept the Bolshevik terms—the Poles, with an assist from General Weygand, triumphed in the battle of Warsaw and in effect saved themselves. The subsequent acclaim accorded Weygand for his stand on the Vistula should not be allowed to obscure the basic fact that the Allies—not only the British, but even the French—were never prepared to undertake a major effort in support of the Poles.

France had indeed been circumspect in defining its interests in eastern Europe. Much of this same caution was apparent in the alliance concluded between France and Poland the following year. In fact, Foch argued strenuously against agreeing to any kind of accord with the Poles. On January 4 and 14, 1921, he addressed memoranda to the government declaring that although France and Poland had interests in common, the latter "would not constitute a real force until it had a

34. British Cabinet Papers, Cab. 23/22: 46/20, appendix 3, August 9, 1920. On the Hythe Conference see *DBFP*, first series, VIII, chap. 9. See also Wandycz, *France and Her Eastern Allies,* pp. 165-171.

35. British Cabinet Papers, Cab. 23/22: 46/20, August 9, 1920.

36. British Cabinet Papers, Cab. 23/22: 46/20, Note to appendix 2, August 9, 1920.

settled policy, clearly marked frontiers, a well-organized army, and stable finances," and that until these conditions were met, a military accord would be premature.[37]

In this instance the politicians, led by Millerand, now president of the Republic, showed less caution than Foch, or rather more willingness to make engagements that might be significant for Polish internal politics but whose military weight was slight. While the political alliance signed in February, calling on the two governments "to get together" (*se concerter*) for the defense of their respective countries in the case of unprovoked aggression, may have been a help to Pilsudski in shoring up his shaky regime, the looseness of the phrase left the French considerable freedom of action. The secret military convention that accompanied the political accord—and which was the result of Polish pressure—though more precise, was of a very limited nature. Under its terms, France would at most supply matériel and technical personnel, but no French troops would be sent to reinforce the Polish army; France would also assure, "so far as its means would permit, the security of communication lines."[38] The French were thus careful not to go beyond the limited commitments they had consented to the previous year. At the same time, Foch insisted, with his characteristic obsession with numbers, that the size of the Polish army be substantially raised. And Poland did, in fact, promise to maintain a peacetime army of nine cavalry brigades and thirty infantry divisions, a considerable increase over the troop totals demanded by the Allies six months earlier.[39]

37. Weygand, *Mirages et réalité*, p. 179; see also Wandycz, *France and Her Eastern Allies*, p. 214.

38. General Maurice Gamelin, *Servir*, II: *Le prologue du drame* (Paris, Plon, 1946), p. 466.

39. Wandycz, *France and Her Eastern Allies*, pp. 217-218.

Whereas Foch was reluctant to provide military support to a regime whose instability seriously undermined its potential usefulness, he was most anxious to conclude a tight alliance with the Belgians. As he put it, Belgium had always been the "meeting ground for decisive battles between France and western Europe on the one hand, and Germany and central Europe on the other. In neutralizing this battlefield, the great powers had thought they were preventing a confrontation and thereby preventing war."[40] Yet neutrality had proved a weak reed; it had been inadequate as a barrier against a German march to the channel coast and the north of France. A sturdier and more effective bulwark must be found. But this could not be accomplished without Belgian cooperation.

From the outset the prospects of joint military planning were seriously handicapped by Belgium's domestic political problems as well as its international concerns. The internal disputes between the French-speaking Walloons and the Flemings, who spoke a variant of Dutch, played no small role on the diplomatic front; the former eagerly sought close relations with France, while the latter suspected that such ties might involve Belgium in another Franco-German conflict. At the same time Belgian diplomats postponed negotiating with the French alone, hoping that Great Britain could be persuaded to join in guaranteeing their nation's security. And they continued to hesitate even when this proved out of the question. Appreciating the importance France attached to a military convention, Belgium's leaders insisted on a prior settlement of the outstanding political dispute between the two countries, the question of Luxemburg's railway system. Only when this matter had been satisfactorily resolved, did the

40. See Foch Cahiers, Dossier E, July 5, 1920.

Belgians set about in earnest to discuss a military convention.[41]

The main lines of the Franco-Belgian agreement were worked out by late June 1920, and the accord was signed in September, with Foch having served as the chief negotiator for France. Foch, however, did not succeed in obtaining as tight an alliance as he would have liked. His original project had called for a union of French and Belgian forces and for the two countries to mobilize armies in proportion to their populations—a demand typical of his concern with numbers. Moreover, the Belgians refused to commit themselves to joint action in response to every violation of the Versailles Treaty. And in the cases in which they would act, the only measures specifically stipulated covered the period when the Allies would still be in occupation of the Rhineland. Each country agreed, for that limited time period, to supply a precise number of troops in the event of a German aggressive threat or in that of a general "taking up of arms" (*prise d'armes*) by Germany. Further provisions and preparations were to be elaborated in the course of joint staff talks that were to implement all aspects of the accord.[42]

What kind of operations would be conducted in response to such German behavior *after* the Allies evacuated the Rhineland was not made clear. The defensive provisions in the agreement, which would become operational after the Rhine-

41. For a detailed account of Franco-Belgian discussions, see Jonathan Helmreich, "The Negotiation of the Franco-Belgian Military Accord of 1920," *French Historical Studies,* 3 (Spring 1964), 360-379; see also Jean Marie D'Hoop, "Le maréchal Foch et la négotiation de l'accord militaire franco-belge de 1920," in *Mélanges Pierre Renouvin: Etudes d'histoire des relations internationales* (Paris, 1966), pp. 191-199.

42. *DDB,* I, no. 175, pp. 405-408; D'Hoop, "Foch et l'accord militaire franco-belge," pp. 191ff.; Helmreich, "The Negotiation of the Franco-Belgian Military Accord," pp. 370ff.

land ceased to be at the military disposal of the Allies, were vague and elusive, calling merely for a coordination of the French and Belgian defensive systems, including the eastern frontier of Luxemburg.[43] The best that can be said for these provisions is that they did not foreclose the possibility of a jointly worked out defensive position, which would provide a bulwark against German aggression. Such, after all, had been Foch's original assessment of what made sense for the long run.

Nevertheless when France's relations with Poland and Belgium are untangled, it becomes clear that its diplomatic efforts had not succeeded in providing guarantees of effective military assistance for the future. Though France might not stand alone, the kind of support that Poland's shaky regime could give, or that would be forthcoming on the basis of the imprecise terms of the accord with Belgium, was far from reassuring. Foch's fear for his country's future—a fear epitomized in the simple statistic of forty million confronting sixty—had not been assuaged. Once again, he concluded, unless and until the reluctant British were induced to enter the conflict, France would be forced to bear the brunt of renewed German aggression.

The Legacy of the First World War

For Foch to summarize his country's long-range military problems in terms of the comparative populations of France and Germany was merely sensible. The experience of total war had made demography and industrial potential the prime data of military thinking. On the level of grand strategy,

43. *DDB,* I, no. 175; D'Hoop, "Foch et l'accord militaire franco-belge," p. 196.

then, Foch accepted, as did nearly all his colleagues, the appropriateness of a basically defensive outlook. The major long-term problem French military planners faced was that of waging a good defensive campaign. How opening operations and maneuvers would be conducted, with what means and in what manner France should deploy its troops at the outbreak of hostilities, would determine whether it would be able to defend itself successfully. These were the crucial questions. And here too, the legacy of the First World War left its mark.

Pétain was in charge of reorganizing the army and laying down the rules for the conduct of operations. Although Foch often objected while the work was in progress and Weygand subsequently claimed that his chief's views had been disregarded with disastrous consequences,[44] it is not at all clear what—in this realm—the former Allied commander-in-chief was suggesting as an alternative. The fragmentary comments in his notebooks that Weygand made so much of reflected a preoccupation with matériel in a quantitative sense, without specifying how that matériel should be used. Above all Foch wanted to postpone decisions about organization and training, leaving these matters in suspense in order to take advantage of further technological developments. But such a wait-and-see policy was not a realistic option: instructions had to be drawn up to train the conscripts and guide the officers, and the army had to be reorganized to conform with the number of peacetime effectives available.

Pétain was best suited for and most interested in thinking on the level of operations.[45] He set about the task with the

44. Foch Cahiers, Dossier F, September 7, 1921; March 24, 1922; May 13, 1922. For Weygand's comments see his *Foch,* pp. 331-334.

45. See Commandant A. M. E. Laure, *Au 3ème bureau du troisième G.Q.G.* (Paris, 1921), pp. 270-275.

same team he had worked with at the end of the war. On the basis of their studies Debeney drew up the military instruction issued in 1921—*Instruction provisoire sur l'emploi tactique des grandes unités.*[46] This document was intended by Pétain and Debeney to be merely a general formulation of principles broad enough to respond to changing circumstances.[47] Much of the work—especially the opening chapter—sounded like a series of platitudes; to abstract a few characteristic phrases from it, such as the "preponderance of firepower," would give only the barest indication of its main thrust. But when phrases like these are set in the context of combat procedures, a general mode of thinking and way of viewing military operations becomes apparent. And though the provisional character of the instruction was underlined in its title, it remained the bible of the French army for fourteen years.

That the general instruction and its companion volume, the *Règlement provisoire de manoeuvre d'infanterie* of 1920, should bear witness to the traumatic effect of the losses in the First World War was only natural. Indeed the prudence with which both these manuals made demands on the troops' bravery was appropriate after the unparalleled and often careless expenditure of lives from 1914 to 1918. The crucial passage in the Infantry Regulation read as follows:

> The advance should take place as soon as gun fire has made it possible to do so with moderate losses [*pertes réduites*], without awaiting a complete destruction or absolute neutralization of the defensive position, which one is never sure of having totally obtained . . .

46. Ministère de la Guerre, Etat-Major de l'Armée, *Instruction provisoire sur l'emploi tactique des grandes unités du 6 Octobre 1921* (Nancy, Paris, Strasbourg, 1932).
47. Laure, *Pétain*, pp. 251-252, 267-268.

Inspired with an offensive spirit that is ever on the alert, always ready to engage the enemy to the full as soon as a rational and deliberate examination of the situation shows that it is possible, the infantry and its supporting forces will never let themselves be stopped by the fear of incurring a few losses, which it would be ... chimerical to hope to avoid completely.[48]

To so moderate and sensible a formulation only those reared in the prewar heroic ideal of infantry charges could object. And it was in fact in such a vein that one French critic phrased his comments; to pay constant attention to minimizing infantry losses, he remarked, might well destroy the spirit of sacrifice.[49]

This was a minority view: the weight of military opinion was on the side of sparing the soldiers, and more particularly replacing manpower by firepower. Throughout the instructions it was apparent how widespread was the support for Pétain's view that the tremendous increase in firepower had drastically altered military realities.[50] The two manuals described the advance of the infantry and its progression from the beginning to the end of an attack as dependent upon achieving dominance in firing capacity. Moreover all forms of combat seemed to be conceived along the same lines, whether it were a *combat de rencontre* or an attack against an organized position—none to be engaged in unless the commander were assured that he had superior forces. The attack might then proceed, slowly and with prolonged halts, waiting at

48. Ministère de la Guerre, Direction de l'Infanterie, *Règlement provisoire de manoeuvre d'infanterie du ler février 1920,* part 1 (Paris, 1920), p. 4 (emphasis in the original).
49. Colonel Alléhaut, *La guerre n'est pas une industrie* (Paris, 1925), pp. 123-124.
50. See, for example, *Instruction provisoire ... grandes unités,* pp. 63, 98; *Règlement provisoire d'infanterie,* part 1, "Rapport au Ministre".

each stage for the preponderance of firepower to make itself felt. Advancing from a fixed line, with the artillery giving support, the infantry would engage in a final assault only if the enemy had resisted the barrage, always taking care not to get too far ahead of their artillery. Once the objective had been seized, the troops would solidly install themselves and reorganize, waiting until their firepower was again ready to give support before moving on.[51] In short the minute preparations prescribed as necessary for an attack made it seem that all actions were to proceed as if in slow motion.

On a more general level what was most striking about the instructions drawn up in the early 1920's was their emphasis on the decisive battle. Military actions were described in terms of an overall plan leading to a direct confrontation with the enemy; it was assumed that unless the main line of the opponent's forces was broken, no further advance could be made.[52] To shake the enemy's will by end-runs or enveloping maneuvers designed to disrupt his rear was not elevated to the level of *major* operations—in large part because the French experience in the First World War, the "race to the sea" of late 1914 and the continuous front it had produced, suggested that such procedures could not bring decisive results. As one would expect, then, French military leaders retained as their chief point of reference the carefully prepared direct assaults that had finally led to victory in 1918.

51. *Instruction provisoire . . . grandes unités,* pp. 88-89, 98-99, 107; *Règlement provisoire d'infanterie* (Paris, 1921), part 2, title 1, chap. 3. See also General Bernard Serrigny, *Réflexions sur l'art de la guerre* (Paris, Charles-Lavauzelle, 1921), pp. 140ff; General Edmond Buat, *Ludendorff* (Paris, 1920), pp. 272-273.

52. See *Instruction provisoire . . . grandes unités,* title 3, chap. 4. Compare Foch's comment: "Dans la guerre, l'acte capital est la bataille," Foch Cahiers, Dossier F, August 21, 1921.

Such a model of an attack, with its soon to be outmoded time sequence and progression, became the framework into which new techniques and machines were fitted. The most interesting case of the pervasive influence of these operational guidelines was the thinking about tanks immediately after the First World War. Originally both Buat and Estienne, the latter commonly known as the father of the tank and the man who had served as Pétain's expert on tank warfare in 1918 and 1919, played with notions of developing a tank so small that each individual could be equipped with one—a modern version of a medieval knight's armor.[53] Such an instrument seemed initially the most efficacious way—though it proved unrealizable—of increasing the protection offered the infantry. The same subservience of matériel to infantry needs was apparent in the manuals for tank operations. Though tanks were to attack in groups, never individually, their chief function was to act as mobile artillery accompanying the infantry.[54]

A more telling example—since it pointed to the future direction of tank studies—was Estienne's conception of the design and use of the combat tank. The weapon, Estienne specified, should be very powerful and very supple, able to cross every kind of terrain, and superior in all these respects to the earlier tanks designed to accompany the infantry. In fact it would function apart from the footsoldiers, preceding the

53. On Estienne see General P. A. Bourget, *Le Général Estienne, penseur, ingénieur et soldat* (Paris, 1956), and the former's memorandum of May 25, 1919, "Etude sur les missions des chars blindés en campagne," in Colonel Georges Ferré, *Le défaut de l'armure* (Paris, Charles-Lavauzelle, 1948), pp. 34-46. On Buat see Laure, *3ème bureau*, pp. 247-248.
54. Ministère de la Guerre, Etat-Major de l'Armée, 3e Bureau, *Instruction provisoire sur l'emploi des chars de combat comme engins d'infanterie* (Paris, 1920), particularly pp. 10-11; *Règlement provisoire d'infanterie*, part 2, pp. 125ff.

infantry and clearing the way for them. These speculations reflected the most advanced French thinking on tank warfare, projecting technological developments that would free the tank from its role of infantry weapon. But what was striking about even Estienne's conception was the way he juxtaposed novel technology and combat procedures with a battle conceived along the orthodox lines of direct confrontation:

> In order to protect our troops, we must launch all our combat tanks to meet the enemy tanks, and we must try to support them, to the greatest extent possible, by artillery, planes, and special equipment. The battle will begin with a tank engagement, as it formerly began with a cavalry combat. In the same fashion as the bulk of the cavalry corps used to seek each other out in order to destroy one another and thus gain freedom of maneuver, the two masses of tanks will hurl themselves upon each other.[55]

Echoes of Estienne's technological imagination can be found in the contemporary military periodicals. Younger men, often attached to the individual services of the War Ministry, contributed articles that suggested a wide range of technical interest and even foresight.[56] Whether these studies

---

55. Ferré, *Le défaut de l'armure*, p. 40; see also "Conférence faite le 15 février 1920 sur les chars d'assaut, par le Général Estienne au Conservatoire National des Arts et Métiers," *Bulletin trimestriel de l'Association des Amis de l'Ecole Supérieure de Guerre*, no. 14 (October 1961), 22-30, in which he accepts the guidelines set down by the military instructions as valid for the present, but imagines a future when tank technology will have advanced so far that a new army organization and new methods of conducting operations will impose themselves.

56. Among the most interesting articles concerned with tanks for the first half of the decade are the following, all of which appeared in the *Revue Militaire française*: Commandant D.-P. Bloch, "L'avenir du char de combat" (no. 7, January 1922, 90-103); Colonel Chedeville, "Les chars de combat actuels et le Haut Commandement" (no. 8, February 1922, 182-196, and no. 9, March 1922, 330-345); Commandant Pigeaud, "L'armée de la sûreté" (no. 21, March 1923,

penetrated the General Staff was unclear; most of the officers on duty there were so overburdened with administrative paper work that it is difficult to see how they could have found the time to keep abreast of the technical literature.[57] But the literature itself indicated that imagination could be pushed only so far. While it offered numerous suggestions for different kinds of tanks designed to perform the usual operations—such as a breakthrough—more rapidly and more efficiently than by the traditional combination of infantry and artillery, few writers showed how all these instruments could be combined in such a way as to revolutionize the notion of an exhausting and prolonged engagement.

The dominant impression that one derives from the military manuals and, to a lesser extent, the military periodicals of the era, is of the clock of the First World War slowly ticking. And in this lay the major difficulty for French military leaders. While their concern for sparing effectives and maximizing the role of matériel was not only understandable but also appropriate after the experiences of 1914-1918, such preoccupation carried the danger of producing a cumbersome and hence inflexible battle plan.

The French military-intellectual establishment, the group that set the dominant tone and might have provided the

---

388-409); Commandant Pigeaud, "Etude sur la sûreté et le combat" (no. 28, October 1923, 60-89); Lt. Col. Pigeaud, "Le problème du char de combat en 1926" (no. 62, August 1926, 219-244); Lt. Col. Velpry, "L'avenir des chars de combat" (no. 26, August 1923, 205-231); Lt. Col. Velpry, "Chars blindés et chars cuirassés" (no. 34, April 1924, 92-119); Lt. Col Velpry, "Le char, moyen de guerre économique" (no. 49, July 1925, 52-72).

57. For a description of the work routine of officers attached to the General Staff by a former high-ranking officer, see Tony Albord, *Pourquoi cela est arrivé ou les responsabilités d'une génération militaire 1919-1939* (Nantes, 1946), pp. 36-37.

impetus for changes in techniques and procedures, was small indeed. In no country did anything resembling the post-Second World War panoply of defense "think tanks," now so prominent a feature of American military life, exist. This smallness of scale should be underlined before one tries to assess the role the French military-intellectual establishment played or should have played in military planning. In fact in both Great Britain and France speculation was never entirely divorced from instruction; for it was the educational institutions—the staff colleges—that bulked largest in the intellectual life of the French and British military.[58]

Whereas in Great Britain the three services had schools of roughly equal importance, in France the dominance of the army assured primacy to its staff training institution, the Ecole Supérieure de Guerre. This school had a very high reputation for rigor and thoroughness throughout the interwar period; indeed part of each class was composed of future military commanders from other countries—notably from those of eastern Europe—whose admission attested both to French prestige and to the French policy of aiding those nations to establish sound military organizations. In addition, a few years before the outbreak of the First World War, the French had set up the Centre des Hautes Etudes Militaires (CHEM) in order to prepare the most promising officers for future roles within the High Command. This institution, as well as the Ecole Supérieure de Guerre, was reconstituted in 1920, and both were placed under the command of General Debeney.[59] Not until 1927, when the British established the Imperial Defense College, did a comparable institution exist elsewhere.

58. On the intellectual life of the British military, see Robin Higham, *The Military Intellectuals in Britain: 1918-1939* (New Brunswick, N.J., 1966).
59. Laure, *Pétain*, p. 269.

In no sense, however, could the CHEM be considered a reservoir or source for military thinking and innovation. Lacking a permanent staff of its own, the CHEM drew largely on civilian personnel to give general courses concerned with economics or politics. Military experts, usually those who had commanded armies in the last war, were called in to handle the technical side of the instruction. This consisted of exercises and studies designed to illuminate the conduct of operations performed on the level of an army or group of armies. In any event the period of instruction was too short— a mere six months—for the students to gain more than a general acquaintance with the material covered. The CHEM apparently served as a refresher course for those eligible for positions within the High Command, supplementing the instruction these officers had received earlier at the Ecole Supérieure de Guerre, while preparing them for the duties that lay ahead. Indeed many of the forty students admitted in each class and chosen from the ranks of colonels or brigadiers—whereas before the war they had been picked from among majors and lieutenant colonels—considered "their stay at the Center as a formality that it was necessary to fulfill in order to attain a [higher] rank."[60]

Nor did the Ecole Supérieure de Guerre supply the mental stimulus required to prod the military imagination. While proclaiming a desire to expand the intellectual horizons of the highly selected junior officers who took its two-year course, its commandant and professors could not but spend the bulk of their time initiating students into the technicalities of their future jobs as staff officers. Following very stiff

---

60. Weygand, *Mirages et réalité,* p. 311. For a description of the center's activities see also pp. 309-315, and Stefan Th. Possony, "Organized Intelligence: The Problem of the French General Staff," *Social Research,* 8 (May 1941), 234.

entrance examinations, which tended to reward the methodical memorization of standard texts and documents, the successful candidate continued his training in the fundamentals of his discipline by spending six months studying the branches of the army he did not already know. Throughout the first year the emphasis was on teaching the officers how to execute orders, while during the second they learned the practical art of command, with special stress on the exact and clear wording of orders. Having been thus prepared to handle such problems of their daily life as supply and gun deployment, the officers had at least a thorough knowledge of the mechanics of the military profession.[61]

To what extent the concentration on military science narrowly defined was due to the inadequacy of the teaching personnel is unclear; for it is difficult to assess the complaints leveled at the professors of the Ecole Supérieure de Guerre.[62] Although a few were singled out as having been particularly imaginative, the majority seem to have been merely technically competent and intellectually limited. This is quite what one would expect, and probably the standard of talent was no different from what it had been before the war. The victory of 1918, however, gave a retrospective luster to the prewar professors—a surprisingly large number of whom subsequently held important command positions[63] — whereas the reputation of their successors came to suffer from the

61. *Ibid.*, pp. 223-224; Lt. Col. G. Guy Waterhouse, "Some Notes on the Ecole Supérieure de Guerre, Paris," *Army Quarterly,* 8 (July 1924), 325-334.

62. See, for example, Albord, *Pourquoi cela est arrivé,* p. 23; J.-R. Tournoux, *Pétain et De Gaulle* (Paris, 1964), part 1, chap. 7. For a more nuanced critique see Colonel Yvon, "La 49e promotion de l'Ecole Supérieure de Guerre," *Bulletin trimestriel de l'Association des Amis de l'Ecole Supérieure de Guerre,* no. 7 (January 1960), 38-60.

63. For example, Foch, Fayolle, and Debeney had all been prominent as teachers at the Ecole Supérieure de Guerre.

defeat of 1940. In any event, their principal function was not the formulation of new military policy, but rather the propagation of established principles, often taught with a plodding uniformity of language and presentation.

Even when the broader aspects of military thinking and planning were studied, the impression of unimaginative instruction remained. The more general statements and precepts, which were handed down in an abstract fashion, epitomized the formalistic and routine quality of the military education offered. Between such statements and the study of the specific operations that might be performed, the intermediate stages were lacking. This intellectual hiatus was apparent in the lectures of the most important course given at the Ecole Supérieure de Guerre, the *Cours de tactique générale d'Etat-Major*.[64] Only in the courses on military history did the general and the concrete seem to find a meeting gound; for here the abstract phrases and concepts came alive as appropriate responses to actual military situations. Here the attention to the complicated and slow mechanism of launching a battle—a fundamental and substantial part of the training given at the Ecole Supérieure de Guerre as well as of the military manuals—was implicitly justified.

In studying military history, the students concentrated their attention on the First World War. The lectures themselves attained their most dramatic pitch in describing the sequence of events that had led to the Allied victory in 1918. In so doing they emphasized the way France had exploited the situation of the stabilized front; for as long as it could stave off a German offensive without suffering too great losses, time, and with it the arrival of American reinforce-

64. *Cours de tactique générale d'Etat-Major, 1928-1929, 49e Promotion,* Marshal Jean de Lattre de Tassigny Papers.

ments, had assured France and its Allies decisive numerical superiority. And while ordering the maintenance of defensive positions, Foch had worked out a general plan calling for powerful ripostes and prepared the reserves necessary for a major counteroffensive. The battle of Montdidier launched on August 8, 1918—the so-called black day of the German army—by General Debeney, now commandant of the two most important military educational institutions, became the model for the proper conduct of such an offensive. In extending the attack in space, through assaults on the two flanks of the battle already underway, and in time, by assuring a constant flow of men and supplies, the French had found the formula for transforming a carefully prepared battle into a general rollback.[65]

While general maxims such as economy of forces and its corollary, concentration of means, could thus be explicitly linked up with the methodical plans for launching a battle, the course on the history of the war also suggested some significant implications. It seemed clear, though it was never specifically stated, that the decisive offensive engagements would come only at the very end of a future conflict and that in its earlier stages a war of stabilization had certain advantages in terms of increasing the contributions made by France's allies and allowing the resulting coalition greater control over the timing of events—with, to be sure, the proviso that the initial defensive positions be maintained at a minimum cost in lives. Indeed, throughout the decade the students at the Ecole Supérieure de Guerre spent a large part of their time studying such a war, despite the oft-repeated claim that a war of movement remained the desirable objec-

65. Ecole Supérieure de Guerre, Colonel Duffour, *Cours d'Histoire—la guerre de 1914-1918* (Paris, 1923).

tive.[66] The advantageous possibilities of a war of stabilization may, in an almost unconscious fashion, have reinforced the willingness of French military leaders to accept an overall defensive war plan. Such a plan would not become strictly necessary until Germany revived militarily. But when that time came, a recognition of the advantages of a war of stabilization and delayed decision could mold future expectations and possibly even military objectives.

The Versailles Treaty and French Military Planning

To a foreign observer at the time, the emphasis French military leaders placed on their country's long-range defense problems and their almost hypnotic concentration on the First World War would undoubtedly have seemed prematurely gloomy. After all, Germany had been vanquished and had been forced to accept a treaty that left it practically disarmed. In the short run, at least, France enjoyed clear military superiority. The nation's army chiefs were obviously not unaware of this fortunate situation. Indeed military and civilian alike shared the belief that Germany would not provoke a war under conditions so favorable to its foe. Witness the fact that no less an authority than General Buat, the chief of staff, did not expect a conflict to break out so long as France and Belgium were in occupation of the Rhineland. This, he maintained, combined with the measures of control imposed by the treaty, would prevent the Germans from organizing a clandestine mobilization and launching an overwhelming attack on the model of 1914.[67]

66. *Cours de tactique générale d'Etat-Major,* p. 198, Marshal Jean de Lattre de Tassigny Papers.
67. *DDB,* I, no. 154, pp. 368-370.

Yet at the same time, France's army leaders remained profoundly skeptical about the long-term efficacy of the document on which the current military equilibrium rested. Foch's own reflections on this subject were of a particularly pessimistic nature. At the Paris Peace Conference he had advocated permitting Germany only a small army—he had specified 200,000—composed of short-term conscripts. Instead the Allied leaders had accepted Lloyd George's proposal of a 100,000 man military force whose members would enlist for twelve years of service, leaving Foch with the unnerving certainty that Germany would always have the highly trained professional cadres necessary for the rapid organization of a new army.[68] It was at this point that he remarked to his friend Sir Henry Wilson that the Allies could "no more limit the number of men trained to arms in Germany than the Germans could limit the output of coal in England." As for "the possibility of checking and limiting guns, rifles, lorries, etc.," Foch again concluded that "it would be quite impossible."[69] Moreover, there was no way to restrict Germany's industrial capacity, and it was this superiority which posed the greatest potential danger for France.[70]

Foch was equally gloomy about the effectiveness of the demilitarization of the right bank of the Rhine. The treaty had stipulated that the Germans could maintain no military installations within a zone extending fifty kilometers east of the river. But the ease with which they had introduced troops into that area in March 1920 to put down the disturbances that had followed the Kapp Putsch led Foch to comment that neutralization was a chimera. Such would also be the

68. *Echo de Paris,* March 11, 1919.
69. Callwell, *Sir Henry Wilson,* p. 166.
70. See Foch Cahiers, Dossier F, August 21, 1921, and October 14, 1921.

neutralization of the left bank, he claimed, when the Allies were no longer in occupation of the Rhineland—and the house of cards erected with the military clauses of the treaty would come tumbling down.[71]

Following this line of reasoning one could not escape the conclusion that the long-range danger of a powerful Germany could only be postponed: it could not be prevented. At the beginning of the 1920's France's leading authority on industrial mobilization formulated his country's future dilemma as follows:

> Our enemy, regardless of all treaties, will certainly find a way of reconstituting its military power. Given the density of its population, we will be able to field equal numbers against it only by drawing heavily . . . on our allies. However free access by air and sea may be, their arrival will require several weeks. Our metropolitan troops will thus have to accomplish the difficult mission of gaining the time necessary for this concentration.[72]

Such a remark suggests the uncertainty that plagued French military policy in the immediate postwar years. Indeed the combination of short-term strength and long-term foreboding gave a peculiar unreality to military planning. To be sure, the mobilization plan that was in effect in the early 1920's, the provisional and offensively oriented Plan P, testified to the military's appreciation of the current balance of armed might. At the same time, the plan's dependence upon the

71. *Ibid.,* Dossier E, April 3, 1920. For similar statements by a French disarmament expert on the ease with which the Germans could reoccupy a demilitarized Rhineland, see "Examen d'une proposition de Lord Robert Cecil relative à l'établissement de zones démilitarisées [July 1923]," General Edouard Réquin Papers.
72. Serrigny, *Réflexions sur l'art de la guerre,* p. 101. For similar views see General Debeney, "La guerre moderne et les machines," *Revue de la semaine,* no. 6 (February 10, 1922), 151-154.

provisions of the Versailles Treaty suggested that it might soon become a historical relic of a happier era rather than an instrument designed for immediate use. Moreover, when one situates it in the context of the way contemporary French military writers discussed the steps that could be taken at the beginning of a renewed conflict, it becomes apparent that France's army leaders were unsure of how they could best bring to bear their country's military superiority.

Plan P, which was drawn up in 1920 and which went into effect in 1921, was based on the assumption of Belgian co-operation and more particularly joint utilization of the Rhineland. In the case of the threat of a major German attack, Foch was to command French and Belgian units north of the Rhineland town of Remagen, while Pétain would lead the bulk of French divisions stationed further upstream all the way to the Swiss frontier at Basel. The first mission assigned to these combined forces was to disrupt the enemy's mobilization, by occupying without delay the closest German industrial regions, the Ruhr basin and the valley of the Main, and thereby to prevent the Germans from utilizing the resources of those areas. By thus gaining both time and space, the allied advances would provide the cover necessary for the further mobilization envisaged in Plan P's successive stages: France fielding sixty-four divisions in a first wave and another twenty at the end of a month, with Belgium ready to supply twelve and having an additional six in reserve.[73]

73. For a sketch of this mobilization plan, see General P.-E. Tournoux, *Défense des frontières: Haut Commandement-Gouvernement 1919-1939* (Paris, 1960), p. 333. See also D'Hoop, "Foch et l'accord militaire franco-belge," pp. 192-193; *DDB*, I, no. 175, pp. 406ff. I am uncertain of the exact number of French divisions. D'Hoop, who was authorized to consult the French mobilization plan, gives the figures cited here, whereas the Franco-Belgian military accord called for fifty-five French divisions initially, with a second wave of twenty-five.

The second mission outlined in Plan P was to realize a common French-Czechoslovak-Polish front, designed to drive a wedge between the southern and northern German states. The inclusion of Poland and Czechoslovakia in the French mobilization plan requires a word of explanation. Indeed, the reference to Poland was very vague. Although it was assumed that Germany would have to deploy a considerable number of troops in defensive positions in the East, what the Poles would do aside from pinning down those forces was not at all clear. The Czechs, on the other hand, who, unlike the Poles, did not at this point have a military alliance with France, had worked out a mobilization plan according to French directions. The Czechoslovak General Staff, headed by the chief of the French military mission in Prague, had prepared Plan N, which called for "a military advance into Germany aiming at a junction with the French in Bavaria."[74]

The Czechs, however, and also the Poles would be unable to carry out their assignments if they were the primary target of a German attack. While the French plan could possibly have been modified to cover the eventuality of a German threat against Czechoslovakia or Poland (on the assumption that French troops were still in the Rhineland), the arrangements with Czechoslovakia had a fatal flaw. Since there was no formal alliance between the French and Czechs, the *casus foederis* was unclear; nowhere was it specified under what circumstances Czechoslovakia would be obliged to come to France's aid or vice versa. Similarly the agreement with Poland had avoided the whole matter of substantial troop support. In short the mention of a common front among all three countries should not be taken as a commit-

74. Wandycz, *France and Her Eastern Allies*, pp. 235, 280-281.

ment on France's part, but rather as an indication of Foch's determination to induce the nations of eastern Europe to come to the help of his own.[75]

Despite the suggestion of far-reaching objectives, it was not at all clear that French army leaders ever foresaw utilizing their forces to decisive advantage. When military writers sketched out more thoroughly how offensive operations at the outbreak of hostilities should proceed, the goals they specified appeared modest indeed. While the weakness of the German army, they speculated, would force it to engage in delaying actions, possibly of a guerrilla nature, on a broad front, the French advance they envisaged seemed designed merely to hinder German mobilization and strengthen their country's diplomatic stance. The French anticipated—if an armistice had not been concluded in the meantime—that at the end of six months or a year, Germany would be fully armed, and their own nation would be called upon to utilize all its manpower and industrial resources.[76]

Yet even such a curious dénouement—after all, France's superior forces should have been hindering German mobilization throughout those six months—was more favorable than what was anticipated once the Rhineland was evacuated. When that time should arrive, military writers speculated that opening offensive maneuvers would be much reduced in

75. In this connection Foch noted in his Cahiers: "La nation Tchec a ses destinés entre ses mains. Elle les assurera, à la condition d'assumer elle-même les charges qu'elles comportent. . . . Elle ne peut compter pour cela sur une conflagration générale du monde mettant en ligne à son profit les puissances les plus lointaines comme les Etats-Unis." Dossier F, July 11, 1923.

76. This war plan was sketched out in Colonel F. Culmann, *Stratégie* (Paris, Charles-Lavauzelle, 1924), pp. 500ff. Throughout the 1920's the author worked very closely with the High Command and in the latter part of the decade was secretary to the commission in charge of devising and developing plans for fortifications.

scope. The operation most frequently mentioned as appropriate for this eventuality would be for the covering troops, which might be the bulk of the standing army, to advance into the militarily unoccupied Rhineland. A number of purposes could be accomplished by such a move, the most ambitious being to prevent "any major concentration of German forces on the left bank of the river, or at least in the more limited zone of Kreuznach, Bingen, Mainz, Worms." Even an advance of only fifty kilometers beyond the northern frontier of Alsace-Lorraine to a line running between Trier and Speyer could forestall a German offensive along the left bank of the Mosel through Luxemburg. By thus diminishing the "total width of the Allies' deployment" and facilitating "liaison between the French and Belgian armies," this operation would protect Luxemburg itself, as the Franco-Belgian accord had specified.[77] At the very least such an advance would gain the space required for an eventual withdrawal, if this should prove necessary, over territory that was not France's own.[78]

The profound hesitation of France's army leaders in developing plans to take full advantage of their country's initial superiority meant that for the better part of a decade their military machine remained stranded without a clear objective. Quite obviously the French did not expect to launch a major assault against an antagonist that would offer no resistance. Nor did they plan an attack that might cost them potential allied support. It was equally apparent to France's army chiefs that the Reich would become an appropriate target in an armed conflict, that Germany would act in such a

---

77. *Ibid.,* pp. 465-466.
78. Serrigny, *Réflexions sur l'art de la guerre,* p. 103.

fashion as to justify a renewal of hostilities, only when their own nation no longer enjoyed decisive military superiority.

Despite his pessimism about the efficacy of the Versailles Treaty's military clauses, Foch prepared for his new assignment as France's chief international military representative with undaunted determination to make the Germans fulfill all their obligations. If Foch had been alone in his combination of a realistic estimate of his country's weaknesses and a resolve to defend its rights, his personal reactions to the diplomatic situation would be of little interest. But in fact his behavior was not atypical, and it suggested one mode of response to France's difficulties, which was echoed by other French leaders and reverberated throughout the decade. A part of their minds recognized the long-range limitations on France's position and another part was determined to resist all treaty violations, while the men themselves rarely permitted these two attitudes to confront each other.

So long as the French did have a breathing space, their determination to enforce the treaty could be put into practice at very little military cost. Indeed the coercive actions that Foch executed in the early 1920's cannot appropriately be considered military operations at all. No real armed resistance was anticipated, and aside from a certain reshuffling of troops in order to reinforce the Rhine Army, from a technical point of view these actions proceeded in a semi-automatic fashion. Such operations thus offered no military experience or organizational precedents; in no sense can they be assimilated to a strategy of limited war. The result was a compartmentalization—a separation between long-range military problems and those connected with the execution of the treaty. In these circumstances the demands that Germany fulfill all its obligations took on a life of their own without altering the potential imbalance between France and its powerful neighbor.

Such compartmentalization was reinforced by the prevailing attitudes toward the financial clauses of the Versailles Treaty. Almost as if to compensate for frustrations and failures in trying to provide for their country's security, French political leaders transferred their energy to enforcing the financial provisions of that document. For German reparations offered some immediate hope of alleviating pressing monetary and budgetary difficulties. Or so it seemed to the vast majority of French conservative and moderate opinion, and political leaders could ill afford to ignore this sentiment. Foch, even when most discouraged about the possibility of preventing Germany's eventual military recovery, never wavered in his conviction that the Germans must be made to pay for the damage and destruction they had wrought in the First World War.[79] Indeed after April 1920—when French troops, joined by a Belgian battalion, had occupied Frankfurt and Darmstadt in response to Germany's violation of the demilitarization provisions—the primary objective of French coercive actions shifted from the enforcement of the military clauses of the treaty to the collection of reparations.

In attempting to enforce the reparations agreements, Foch acted as the military executor for the three significant prime ministers of the early 1920's, Alexandre Millerand, Aristide Briand, and Raymond Poincaré. And as these three figures elaborated their policies toward Germany, the tendency to

79. See, for example, Foch Cahiers, Dossier E, January 1921; Dossier F, February 6, 1921.

suspend consideration of major military problems while concentrating on making Germany pay became more pronounced.

Of the three, Millerand was temperamentally closest to Foch. Born in 1859 and coming from simple origins—his father had been a draper and his grandfather a peasant—Millerand got his first leg up into the French establishment by attending a proper Parisian lycée. He then went on to become a lawyer but soon turned his enormous energies to politics. His humanitarian sentiments, as well as—one might speculate—his marginal class position, led him in the direction of socialism. Influenced more by John Stuart Mill than by Karl Marx—of whom he never had more than an imprecise knowledge—Millerand was concerned with humanizing economic liberalism and promoting solidarity among all classes rather than with reconstituting society on a new social and economic basis. He began to fulfill his personal political ambitions at an early age—having been elected a deputy from Paris at twenty-six. Millerand's entry into Waldeck–Rousseau's ministry in 1899 and subsequent expulsion from the Socialist party did not represent a sharp break with his earlier political ideals; rather his vague political principles seemed to allow quite comfortably for a steady shifting of priorities and a slow evolution toward the Right.

Millerand did not become involved in military affairs until 1912, when he served as minister of war in Poincaré's cabinet. There he came into close contact with army chiefs such as Joffre and Lyautey, formed his lasting friendship with Buat, and acquired his permanent affection for the military. There he also caused a considerable tempest by destroying the *fiches* which War Minister André had collected and used to block the advancement of officers tainted with antirepublicanism or devout Catholicism, and by carrying out the administrative steps to rehabilitate Paty du Clam, who had been dismissed as an outspoken anti-Dreyfusard. In so doing Millerand claimed that he was not championing any particular political cause but simply redressing past grievances in an effort to restore self-confidence to the army. Whether these assertions were entirely accurate is here of minor importance; for what the incidents suggested above all, was that once Millerand had fixed on a course of action of whose rightness he was convinced, he was determined and courageous in carrying it out, regardless of attendant political unpleasantness.[80]

It was with this kind of unwavering conviction that Millerand took up the task of enforcing the treaty. As leader of the victorious Bloc National in 1919, he became president of the Council on Clemenceau's retirement in January 1920. At the end of the year, when Paul Deschanel, who had defeated Clemenceau for the presidency of the Republic, became too incapacitated to carry out his functions, Millerand was elevated to that post. In this new position he continued to play an important role in French foreign policy, until he was unceremoniously forced to resign after the elections of 1924.

The occupation of Frankfurt and Darmstadt in April 1920—when Millerand was still prime minister—showed him at his best. Not only could the operation be considered a technical success, in that German troops were within a short time withdrawn from the demilitarized zone, but it was also handled adroitly from the diplomatic standpoint. At the very time that Foch was proving unable to wrest from the Belgians

---

80. Alexandre Millerand, "Mes souvenirs: contribution à l'histoire de la Troisième République" (unpublished manuscript); interviews with his son Jacques Millerand, October 11, 1966, and October 23, 1966.

a specific commitment for joint action in the case of any German resistance to the Versailles Treaty,[81] Millerand succeeded in persuading them to send a battalion to join the occupation forces. Moreover, this support enabled Millerand to counter the objection of the British, who opposed the whole operation, that his country's independent action was disrupting harmony among the erstwhile allies. The occupation of Frankfurt and Darmstadt in fact settled nothing: the problem of German disarmament continued to plague interallied conferences. But in the short run Millerand had been strengthened in his belief that decisive action could produce quick results.[82]

So self-confident was he and so imbued with an ethic of vigor that it sometimes seemed as if he reflected little on the long-range significance or effectiveness of his endeavors. His exertion on behalf of the Franco-Polish alliance might be cited as one case in point, his attitude toward the question of reparations as another. Always optimistic about the possibility of making Germany pay—through a combination of force and agreements between the industrialists of the two countries—he seemed unwilling to admit the financial and diplomatic obstacles to such a course. To be sure, by the time reparations became the central problem facing French leaders, Millerand was no longer in charge of the day-to-day negotiation and formulation of foreign policy; behind the protection of the Elysée he could allow himself a certain imprecision. While Millerand's accusations of vacillation and lack of will directed at other French political leaders became something of a reflex, it is not at all clear that a reasoned alternative lay behind these charges.

81. D'Hoop, "Foch et l'accord militaire franco-belge," pp. 196-197.
82. Millerand, "Souvenirs," annexe no. 8; British Cabinet Papers, Cab. 23/22: 18/20, April 8, 1920; *DBFP*, first series, VIII, no. 3.

The fact was that the outlines of Millerand's foreign policy did not differ from the course pursued by his successors, Briand and Poincaré—that is, to enforce the treaty in concert with France's allies, notably the British. Though Millerand had acted independently in occupying Frankfurt and Darmstadt, though Briand was prepared to behave similarly the following year, and Poincaré, after much hesitation in January 1923, felt that there was no other recourse, all three worked conscientiously for an understanding with Great Britain. In the long run they all knew that France could not face a revived Germany without British support; it was only the breathing space provided by the military clauses of the treaty which permitted these French political leaders to be as independent as they were.

In manner and behavior Briand cut a very different figure from Millerand and Poincaré. Coming from a petit-bourgeois provincial family, Briand never felt entirely at home in proper Parisian society. There was a looseness about him in dress and in temperament which contrasted sharply with the moral rectitude that Millerand and Poincaré, in their different ways, both exuded. Nor did he share their ethic of work; Briand was often accused of being uninformed and almost unconcerned. Above all, he was an astute practical politician; Millerand early conceded that he was "very clever, perhaps too clever at intrigue."[83] Briand's appearance and general laxness—as well as the convenient political position into which he had slowly modulated—suggested that he would not join in the chorus demanding that France maintain constant vigilance over German execution of the Versailles Treaty.[84]

83. Millerand, "Souvenirs," p. 60.
84. On Briand's early career see Georges Suarez, *Briand,* I (Paris, 1938). For the most evocative sketch of Briand's working habits in the early 1920's, see Comte

To those who considered the wisest path the French could follow one of concessions to Germany in order to strengthen embryonic democratic forces, Briand seemed a great statesman; to those who thought that unless constrained, Germany would never relinquish dreams of European hegemony, Briand appeared a fool. Neither view was correct, for each failed to take into account the continuity of French foreign policy, regardless of changes in rhetoric. Though Briand often exhibited a tendency to use pacifist terminology, in March 1921 he proved steadfast in trying to get the Germans to pay. It was then, after obtaining British backing, that Briand sent French troops to occupy Düsseldorf, Duisburg, and Ruhrort. Two months later he had the class of 1919 recalled, again with the consent of the British—this time in large part because he had convinced them he would act whether or not their support was forthcoming; he was determined to give substance to his threat of further occupations if Germany failed to fulfill its agreements with regard to both reparations and disarmament.[85] Foch subsequently contrasted Poincaré's lack of action (before he moved troops into the Ruhr) with Briand's resoluteness in carrying out a prearranged plan.[86]

The usual comparison between Briand and Poincaré—the former dealing in hollow phrases and the latter strictly adhering to precise and narrow definitions—was more apparent in the way they handled negotiations with the British for an Anglo-French alliance. Both had the same objective: to get Great Britain to consider violations of the military clauses of the Versailles Treaty a *casus foederis.* Neither wanted an

de Peretti de la Rocca, "Briand et Poincaré (Souvenirs)," *Revue de Paris,* 43, no. 24 (December 15, 1936), 767-789.

85. British Cabinet Papers, Cab. 23/25: 24/21 (5), April 19, 1921; Cab. 23/25: 31/21, April 30, 1921; Cab. 23/25: 32/21 and appendices, May 1, 1921.

86. Foch Cahiers, Dossier F, September 9, 1922.

agreement that would simply guarantee France's frontiers—the war must not again be waged on French soil. And to implement the desired accord, both were insistent on the necessity of joint military planning. Lloyd George, however, had no intention of committing his country in so precise and far-reaching a fashion. He would agree to come to France's assistance if French soil were attacked, but would merely consult with the French if the military clauses were violated. Primarily the British wanted to use the promise of such an accord as a means to put pressure on the French to settle—on British terms—the outstanding differences between the two nations, such as submarine building, Near Eastern problems, the situation in Tangier, and the economic reconstruction of Europe.[87]

Despite the gaps between the French and British objectives, it seems clear that Briand, unlike Poincaré, was prepared to go ahead with an accord. For besides a precise military alliance between the two countries, to which the British would not agree, Briand wanted to arrive at a more general understanding to deal with all European affairs. By getting the British to take a first step toward closer cooperation with France, he hoped to set in motion the mechanism of a two-power peace-keeping system.[88] Such a maneuver was characteristic of Briand's diplomatic style: accepting vague agreements at the outset with a view to building up precedents and thereby ensnaring his partner into firmer commitments. The

87. British Cabinet Papers, Cab. 23/29: 1/22, January 10, 1922; Great Britain, *Cmd. 2169: Papers Respecting Negotiations for an Anglo-French Pact* (London, 1924), part 2 (henceforth cited as *Cmd. 2169*); France, Ministère des Affaires Etrangères, *Documents diplomatiques: Documents relatifs aux négociations concernant les garanties de sécurité contre une agression d'Allemagne* (Paris, 1924), nos. 20, 21, 22 (henceforth cited as *Doc. dipl.: Garanties de sécurité*).
88. Georges Suarez, *Briand*, V (Paris, 1941), chap. 10.

entente between France and Great Britain before the First World War had developed in this way, and it was with similar incremental tactics in mind that Foch had accepted the alliance with Belgium—in spite of its vagueness about the enforcement of the Versailles Treaty.[89]

Poincaré refused to behave in a similar manner. Assuming the presidency of the Council following Briand, he made a further attempt to wrest a meaningful commitment from the British, and having failed, let the matter drop. Where France's vital interests were concerned—as with preventing a German attack from reaching French soil—he would not tolerate vagueness, though where he felt that there was no imperative for French action—as in the case of Poland—he seemed willing to accept formulas worthy of Briand.[90] Great Britain, he assumed, would act if France were invaded even if there was no pact; thus nothing would be gained by accepting the unsatisfactory British offer.[91]

Indeed both he and Millerand feared that much could be lost in the process of making such an agreement. At Cannes in January 1922, where the discussions between Lloyd George and Briand came closest to ending in an accord, Briand seemed about to make concessions to the British that were intolerable to the other two French political figures. What angered Millerand the most was Briand's willingness to invite the Bolshevik leaders to participate in the forthcoming international economic conference; but both he and Poincaré were almost equally concerned lest Briand's desire for an alliance with Britain lead him to make concessions on German reparations. Together they successfully conspired to

89. D'Hoop, "Foch et l'accord franco-belge de 1920," p. 197.
90. *Doc. dipl.: Garanties de sécurité,* no. 23.
91. *Cmd. 2169,* no. 48.

bring about Briand's resignation.[92] For the next two years France's long-range security problems faded into the background, while the government's energies were focused on the immediate problem of forcing Germany to pay.

Poincaré was both more prudent and narrow in his outlook than either Millerand or Briand. Marked for life by his training in the legal profession, he approached the formulation of French foreign policy as a lawyer would work up a complicated brief. He did his homework meticulously, taking special note of the legal ramifications of a particular problem, and, thus prepared, he faced his own conscience and the rest of the world. Poincaré was also sustained by a sincere and often selfless devotion to his country. Born in Lorraine in 1860, of solid bourgeois stock, he had passed part of his childhood under German guns, and then continued his education at Louis-le-Grand before taking up the study of the law. He brought with him into politics and state service a kind of integrity and moral probity that inspired confidence among large numbers, while often disconcerting his fellow politicians. And unlike many of his colleagues, Poincaré remained faithful to the political views he had worked out in his early manhood. Though his backing came increasingly from the Right, he was careful to delineate the differences that separated him from his supporters; in contrast to Millerand, he never renounced the laicism of his youth. While he might not always remain loyal to a friend—Millerand had numerous complaints on this score—he was unswerving where principles were concerned.[93]

92. Suarez, *Briand,* V, chap. 11.
93. For the most evocative portrait of Poincaré see Pierre Miquel, *Poincaré* (Paris, 1961), particularly pp. 609-617; also Peretti de la Rocca, "Briand et Poincaré." For Millerand's attitude toward Poincaré see his "Souvenirs," p. 74.

It was with his objectives narrowly conceived and rigorously justified on legal grounds that Poincaré ordered French troops to occupy the Ruhr in January 1923. Throughout the previous year he had hesitated and negotiated, reluctant to assume responsibility for the operation without British backing. When it became clear that such support was out of the question, Poincaré felt compelled to act alone. It was inconceivable to him that France could be asked, or be forced, to relinquish its legitimate claim to reparations. And it was to make Germany pay and for that reason alone that Poincaré sent troops into the Ruhr. Both Poincaré and Foch insisted that the occupation was not necessary for France's security.[94] Even when in September 1923 Germany was obliged to renounce passive resistance, and Foch hoped to take this opportunity—with the aid of Rhenish separatists—to reopen the Rhineland question, while Millerand wanted to force industrial concessions from the Germans, Poincaré persisted in pursuing his more modest goal.[95]

In part Poincaré refused to deviate from his original intention for fear that acting on Millerand's and Foch's suggestions would lead to a final rupture with Great Britain. Willing, though reluctant, to strain relations between the two countries in the present, he refused to jeopardize the future. The situation was not unlike that of 1919, this time with Poincaré playing the role of Clemenceau. Foch, once again unable to persuade his political superior to wrest the Rhineland from Germany, could not but agree that in these circumstances British friendship was vital for France. Though disappointed by the failure to create an Anglo-French military alliance,

94. Foch Cahiers, Dossier F, May 31, 1922, and July 19, 1922; *Cmd. 2169,* No. 51; Miquel, *Poincaré,* pp. 441-485.

95. Foch Cahiers, Dossier F, September 21, 1923, and November 15, 1923; Millerand, "Souveniers," annexe no. 10.

Foch, like Poincaré, counted on Great Britain coming to France's aid in the event of all-out war. And no matter how preoccupied with and determined to enforce the Versailles Treaty he might be, concern for the distant future was never far from Foch's thoughts.

When Foch turned his attention to the problem of future military organization, it was clear that he saw no real chance, except through diplomacy, for France to attain a strategic position equal to what it had enjoyed in 1914. For at best he made only tentative links between coercive operations and overall military planning; these links were never emphasized, and the general thrust of his thought was to keep the two problems separate. To be sure, detailed, plodding organizational work had never been his forte—he was a dashing strategist who tended to rely on improvisation. Moreover, all the tentative organization plans of the early 1920's would have provided a sufficient number of troops for coercive actions—and quantity was all that the military weakness of Germany required. These essentially economic operations were not calculated to evolve into an instrument for forestalling Germany's eventual military recovery.

Led thus to shuttle mentally back and forth between enforcement of the Versailles Treaty and France's long-range military problems, Foch could not but feel dissatisfied with what had been accomplished in both areas. The occupation of the Ruhr and the military provisions of the treaty had solved nothing; France's alliance system was manifestly weaker than it had been before the First World War. Determined and energetic though he was, refusing to succumb to pessimism, Foch nonetheless seemed unable to escape from his nightmare—to find a way for France with its decimated population and weakened finances to win another war.

3 | Pétain and Parliament: The Formulation and Passage of Military Legislation

Military-Civilian Relations: The Institutional Setting

One of the implicit or explicit themes in writings on French military history of the interwar period has been the presumed struggle between military and civilians over the shaping of policy. To a large extent this assumption derived from the defeat of 1940 and its aftermath of apologia and self-justification. The catastrophe required a search for responsible agents, and for the military the natural place to look was among civilian policy makers, heads of government and their cabinets, parliament, and, more generally, politicians whose practices had impaired the effectiveness of French representative institutions. The underlying thread was the way political figures had ignored or failed to satisfy the legitimate demands made by the military and had thus, in an almost treasonable fashion, undermined French security. Civilian writers, on the other hand, while castigating the military establishment for being stuck in an outmoded routine, have judged the incompetence or misjudgment of only a few individuals as equivalent to treachery.[1]

---

1. For a discussion of the literature about the fall of France, see John C. Cairns, "Along the Road Back to France 1940," *American Historical Review,* 64 (April 1959), 583-604.

Both these views have elements of truth in them, but their partial accuracy is more misleading than helpful. The penchant for depicting French military history as a struggle between military and civilians, regardless of who ends up bearing the burden of responsibility for the defeat of 1940, has obscured the large areas of agreement between the two. In fact, this agreement was the dominant note of the 1920's and was crucial to the formulation of military policy. In the first part of the decade such consensus rested on two very firm foundations: a common understanding of France's diplomatic-military situation—the need to enforce the Versailles Treaty, whose provisions, while assuring a breathing space, could not compensate for French demographic and industrial weaknesses—and a shared desire to reduce as much as possible the military burdens imposed upon the war-weary nation.

To be sure, disagreements could and did arise within this broad framework, but the individuals involved did not necessarily line up according to their military or civilian status. The usual assumption that the military chiefs and civilian leaders acted as two separate blocs does not hold up under a more detailed analysis of the workings of the institutions that formulated military policy. One finds instead that the ties binding co-workers together were substantially more important than whether or not a particular person wore a uniform.

The war minister himself could not but turn to the military for advice. His own insecurity of tenure—more pronounced in the 1930's than in the 1920's, when Maginot and Painlevé each held office for a total of over three years—and relative lack of expertise made him dependent upon the military who largely staffed the War Ministry's bureaucracy. Indeed there was one man whose advice, by virtue of his position, could not easily be ignored. This was the chief of the French Gen-

101

eral Staff. Though his initial appointment rested with the war minister and prime minister—Buat had been named in early 1920 when his good friend Alexandre Millerand became president of the Council—the chief of staff's tenure in office far exceeded that of his immediate political superior. In general it went on indefinitely, that is, until the incumbent died, reached the retirement age, or was promoted to some higher function. More familiar with the bureaucracy and the army than the war minister, the chief of staff was central to the minister's job of presenting military matters to the Chamber and Senate. He prepared answers to parliamentary interpellations and frequently accompanied the minister when the latter appeared before the Chamber or Senate Army Commission. When pressed on a technical point, the minister would often turn to his aide and allow him to supply the response. For the matters that most directly concerned the parliamentary commissions, such as army recruitment and organization, were under the aegis of the chief of staff. It was within the General Staff that the details of French military policy were worked out—mobilization plans, initial deployment of troops, and transportation schedules, as well as gathering intelligence reports on enemy intentions and capabilities.[2]

While the need to collaborate closely on a day-to-day basis—both on matters of military legislation and on a wide variety of long-range projects—led to a modicum of understanding between the war minister and the army officers on the General Staff, the relations between the former and the Conseil Supérieur de la Guerre (CSG) were subject to greater

2. The First Bureau was officially charged with mobilization and organization, the Second with supervising foreign missions and intelligence, the Third with operations and instruction, and the Fourth with transportation.

variations.[3] Composed of the marshals of France, those generals maintained beyond the prescribed age limit, and a maximum of twelve generals designated to become army or army group commanders at the outbreak of hostilities, including the chief of staff, this body was the glittering and prestigious summit of the French High Command.[4] The CSG met, however, only when called into session by the war minister, who acted as its presiding officer. Though charged with advising the minister on all matters relating to army organization, troop instruction, the essential outlines of mobilization plans, programs for weaponry development, and frontier defenses, this august body was often presented with projects already worked out, leaving little opportunity for its members to demand major revisions.[5] Preoccupied with other duties, such as sitting on various commissions within the ministry, where their influence was felt in the first instance, or overseeing the command posts they would assume in case of war, they did not have the time to scrutinize and make detailed suggestions on all matters that came before them. There might indeed be a good deal of dissent, yet it was unlikely that those opposing a particular item would constitute the majority necessary to obtain substantial modifications.[6]

The vice-president of the CSG (no other than Pétain him-

3. For further information on the organization of the War Ministry, see Ministère de la Guerre, Ecoles Militaires, *Cours d'organisation et législation* (Paris, 1921), pp. 33ff.; Contrôleur-général Chareyre, "Organisation de l'administration centrale du Ministère de la Guerre," *Revue militaire française,* no. 10 (April 1922), 47-62.

4. General Maxime Weygand, *Mémoires,* II: *Mirages et réalité* (Paris, 1957), pp. 315-317.

5. *Ibid.,* p. 316.

6. On the frustrations of being a member of the CSG, see the letter from Marshal Lyautey to General Guillaumat, dated November 11, 1926, and published in Léon Noël, *Témoignage d'un chef: le Général Guillaumat* (Paris, 1949), p. 125n.

self) would be named commander-in-chief of the French armies when mobilization was declared, though it was the chief of staff who was charged with preparing the military establishment for an eventual war. Throughout the 1920's there was a certain amount of criticism of thus splitting peacetime and wartime responsibilities between the chief of staff and the vice-president of the CSG. From 1912 to 1914 these functions had been united in the person of Joffre, who had held simultaneously the posts of chief of staff and vice-president of the CSG, and was generalissimo-designate. This system of unified command was not reintroduced until 1935, when Joffre's protégé General Maurice Gamelin was given the multiple positions his former chief had occupied. Yet throughout Pétain's tenure as vice-president of the CSG, relations between him and the chiefs of staff seem to have been smooth.[7] During the war he had worked closely with the two men who were to hold that post in the 1920's, Generals Buat and Debeney. And while it would have been considered demeaning to a marshal of France for him to perform the duties of the chief of the General Staff, "to compel him . . . to dance attendance" on the minister, Pétain's constant contact with that officer—he maintained an office at staff headquarters—meant that he could give his advice or approval before projects became faits accomplis.[8] And of all the members of the CSG Pétain was listened to most attentively and had least reason to be dissatisfied with the advisory role that the CSG was assigned.

The CSG was not the only high level body consulted on war preparations. When questions relating to such measures

7. For Pétain's relations with the chiefs of staff and war ministers, see General A. M. E. Laure, *Pétain* (Paris, 1941), pp. 243-246.

8. War Minister Maginot to the Senate Army Commission, Procès-verbal, February 1, 1922. See Senate Army Commission, Procès-verbal, February 23, 1921.

became involved with the broader issues of industrial mobilization and coordination of the nation's resources—the necessity for which had been driven home by the protracted character of the First World War—decision-making moved from the War Ministry to the Conseil Supérieur de la Défense Nationale (CSDN). An interministerial body attached to the presidency of the Council, the CSDN was specifically empowered to deal with these general problems. It had been created in 1906 with a mixed civilian-military membership and was substantially reorganized after the war. In the early 1920's it included the president of the Council, the service ministers, and those such as the ministers of colonies, foreign affairs, interior, finance, and public works, whose duties impinged on military matters. Throughout the decade it was successively enlarged until it became practically the equivalent to the "Council of Ministers deliberating on questions of national defense."[9]

When the CSDN was thus transformed, the military figures who had sat on it before the war were excluded. The two remaining leaders who were allowed to attend meetings, the vice-president of the Conseil Supérieur de la Guerre and his counterpart for the navy, were granted only consultative rights. Yet a body as unwieldy as this was in no sense equipped to study or oversee the means for executing general policy. And in the different commissions and subordinate bodies that formed the core of the complicated structure, military advisors were once again in a crucial position. The Commission d'Etudes, an organization that was itself divided into numerous sections, prepared the questions that were then considered by the CSDN and was largely staffed by

9. J. Vial, "La défense nationale: son organisation entre les deux guerres," *Revue d'histoire de la Deuxième Guerre Mondiale,* 5, no. 18 (April 1955), 14.

military men. Of even more importance was the secretariat-general, since it had the responsibility not only of coordinating the work of the Commission d'Etudes, but of overseeing the execution of the CSDN's decisions. The secretariat-general became the motor force for studying the problems of how to utilize all of France's resources in wartime. It was directed initially by General Bernard Serrigny, who had been a close associate of Pétain during the war and had been one of the rare officers who even before 1914 had been passionately concerned with industrial mobilization, and subsequently by General Louis Colson. Both men were widely respected and worked harmoniously with their immediate civilian superiors.[10]

This close intermeshing reinforces the observation already made, that the crucial distinctions did not coincide with military as against civilian status. As was true in the War Ministry, political leaders were perforce dependent upon military advice, though to whom they listened was a matter of choice. It thus becomes relevant to ask what qualities enabled a military chief to gain such a favored position. Here, personality and temperament seem to have been crucial. To work smoothly with civilian colleagues, a military man had to give evidence of a breadth of view embracing political as well as military realities; he had to show that he saw beyond the boundaries of his profession and understood the public pressures that impinged on the ministers and men in parliament. Even when substantive issues seemed to divide some members of the government from a few military figures, as when Paul-Boncour disagreed with Weygand in 1932 over French dis-

10. *Ibid.,* pp. 11-33; see also Senate Army Commission, Procès-verbal, December 2, 1921; "Le mois militaire," *Revue militaire française,* no. 2 (August 1921), 241-247; no. 7 (January 1922), 103-110; no. 13 (July 1922), 116ff; and Laure, *Pétain,* pp. 266-267.

armament proposals, temperamental incompatibilities and differences of job definition made a large contribution to the acerbity of the discussion.[11]

No matter how close an understanding existed between the war minister and his most intimate military collaborators, such rapport did not insure the final realization of their plans. These plans could not be carried out until the Chamber and Senate had their say. It was in the parliamentary setting, more specifically in the relations between the War Ministry and the Senate and Chamber Army Commissions, that deference to military advice and the recognition of common concerns acted as a kind of cement, binding together a sizable group of military and civilians alike.

The Chamber and Senate Army Commissions that were formed after the elections of 1919 were distinctive in their high percentage of members who had had military experience. These retired officers maintained numerous contacts with former colleagues and thus were kept abreast of army life—all of which augured well for the army's chances of finding a sympathetic response to its desires and difficulties.[12] But even without this complement of former military men, the commissions would have been disposed to consider favorably the demands of the war minister. The experience of sitting on these particular bodies for some time induced many members to assume a protective attitude toward the army and to defend the military establishment as their special

11. For an excellent discussion of this incident, see Philip Charles Farwell Bankwitz, *Maxime Weygand and Civil-Military Relations in Modern France* (Cambridge, Mass., 1967), chap. 2.
12. For a discussion of military men's adaptation to political careers, see Mattei Dogan, "Les officiers dans la carrière politique du Maréchal Mac-Mahon au général de Gaulle," *Revue française de sociologie,* 2, no. 2 (April-June 1961), 88-99.

interest. Within the Senate Army Commission, at least, there was no echo of the more intangible antagonisms that led the military to be mistrustful of politicians as a whole. Such a co-operative ambiance and such mutual concerns prompted the minister to be quite open before the commissions—though in this regard there was a notable difference between the Chamber and the Senate. While considering the majority of the Chamber group trustworthy, and collaborating closely with a number of its members, the minister was wary before the body as a whole, lest its few antimilitary deputies leak information or create difficulties. Such anxieties seemed to weigh much less heavily on the minister when he appeared before the Senate Army Commission, where no such extremists sat.[13]

The cooperative relations based on shared values were strengthened by the senators' acceptance of the military's estimate of defense problems. Although many members of the Senate Army Commission were versed in the technicalities of military legislation and frequently wrote their own proposals concerning army organization and the length of military service, they did not have a comprehensive vision of strategic and tactical planning. And rarely did the minister or his military advisors present a fresh outlook or raise unexpected considerations before that body. In fact the military's presentation tended to reinforce the senators' narrow perspective. On the occasions when Chief of Staff Buat appeared before the group to discuss army organization, he shaped the conversation in terms of finding the effectives for manning the divisions needed at the start if mobilization were to proceed successfully.[14] With such guidance it is not surprising

13. War Minister Barthou to the Senate Army Commission, Procès-verbal, June 8, 1921.
14. Buat's testimony before the Senate Army Commission, Procès-verbal, February 23, 1921 and October 13, 1922.

that the commission members never went beyond considering the problem as one of numbers, and simply relied upon the minister and his staff to make the appropriate decisions in matters of strategy and tactics.

To ascertain the army's needs and to defend its honor were these senators' primary concerns. More particularly the commission members were ever on the alert to bring to the minister's attention difficulties afflicting the officer corps, the non-coms, and the ordinary conscripts. Yet on questions such as age limits and those related to the rejuvenation of the officer corps, the members wavered back and forth, caught between their sympathy for the plight of the older officers and recognition of the difficulty of satisfying their demands. Similarly while the recruitment of young officers and even more of non-coms was a continual source of concern, the Senate Army Commission rarely ended its discussions with unequivocal suggestions for assuring it.[15] As for protecting young soldiers, one heated exchange occurred when War Minister Louis Barthou made it clear that commission members would not be allowed to go themselves to interrogate the troops serving in the Rhineland about their living conditions.[16]

Indeed, pressing the minister on the malaise that afflicted the army and the state of matériel epitomized the senators' conception of overseeing the military establishment and exercising civilian control. A significant example of this attitude was the commission's examination of aviation production—a subject to which numerous meetings were devoted. Even though several commission members exhibited considerable virtuosity in discussing the characteristics of the various airplane models then in use, such displays of knowledge were

15. Senate Army Commission, Procès-verbal, June 9, 1920.
16. *Ibid.*, June 8, 1921.

incidental to their main concern. The senators repeatedly demanded to know how many frames and how many motors were operational. Above all they hoped to make sure that the army would have the necessary equipment, that the experience of 1914, when artillery ammunition had been in short supply, would not be repeated.

At the same time the senators wanted assurances that the money appropriated would be well spent. In these matters the commission and the war minister alike shared what could be considered by today's standards rather antiquated notions of industrial production. Recognizing that modern equipment rapidly became out of date, they sought to limit as much as possible the investment in a potentially obsolete item—even to the point where orders fell below the minimum necessary for economical mass production. Stockpiling of inventories, now so accepted a part of both our economy and our military industry, was quite alien to their way of thinking. Linked to this antipathy for waste were plans to restore old matériel, mostly artillery equipment, or, as with airplanes, to use old parts in new models. Lest the slowdown of war production that followed the end of hostilities leave too many trained hands idle, War Minister André Lefèvre suggested utilizing these people to manufacture typewriters or sewing machines, with the proviso that plans be made for a speedy conversion back to producing war matériel.[17]

Throughout the 1920's both the Senate Army Commission and the war minister operated within straitened financial circumstances that hampered armament programs as well as

17. *Ibid.,* June 9, 1920; compare Lefèvre's testimony before the Senate Finance Commission, Procès-verbal, July 15, 1920. See also joint meetings of the Senate Army and Navy Commissions, Procès-verbal, May 31, 1922, and June 7, 1922.

attempts to redress the grievances of the officer corps and stimulate long-term enlistments. Budget cutting was the order of the day—to counteract years of inflationary deficit spending and to shore up a precarious exchange position.[18] But because it was the commonly agreed-upon cure to French financial ills, this imperative did not set ministry and parliament at odds. In fact War Minister Barthou told the Senate Finance Commission that he considered "reduction in the budget of the War Ministry as a form of national defense . . . ; contributing to the reduction of expenses" meant "contributing to the national defense."[19] To be sure, such consensus did not rule out haggling over specific items, but an atmosphere of camaraderie suffused most Senate Finance Commission discussions, and rarely did the members cut an appropriation over the minister's firm insistence.[20]

Thus when the Senate Army Commission failed in its mission of relieving the army's distress, it was not for lack of care; it was rather because financial and political considerations seemed to the senators as well as to the military to form insuperable obstacles. In short, military leaders had little reason to complain about and much to be satisfied with their reception by the Senate Army Commission. And in confronting the overwhelming political pressure for reducing the length of military service, the senators and military men would show once again a solidarity in practice that belies the sterotype of civilian-military hostility that historians have subsequently imposed upon them.

18. For the clearest and most comprehensive discussion of French financial mismanagement in the early 1920's, see Stephen A. Schuker, "The French Financial Crisis and the Adoption of the Dawes Plan" (Ph.D. diss., Harvard University, 1968), chap. 2.

19. Senate Finance Commission, Procès-verbal, December 17, 1921.

20. For example, see the discussion of armament expenditure, *ibid.*, December 20, 1921.

Fixing the Limits of Disagreement and Debate

Ever since 1919 the cry to reduce the length of military service had arisen from every segment of the political spectrum. In the wake of victory, French political and military leaders had foreseen the possibility and desirability of a one-year term of service. As foreign policy commitments sorted themselves out, and more particularly, as the difficulties in making Germany fulfill its treaty obligations became apparent, the feasibility of such a drastic shortening of the time spent under the colors became doubtful. Although government leaders never relinquished the ideal of one-year service, they agreed that its implementation would have to be postponed. In the early 1920's their immediate concern was to decide upon a term of service and an organizational structure that would enable French leaders both to cope with current foreign policy difficulties and at some future date to reduce still further the country's military burdens.

The impact such decisions would have on the future military position of France should have been a crucial consideration. While German recalcitrance in complying with the treaty was troublesome and politically and financially vexing, the real threat posed by France's powerful neighbor would not appear for a number of years. Yet when the length of military service became a public issue, French politicians were careful *not* to grapple with this problem or did so in an ambiguous and gingerly fashion. Unable to face potential dangers and equally unable to deny them altogether, the men attempting this delicate balance needed the reassurance that consensus alone could provide. What emerges, then, from examining the initial stages of French military legislation is the variety of ways such agreement was reached, and, simultaneously, the drama of men guarding themselves against too complete and too devastating a recognition of future intractabilities.

Above all France's leaders had to find a way of handling the Cassandras who insisted on envisaging a too-harsh reality. Since all agreed that Germany would remain a continual threat to French security, blatant disregard of those who warned persistently against any lessening of vigilance vis-à-vis Germany was not entirely feasible. It was impossible for the majority who wanted to relax after the strains and sacrifices of the war to dismiss out of hand, as belonging to another mental universe, the minority among their colleagues who maintained that no respite could be permitted.

Moreover the warnings of some figures, by virtue of their prominence and the positions they held, could not be totally ignored. In fact, the most serious public dissenter to a hasty reduction in the length of military service was the war minister himself, André Lefèvre. Appointed in January 1920, he owed his position to his long-time friend, the new Prime Minister Alexandre Millerand. Like Millerand he had moved from the Left in the course of his career—largely because of his growing concern with problems of national defense; unlike Millerand, however, he did not develop the social and domestic political attitudes consonant with such an evolution. His commitment to the Right remained narrowly defined. Indeed, his obsessive and exclusive concern with his country's defense prevented him from becoming a member of the inner group of parliamentarians among whom ministerial posts were so often traded. Temperament, too, foreclosed such a role. Simple and direct in manner, Lefèvre lacked the polish of his more prominent colleagues. Before the Senate Army Commission he always appeared a little hesitant and almost self-deprecating. He seemed most at ease and self-assured when he could quote facts and figures or elaborate on the technical aspects of armament manufacture—perhaps an outgrowth of the education he had received at the Ecole des Mines.[21]

The first public hint that all was not well between Lefèvre and his cabinet colleagues appeared in October 1920. Early in the month he had laid before the Chamber Army Commission a recruitment proposal calling for a two-year term of service. This plan not only ran into opposition in the Chamber group but failed to gain support from his fellow ministers. The discussion within the cabinet was heated, with both Georges Leygues, who had taken Millerand's place as prime minister when the latter became president of the Republic, and Millerand himself opposing the minister of war. Lefèvre offered his resignation, which was refused, the cabinet attempting to keep its internal disagreements private rather than to provoke a public discussion.[22]

The issue that divided Lefèvre from his colleagues was one of numbers: would eighteen-month service provide enough men to enable France to enforce the treaty as well as fulfill its colonial obligations? Behind this quantitative dispute lay Lefèvre's pessimistic assessment of Germany's current military capabilities; far from disarming, he claimed, France's traditional enemy was manufacturing arms and ammunition and might at any moment fall upon the victor of 1918. Throughout October and November, the debate over the

21. Interviews with Jacques Millerand, October 11, 1966, and October 23, 1966; Senate Army Commission, Procès-verbal, 1920, *passim.*
22. *Echo de Paris,* October 8, 1920; October 20, 1920.

length of military service continued behind closed doors. Nevertheless the occasional leaks in the press indicated that Lefèvre was wavering between accepting the cabinet's demands and doggedly maintaining his own position. And at the end of November he publicly announced his acceptance in principle of an eighteen-month term of service.[23]

Lefèvre gave way very reluctantly. Pressure from his cabinet colleagues was obviously an important factor in his decision. More particularly, the repeated interventions on behalf of eighteen-month service by his long-time friend Millerand must have weighed heavily. Finally Lefèvre's failure to gather influential military support behind him must be added to the balance. Indeed, one might speculate that this was the crucial element, for he earlier had had reason to believe such assistance would be forthcoming. Lefèvre had received corroboration for his gloomy estimate of current German military strength from no less a figure than Marshal Foch. The latter's cahiers are dotted with the kind of pessimistic assessment of Germany's failure to disarm that lay at the heart of Lefèvre's contentions. Moreover, Foch too remained skeptical about France's ability to carry out coercive actions against a recalcitrant Germany with less than two classes available and trained. And it was to Foch that Lefèvre looked most often for military advice.[24]

To what extent Foch did or did not actively second Lefèvre's initial stand in favor of two-year service is unclear. The circumstantial evidence suggests, however, that the marshal did

23. *Ibid.,* October 28, 1920; November 15, 1920; November 17, 1920; November 18, 1920.
24. See, for example, Foch Cahiers, Dossier E, December 2, 1919; June 2, 1920; December 11, 1920. That Lefèvre relied heavily on advice from Foch is clear from the gossipy news reports published in the *Echo de Paris* during the last quarter of 1920.

not interfere with the government's wishes. In fact, Lefèvre made his announcement accepting the principle of eighteen-month service directly after a meeting with Foch.[25] Even if the marshal had been obstinate in resisting the proposed reduction in the length of service, he would almost certainly have been in a very small minority within the Conseil Supérieur de la Guerre. Although reports that this body was unanimously in favor of an eighteen-month term might be taken with a grain of salt, the constant repetition of these claims suggests that a substantial majority backed the government.[26] Whatever misgivings the military may have felt were quieted by assurances that the length of service would not be reduced until a corresponding reorganization of the army had been worked out.[27] In addition, it was specifically stipulated that the new term of service would be dependent on a substantial increase in the number of career military men (not including officers), native Africans or Indo-Chinese serving under the colors, and civilian employees replacing soldiers in essentially nonmilitary jobs.[28]

Having been thus led to agree to the principle of eighteen-month service, potential army or governmental dissenters found that their original objections could no longer be invoked. Lefèvre himself fell victim to this stratagem, for when he abruptly submitted his resignation in mid-December the force of his act was undercut by his earlier agreement in

25. *Ibid.,* November 18, 1920.
26. *Ibid.,* December 14, 1920. See also Prime Minister Leygues' speeches to the Chamber of Deputies, JOC *Déb.,* December 17, 1920, p. 3727; December 24, 1920, p. 3986.
27. The length of military service had already been reduced from three to two years. The bills calling up the classes of 1921 and 1922 had incorporated this reduction. At the same time, through clauses in various finance bills, a start toward de facto reorganization of the army had been made.
28. *Echo de Paris,* December 15, 1920, p. 3.

principle to eighteen months. What had happened was the following. After considerable prodding by the Chamber Army Commission, the government had undertaken to place before parliament within a few days legislation concerning army recruitment and organization. The cabinet's decision to expedite the transmission of these proposals to the Chamber had in fact been made in Lefèvre's absence. Tired and ailing, he had gone to take the cure at Vichy. When he heard of the cabinet's action, he rushed back to Paris, and upon Millerand's urging he presented the legislation. A week later he resigned.[29]

Although Lefèvre's resignation caused a stir and Prime Minister Leygues was questioned sharply in the Chamber on the day the news broke, the latter was able to side-step the issues that had caused difficulties between Lefèvre and his cabinet colleagues.[30] Lefèvre himself, wishing to avoid a direct confrontation with his former ministerial chief, did not attend the session. He bided his time for another week while the press continued to debate the matter, waiting until the discussion of the war budget was underway before making his appearance. Even then he refused to challenge the government directly. He did not, as he had done earlier in cabinet discussions, insist on the fragility of France's current military position. Instead he gave a rambling speech elaborating on the demographic superiority of a malevolent Germany and the possibility of joint German-Bolshevik action in eastern Europe.[31] But having accepted the proposed reduction in the length of military service, which he scrupulously refused to

29. *Ibid.,* December 4, 1920; December 8, 1920; December 9, 1920; December 10, 1920; December 17, 1920.
30. JOC *Déb.,* December 17, 1920, pp. 3727ff.
31. *Ibid.,* December 23, 1920, pp. 3942ff.

renounce, Lefèvre could not openly deny the argument made by Lt.-Col. Jean Fabry, the chief spokesman on military matters for the moderate Right, that eighteen-month service would cope with whatever danger Germany posed at that time.[32] With no alternative plan, Lefèvre laid himself open to Leygues' well-aimed retort: "Systematic criticism is easy; but it leads nowhere. To raise an alarm is also easy, but that's a more serious matter."[33]

Indeed it was as an alarmist that the press dealt with Lefèvre, and the efforts to undercut his dissent took the form of psychological criticism.[34] As early as October 1920, his disagreement with the other ministers had been minimized as the product of a pessimistic imagination. "It is no secret," wrote Marcel Hutin, the editor of the *Echo de Paris,* "that André Lefèvre . . . is . . . an extremely nervous man and that his nervousness, according to his colleagues, leads him to take a gloomy view of things."[35] *Le Temps,* on the other hand, attributed Lefèvre's estimate of the danger posed by Germany to his scientific education, which made him deduce a certainty from a mere possibility. Whatever one may think of this notion of scientific reasoning, the inference that possibilities might be dismissed because future events could prevent their coming to fruition was rather bizarre. The writer did not, however, rest content with this conclusion, but buttressed his discounting of Lefèvre's opinions by invoking the authority of the Conseil Supérieur de la Guerre and the cabi-

32. *Ibid.,* December 23, 1920, pp. 3948-3949.
33. *Ibid.,* December 24, 1920, p. 3988.
34. Lefèvre had exposed himself to this kind of attack when he maintained in his letter of resignation—evidently composed for the historical record—that a differing perception of the German threat was the real issue between him and his former colleagues. The letter appeared in the *Echo de Paris,* December 17, 1920.
35. *Ibid.,* October 20, 1920.

net.[36] In similar vein the *Echo* cited assurances that had been given by Leygues as settling "the eternal quarrel of . . . *tant-pis* with . . . *tant-mieux.*"[37]

What thus emerged from Lefèvre's resignation was not only a general agreement that an eighteen-month term of military service would be the maximum demanded of the country, but a pattern of justification, or, if you will, rationalization. The dangers posed by Germany, while not denied, were pushed into the background: since they were not an immediate reality, reckoning with them could be postponed or avoided. General de Castelnau, an outstanding military leader during the war and after 1919 a rightist deputy and president of the Chamber Army Commission, summed up the prevailing mood when he declared: "I should not like to carry for thirty years a burden that weighs heavily on my shoulders, in order to forestall an eventuality that will materialize in fifty years; I shall simply ask you for a 'breathing space' if that is at all possible."[38]

The two men who followed Lefèvre as war minister, Louis Barthou and André Maginot, showed a dexterity or flexibility that Lefèvre had so obviously lacked. They succeeded in keeping in equilibrium a recognition of France's external peril and politically acceptable length of military service. Indeed at the time of Lefèvre's resignation, Barthou, quite apparently maneuvering to resume a ministerial portfolio, had questioned sharply Leygues' soothing assessment of the current German threat. Yet in almost the same breath the statesman who had achieved his place in French history as

36. *Le Temps,* December 18, 1920.
37. *Echo de Paris,* December 25, 1920.
38. JOC *Déb.,* December 23, 1920, p. 3944.

the champion of the three-year service law of 1913 had taken pains to underline his acceptance of the government's proposed military legislation.[39] Such careful balancing, while assuring Barthou's acceptability in Center and Center-Right coalitions, still managed to give the impression of resoluteness and determination.

Similar talents were displayed by Maginot, who had served as minister of pensions in 1921, the year in which Barthou was at the Rue Saint-Dominique. When Poincaré formed his ministry early the following year and combined the pensions post with the War Ministry, giving them both to Maginot, the appointment was widely approved. Indeed Maginot's mere personal presence helped gain confidence and support from the Right and moderate Right. His imposing physique, carried somewhat awkwardly on two crutches, but with a certain majesty, made a deep impression. Early in the war, one of Maginot's legs had been severely injured and was thenceforth stiff and unusable. His incapacity did not, however, prevent him from pursuing an active and amorous Parisian social life, and it proved to be an invaluable trump in his political career. Sergeant Maginot became something of a folk hero and the natural leader of veterans' organizations, while the physical courage he had displayed in overcoming his handicap led people to believe that similar perseverance would characterize his handling of military affairs.[40]

39. *Ibid.,* December 17, 1920, p. 3731. For a short but evocative sketch of Barthou, see Ignotus, "Etudes et portraits: M. Louis Barthou," *Revue de Paris,* 29, no. 21 (November 1, 1922), 77-82.

40. It should be noted that Maginot had served briefly as under-secretary in the War Ministry before 1914. Two very laudatory and superficial treatments of Maginot's life are: Pierre Belperron, *Maginot of the Line,* trans. H. J. Stenning (London, 1940); Marguerite Joseph-Maginot, *The Biography of Andre Maginot: He Might Have Saved France,* trans. Allan Updegraff (New York, 1941).

Maginot, moreover, was careful to cultivate, or perhaps merely fortunate to find, suitable military support for his neat balancing act. In January 1922, when he replaced Barthou as war minister, Maginot simplified or regularized his relations with the technical experts of his ministry by interposing Marshal Pétain between himself and the other military leaders, more particularly the chief of staff. By a decree dated January 18, 1922, Pétain was named inspector-general of the army and given supervisory powers over all questions relating to war preparation. Henceforth the chief of staff was obliged to submit to Pétain, for the latter's endorsement, all pertinent documents before passing them on to the war minister.[41] By simply following Pétain's recommendations, which would be laid before him in tidy form, Maginot could be spared the difficult task of immersing himself in the complex workings of the French military establishment.

The decree provoked lively discussion within parliament and the press. Senators and deputies expressed concern lest civilian control over military affairs be undermined.[42] In response, Maginot claimed that this new arrangement constituted a partial return to the prewar system, in which the generalissimo-designate had also been chief of staff, and that

41. AN, 130 AP 18: Décret nommant le vice-président du Conseil Supérieur de la Guerre, Inspecteur général de l'armée. Article V, which was the crucial article, read as follows: "Vis à vis de l'état-major général, l'Inspecteur général de l'armée exerce une direction supérieure. Il donne au chef d'état-major général toutes directions utiles. Inversement, le chef d'état-major général soumet à l'examen de l'Inspecteur général de l'armée toutes les questions visant l'organisation, l'instruction et la mobilisation. Les pièces correspondantes, dont la signature est réservée au Ministre, portent le visa de l'Inspecteur général. Ce dernier peut, en outre, être consulté par le Ministre sur les travaux émanant des divers services de l'administration centrale autres que l'état-major général." Jacques-Louis Dumesnil Papers.

42. Senate Army Commission, Procès-verbal, February 1, 1922; JOC Déb., January 19, 1922, pp. 57ff; Echo de Paris, January 18, 1922; January 21, 1922; January 26, 1922; January 27, 1922.

it quite properly gave Pétain additional control over the preparation of the forces he would command in the field. At the same time, Maginot clearly distinguished between the technical and the political aspects of his own job. Pétain's new authority, he argued, would be exercised exclusively in the former domain: "It is a matter . . . only of purely technical questions, those that are within the sphere of action of the General Staff and on which the vice-president of the Conseil Supérieur must be consulted. His endorsement is required for these matters alone. For other questions . . . the endorsement of the inspector general is not mandatory."[43] Maginot, at least, had no fear that technical decisions would undermine political choices already made.

Pétain may well have shared the view of his own job that André Lefèvre advanced in the course of the Chamber debate. Lefèvre objected to the decree on the grounds that the marshal might jeopardize his prestige by being forced to enter into discussions of detail; rather, Pétain's stature should be safeguarded to facilitate his future wartime role.[44] In fact Pétain was never one to be obstinate over minor points. He did his utmost to synchronize army reorganization with the political imperative of a reduction in the length of military service. His cooperative and comprehending attitude maximized the possibilities of an effective relationship between High Command and civilian leadership. No wonder successive war ministers worked so closely and harmoniously with the hero of Verdun.[45]

In fact, Pétain's intervention on military questions suggested that he adopted as his own the tactics that had enabled politi-

43. JOC *Déb.*, January 19, 1922, p. 58.
44. *Ibid.*, January 19, 1922, p. 57.
45. See Laure, *Pétain*, pp. 244-245.

cal leaders to undercut the force of Lefèvre's dissent: achieve agreement on principle first and thus reduce opposition to a quibble. Thereafter one could concentrate on whittling down the conditions on which this agreement had been based—if the fulfillment of such conditions should prove impracticable.

On the crucial question of proceeding with the proposed reduction in the length of military service despite the failure to recruit additional professional cadres, it is quite clear that Maginot had the marshal's support. At the end of 1920 the CSG had agreed to eighteen-month service on certain technical conditions, notably that the number of professional military men be substantially increased. By 1922 it had become apparent that the government could not in the present or the near future fulfill this condition. Low pay, outside economic opportunities, and uncertainty about retirement benefits were hindering the recruitment of the required number of cadres. Yet Pétain made it clear that such noncompliance with the earlier stipulations should not stand in the way of the proposal to cut the term of military service.[46]

The marshal actually used this very failure to give further support to his argument that only a division composed of three infantry regiments was practicable. The controversy within the CSG over the organization of the individual division may have seemed a minor technical question, but its resolution highlighted how Pétain managed to reinforce a political choice already made. The CSG had initially favored a division composed of four rather than three infantry regiments, that is, a "square" as opposed to a "triangular" division. Each type had its advantages and disadvantages. The square division, with its corresponding artillery, had greater

46. Senate Army Commission, Procès-verbal, October 19, 1922.

firepower than the triangular, and its higher complement of men enabled it to remain longer in the line. In fact, it was only in 1917, when France had been desperately short of effectives, that Pétain had instituted the triangular formation. Subsequently he became a firm advocate of this organization, arguing that the lighter division could be more readily deployed by the High Command.[47] Whatever the relative merits of these two types of division, or the possible value of employing the two simultaneously—the lighter one to move rapidly in initial operations, the heavier one to hold the ground taken—discussion was foreclosed by the decision in favor of eighteen-month service.[48] For if the CSG were to stick to its initial preference for the square division, and if this view were to be accepted, an eighteen-month term of service would be indefinitely postponed.[49] On two occasions, nevertheless, more than half the members of the CSG voted in favor of the square formation. Subsequently, Maginot justified his overriding of the majority opinion by citing a memorandum prepared by Marshal Pétain. In this particular instance, in order to discount the slight majority, Maginot had given triple weight to Pétain's advice.[50]

With technical objections foreclosed and with a term of eighteen months long since agreed upon as the maximum length of service, Maginot might well feel satisfied and secure. The government and its chief spokesman for military affairs had gained the confidence and solidified the support of the Right and moderate Right. Such self-assurance would be

47. Commandant A. M. E. Laure, *Au 3ème bureau du troisième G.Q.G.* (Paris, 1921), pp. 254-259.

48. For interesting suggestions about simultaneous use see the article by Jacques de Prechac, *Echo de Paris,* September 28, 1923, p. 4.

49. War Minister Maginot to the Senate Army Commission, Procès-verbal, October 19, 1922.

50. Senate Army Commission, Procès-verbal, October 19, 1922.

much in demand when the military legislation finally came to the Chamber floor. For here new challenges threatened to unmask the fears that lay behind the general reluctance to grapple with France's long-range military problems.

Apprehensiveness Unmasked

By the time the recruitment legislation reached the floor of the Chamber in February 1922, fourteen months after it had been transmitted to that body's Army Commission, the terms of the debate had changed. The task confronting the government and its parliamentary spokesmen was no longer one of rallying support for eighteen-month service but of staving off a still further reduction, to one year or less. Such was the essential element of the counterproposals presented by Radicals, Socialists, and scattered members of Poincaré's own coalition. Accompanied by differing organizational schemes, the proposals had the common effect of reopening questions that had long since seemed resolved. To justify eighteen-month service as a present necessity, the government and its backers in the Chamber were forced to recall the international situation and France's foreign policy, and more significantly to elaborate on the nature of the military operations that the reorganized army would be in a position to undertake.

It was ironic that what Lefèvre had been unable to do, that is, to provoke a serious discussion of French military policy, the Left should now succeed in accomplishing. For the assault on the government's legislation was by no means simply a rhetorical display of antimilitarism. Although political motives certainly lay behind the advocacy of one-year service, those who presented counterproposals were raising serious questions about military organization and operations. And these were the grounds on which they had to be answered.

In so doing the government and its defenders exposed their profound desire to avoid another war. Both Right and Left were haunted by the same nightmare: a second holocaust that would result in the sacrifice of still another generation of young Frenchmen. Yet at the same time as these shared sentiments were being expressed, the ostensible assurance of the Right remained unimpaired. Their very stand against a further reduction in the length of military service confirmed their feelings of self-confidence. They were thus able to screen from full consciousness the impact their emotional revulsion from the idea of another war would have on their own determination.

The first move of the government's spokesmen in defense of eighteen-month service was to renounce the arguments they had used against André Lefèvre and to take that champion of military preparedness into camp. What had once been accepted, that Germany's present state of weakness permitted France a breathing space during which military burdens could be drastically reduced, was now denied.[51] While thus persuading the public at large, and most of all themselves, that they were alert guardians of France's security, the government and its supporters demonstrated that their watchfulness was intermittent. The debate suggested, as had the incident of Lefèvre's resignation, that rather than relentlessly facing present or future dangers, they might summon

51. See Fabry's speech, JOC *Déb.*, March 22, 1922, p. 1006. Also note the difference in tone between Fabry's first and second reports on the recruitment legislation presented on behalf of the Chamber Army Commission, JOC *Doc.* 1921, annexe no. 2710, pp. 1713ff., and *ibid.*, 1922, annexe no. 3776, pp. 37ff.

up or ignore these terrors depending upon the extent to which such invocation was necessary to buttress arguments for a military policy deemed the maximum that was politically feasible.

In the course of the debates, Lefèvre himself returned to the attack, offering an amendment that would continue two-year service during an indefinitely stated transition period. Repeating his now familiar warnings, he emphasized Germany's manpower and industrial resources, which he claimed could be mobilized with great rapidity at the beginning of hostilities. His remarks were greeted with enthusiasm and the public posting of his speech was voted by a large majority. [52]

The previous day Maginot had stressed the related problem of German disarmament. Progress in that area, he had pointed out, was shrouded in uncertainty: Germany still had more than six million trained veterans, and France had been unable to bring about the "moral disarmament" of its former enemy.[53] At the same time as government spokesmen emphasized Germany's war potential and the evidence of its failure to disarm, they expressed the hope that even partial compliance with the treaty, by disrupting the continuity of military training in the Reich, might break the spell of German militarism. A policy of firmness, they argued, if practiced long enough, might effect a transformation in German mentality; yet they admitted that this line of conduct, followed since 1919, had to date produced no such change.[54] Having stressed the present lack of success in enforcing German disarmament, the government and its supporters could

52. JOC *Déb.,* March 17, 1922, pp. 894-902; see also Lefèvre's speech, *ibid.,* June 22, 1922, pp. 1930ff.

53. *Ibid.,* March 16, 1922, p. 860.

54. See Fabry's speech, *ibid.,* February 28, 1922, p. 561; also Poincaré's remarks, *ibid.,* April 6, 1922, p. 1424.

not help but see that this failure was simply a premonitory sign of future perils.

Though underlining the dark side of France's situation vis-à-vis Germany, ministers and deputies still refused to let their own forebodings determine current policy. Fabry, the *rapporteur* for the military legislation, while arguing that the international outlook demanded vigilance and the maintenance of a powerful military force, refused to speculate on what future dangers might require. He pointed out that French security was presently at a maximum; when the time came to evacuate the Rhineland, the situation would be vastly altered. Yet the Chamber's Army Commission, he reported, had refrained from "seeing beyond the occupation of the Rhine." It has said: "I am building my system on this occupation. This occupation is in effect for fifteen years; I refuse to look farther."[55]

Despite its applause for Lefèvre's arguments, the government had no intention of accepting his substantive proposals. At no time did the ministers even admit the possibility of putting off eighteen-month service until the conditions initially laid down by the Conseil Supérieur de la Guerre had been carried out. These commitments had been undercut by the government's decision to push for the immediate enactment of an eighteen-month term.[56] The Cabinet went still further to accommodate those who favored proceeding directly to a reduction in the length of service to one year. Both Maginot and Poincaré repeatedly affirmed the government's understanding of its present proposal: eighteen-month service was merely a stage on the way to a one-year term. They readily accepted the clause in the legislation that com-

55. *Ibid.,* March 2, 1922, p. 593.
56. See Maginot's remarks on this point, *ibid.,* March 21, 1922, p. 967.

mitted the government to review the feasibility of one-year service in 1925.[57] The contrast between accepting Lefèvre's arguments and such pronouncements was starkly apparent when Poincaré remarked that everything André Lefèvre had said, all the statements that the deputies had applauded, argued "even more strongly against a too precipitate descent toward one-year service," while simultaneously reaffirming his own desire for that minimum term.[58] In such a fashion were assessments of the menace from across the Rhine manipulated to accord with the dictates of popular political demands.

On the basis of so ambiguous an evaluation of the international situation, the government could not, nor did it try to, rest its case for specific military proposals. Jean Ossola, a Left Republican deputy and the drafter of a counterproposal for one-year service, pointed out quite rightly that the bleak side of the cabinet's presentation, if consistently maintained, should lead to recommending two- or three-year service.[59] Although it was clear that political concerns and not overall military assessments set a maximum limit on the length of service, the government and its supporters did argue that the immediate goals of French foreign policy currently ruled out the possibility of going below an eighteen-month term. Such a term was essential if France was to continue its course of enforcing the Versailles Treaty. This point was made over and over again and became a staple of the government's case.

Just as in 1919, at the time of the Rhineland controversy, when Foch had claimed that the Rhine frontier would enable

<hr>

57. Maginot's testimony before the Senate Army Commission, Procès-verbal, March 24, 1922; October 13, 1922.
58. JOC *Déb.*, April 6, 1922, p. 1424; April 4, 1922, p. 1404.
59. *Ibid.*, March 22, 1922, p. 995.

France to enforce the treaty in semi-automatic fashion, so now the government and its spokesmen argued that eighteen-month service alone would provide what amounted to a reflex response. France must have troop superiority over Germany, General de Castelnau asserted, in the event that the kind of pressure exerted in 1920 and 1921 should have to be renewed or extended; such measures might continue to be necessary to enforce France's just claim to reparations.[60] Without the requisite troops, Fabry maintained, German violation of the treaty would place France in a difficult dilemma, compelling it either to retreat or to call up large additional forces to settle a minor incident.[61] In the course of the parliamentary discussion, however, the restricted character of such measures was made even more explicit.[62] And in defining their conception of these police actions, the deputies and senators half-consciously exposed doubts and hesitancies about their own loudly proclaimed prescription for French policy—the strict enforcement of the Versailles Treaty.

Coercive operations had initially received the firm backing of the Senate Army Commission. Its members had assumed that with the effectives available, such tasks could be easily handled. Indeed it was on this understanding that the Senate Army Commission had readily supported the government when it had decided upon coercive actions. War Minister Louis Barthou had been careful to reassure the commission members, shortly before Düsseldorf, Duisburg, and Ruhrort were occupied in March 1921, that the operation was a simple matter that could be accomplished "very rapidly and in the most auspicious fashion."[63] Barthou's prediction had

60. *Ibid.,* March 21, 1922, p. 963.
61. *Ibid.,* March 2, 1922, p. 598.
62. Compare above, "The Versailles Treaty and French Military Planning," in Chapter 2.
63. Senate Army Commission, Procès-verbal, February 23, 1921.

proved correct so far as this particular maneuver went. In May 1921, however, he and Prime Minister Briand had found it necessary to recall the class of 1919, recently liberated from the colors, in order to back up the government's threat of further occupations if the Germans did not fulfill their reparations and disarmament agreements. This partial mobilization had run into a certain amount of difficulty. Not only was it the first time that such a step had been taken, but the measure involved, simply recalling one class, had proved to be a particularly unsatisfactory expedient. A solitary class lacked the encadrement necessary for active participation in military operations—several classes, at least, would have had to be called up before any of them would be ready for action. Barthou had found himself in the embarrassing, if not ironic, quandary of having recalled a class and then being uncertain what to do with it.[64]

The Senate Army Commission had been dismayed by this dénouement, and throughout the Chamber discussion of early 1922 the deputies insisted again and again that the experience of 1921 must not be repeated. Although the Left pointed out that fewer effectives would be provided by the proposed legislation than were currently available, the government's spokesmen continued to maintain that eighteen-month service, accompanied by the reorganization of the army, would be adequate. With the number of standing units reduced, they claimed, the divisions designated to participate in such actions (six stationed in the Rhineland and six of ready reinforcements) would be able to perform their duties without the recall of any reserves.[65] France was thus led,

---

64. Barthou to the Senate Army Commission, Procès-verbal, June 8, 1921.
65. See dispute between Daladier and Fabry, JOC *Déb.*, March 15, 1922, pp. 831ff.

Castelnau argued, "to maintain [the necessary forces] on a permanent footing" so as "to avoid frequent, upsetting, and sometimes useless call-ups," which the enemy would "contrive to provoke . . . in order to spread . . . lassitude, debilitation, and discouragement and to bring about the abandonment of our just claims."[66]

The restrained character of coercive actions was further and more significantly emphasized by Maginot when he underlined the pacific quality of these police operations. Such actions, he maintained, had "nothing in common with plans for war or annexation, and their only aim" was "to assure us, in expectation of payments due . . . , the temporary possession of certain securities."[67] The i's were dotted and the t's were crossed when Ossola claimed, and the government concurred, that "the Rhine Army must suffice" if an operation was going to be "legal and peaceful"—otherwise the country would no longer be in a peacetime situation.[68]

Above all, deputies and senators alike were unambiguous in insisting that coercive operations not be a prelude to war. War Minister Maginot readily understood these doubts and reassured his parliamentary colleagues that he had no intention of allowing France to be sucked into a military confrontation with Germany. For while deputies and senators clearly supported such actions against Germany, they did not want to unleash the French military machine for essentially nonmilitary operations. Similar doubts about the political feasibility of using military means for nonmilitary ends were shared by the army leaders themselves. Foch chafed at

66. *Ibid.,* March 21, 1922, p. 963; see also Fabry's speech, March 2, 1922, p. 598.
67. JO Sen. *Déb.,* March 22, 1923, p. 465.
68. JOC *Déb.,* March 22, 1922, p. 994.

France's inability to force Germany to execute the treaty, yet at the same time recognized that military measures more drastic than those actually employed would be inappropriate.[69] Thus, although it was a commonplace that a strong military establishment was essential to intimidate Germany, the parliamentarians insisted, and Maginot agreed, that coercive operations should be performed without recourse to mobilization.[70]

Such views were explicitly stated; their implications, however, were not. Clearly coercive actions to enforce the treaty must be a limited liability, militarily, and politically and financially too. Such measures would be acceptable only so long as Germany remained militarily passive. How myopic were British diplomats of the period in viewing France as a militarist power aiming at European hegemony![71] Similarly, how misguided were future historians in describing the abandonment of coercive operations after 1924 as a fundamental change in French policy.[72] Correctly understood, these actions were something of a luxury that could be dispensed with if they proved too costly or dangerous.

In almost the same breath as government spokesmen insisted that coercive actions should not be prelude to war, they asserted the vital necessity of taking advantage of the initial superiority, in effectives and matériel, with which the Versailles Treaty had provided their country. The govern-

69. Foch Cahiers, Dossier E, January 1921; and Dossier F, March 1923.
70. Senate Army Commission, Procès-verbal, June 7, 1922; October 13, 1922.
71. See, for example, British Cabinet Papers, Cab. 23/25: 40/21 (4), May 24, 1921, and Cab. 23/30: 44/22 (1), August 10, 1922.
72. See, for example, Frederick Lewis Schumann, *War and Diplomacy in the French Republic* (Chicago, 1931); Bertrand de Jouvenel, *D'une guerre à l'autre,* I: *De Versailles à Locarno* (Paris, 1940); René Albrecht-Carrié, *France, Europe and the Two World Wars* (New York, 1961).

ment and its backers repeatedly contended that French security rested upon maintaining their country's military superiority; the prewar balance of armed power—which because of Germany's greater resources was potentially a serious imbalance—must not be re-established. As Fabry expressed it:

The victory [of 1918] tipped the [prewar] balance in our favor. On the day you should allow this balance to be re-established, and if by chance you gave Germany the impression that the new balance was once again tipped against us, you would have fulfilled the most cherished wish of a large part of German opinion. For Germany, owing to its population, which is much larger than ours, and its extraordinarily developed productive capacity, would once more . . . escape all control.[73]

The means prescribed for fulfilling this imperative were seriously flawed. Just as contemporary military writing indicated that France's army leaders were unsure of how they could best bring to bear their country's military superiority, so the Chamber discussion echoed the same uncertainty. The concreteness with which various operations were outlined should not obscure the profound hesitancy about taking the military initiative. Indeed the precision itself was largely specious, and while it merely heightened the sense of unreality that pervaded the debates, it helped convince the government and its supporters that they had insured France's safety.

In early 1921 Barthou had testified before the Senate Army Commission that both the Conseil Supérieur de la Défense Nationale and the Conseil Supérieur de la Guerre had agreed upon thirty-two divisions as the basis of the army's reorganization.[74] Though Foch suggested in his private notebooks that this number had been arrived at in a rather arbi-

73. JOC *Déb.*, February 28, 1922, p. 559.
74. Senate Army Commission, Procès-verbal, February 23, 1921.

trary fashion, he did not make his disagreement public.[75] Indeed, figures designating effectives for the different theaters of operation, that is, metropolitan France, the Rhineland, North Africa, and the colonies, were frequently added to and subtracted from with arithmetical dexterity but with little detailed justification.[76] Now, however, this figure of thirty-two took on almost magical qualities.[77]

The peacetime deployment of these divisions was clear enough: six to be stationed in the Rhineland, six in reserve to furnish reinforcement for coercive operations or cover for the arrival of additional troops, and twenty to be distributed among the corresponding number of military regions into which France was divided, there to provide the nucleus for training conscripts and for eventual mobilization. Only the first twelve were to be maintained at full strength, though it was claimed that the others could be brought to combat readiness with a minimum infusion of reserves. While the regionally based divisions moved forward, certain elements would remain behind to provide for the mobilization of a second, and possibly even a third and a fourth wave. In order to man the full complement of divisions, an eighteen-month term of service was essential; in fact, to descend below this minimum would render impossible the maintenance of the magic thirty-two.[78]

The majority supporting the government was in fact easily

75. For Foch's comments about army reorganization and the length of military service, see his Cahiers, Dossier E, February 1919; October 25, 1920; November 25, 1920; December 10, 1920; January 10, 1921; Dossier F, February 11, 1922; February 17, 1922; March 24, 1922; July 19, 1922.
76. See, for example, JOC *Déb.*, March 2, 1922, pp. 596-597.
77. See, for example, Buat's testimony, *ibid.*, April 4, 1922, p. 1399.
78. Senate Army Commission, Procès-verbal, February 23, 1921; see also Maginot's testimony before the Senate Army Commission, Procès-verbal, October 13, 1922.

convinced that thirty-two divisions were the minimum necessary both to coerce Germany and to maintain their country's advantage. At the same time they agreed that an eighteen-month term of service was the maximum that was politically acceptable. Caught between these two requirements, the parliamentary defenders of their nation's security could not effectively question the strategic assignment of France's military forces; to do so would threaten one or the other of their two fixed points. Thus the most incisive questions came from those outside the consensus—from those who doubted the advisability of any offensive maneuver at all.

The opposition in the Chamber was quick to point out that with a standing army consisting of only thirty-two divisions, whatever operations were to be launched at the outbreak of hostilities must be limited in scope. A decisive victory with such a force was out of the question: the Radical spokesman Edouard Daladier doubted that it would be "possible . . . to root out the German concentration on the banks of the Weser or the Elbe or in the region of Magdeburg"; if the French should try to do it, they "would risk falling into a trap."[79] Indeed the spokesmen of the opposition were skeptical that the full thirty-two divisions, which the government referred to as the covering army, could be utilized for initial operations. Only the twelve divisions kept at full strength in peacetime would, they claimed, be capable of undertaking immediate action. And to engage these forces before the rest of the troops stationed in metropolitan France had been transported to the front they considered much too hazardous.[80]

Far from suggesting that France should maintain larger

79. JOC *Déb.,* March 15, 1922, p. 826.

80. In JOC *Déb.* see the remarks of Bénazet, March 10, 1922, p. 740; Ossola, March 10, 1922, p. 751; Paul-Boncour, March 28, 1922, pp. 1189-1190. And also Fourment, JO Sen. *Déb.,* March 2, 1923, p. 475.

forces in order to make initial operations less risky, the opposition proposed a further diminution of their country's military strength. The essence of the four counterproposals presented by the Left Republicans Paul Bénazet and Jean Ossola, by the Radical Edouard Daladier, and by the Socialist Joseph Paul-Boncour was as follows: since the forces to insure the success of such operations were not available, the army would be obliged to wait until a substantial proportion of its reserves had been mobilized before engaging in any action. The government in fact admitted that the twenty divisions regionally distributed would not be ready for combat without an infusion of reserves. The opposition simply wanted to increase this percentage, at the same time making clear that until the bulk of the reserves had been mobilized, their nation's posture must be strictly defensive. Indeed, they argued, the task of mobilizing the country's entire manpower and industrial resources should be the prime concern of the French military establishment. Such a complete mobilization, however, could be accomplished with a shorter term of service or a smaller number of standing divisions than the government was proposing.[81]

A more novel and striking suggestion for army reorganization was made by Jacques Duboin, a Radical deputy who had been an aide to General Estienne and who borrowed the latter's most imaginative thinking. Duboin took great pains to outline a new kind of army based on modern technology, arguing that the defenses provided through national mobilization might easily be turned by a well-equipped and highly mobile German army. France could avoid this danger, he

81. See JOC *Déb.* for the views of Bénazet, March 2, 1922, pp. 602-606, and March 10, 1922, pp. 737-746; Ossola, March 10, 1922, pp. 747ff., and March 22, 1922, pp. 944ff; Daladier, April 6, 1922, pp. 1412-1415; Paul Boncour, March 28, 1922, pp. 1181ff.

pointed out, by organizing such a force itself. Composed of 100,000 men, capable of advancing 150 kilometers during a single night, these troops would be much more effective than the 600,000 soldiers who, according to the government's plan, required a week for mobilization. The force proposed by Duboin would be capable of immediate action in enemy territory—a more realistic prospect, he contended, with this kind of army than with the one outlined by the government. Unfortunately Duboin's own suggestions regarding recruitment and training—he ruled out a priori a professional army— were totally inadequate for establishing such a force, resting as they did on one-year service and the calling up of individual reservists.[82]

The defenders of the official legislation ignored Duboin's suggestions, while agreeing that modern technology might well have changed the character of warfare. Sticking, however, to the more traditional forms of army organization, they concentrated on answering the main critical points made by the opposition.

Initially Maginot had argued that if war was *"imposed"* on France, the nation should be prepared to exploit its occupation of the Rhineland as a base for operations designed to hinder German mobilization. The covering army must be ready for immediate action: "from the start of hostilities" it must be "capable . . . of advancing, of occupying certain strategic points . . . necessary to the concentration of the German forces, and of seizing . . . securities which, once in French possession, would make the enemy's industrial preparation difficult and perhaps impossible."[83] In the course of the debates, however, the government and its supporters were

82. *Ibid.,* March 14, 1922, pp. 785ff.
83. *Ibid.,* March 16, 1922, p. 860.

careful to emphasize that such operations would not be risky and that the mobilization of the nation's resources would not be jeopardized. In essence they maintained that the French advance would be so limited in scope as to pose no threat of excessive and possibly dangerous involvement. As Maginot phrased it, there was no question of "adventurous" moves that might "compromise the future . . . through over-hasty engagements." It was a question, rather, "of protective operations of limited range, carried out with prudence."[84] This caution was underlined when Maginot concurred in the interpretation of the extent of these operations given by Hector Molinié, a Left Republican deputy:

Since you certainly have no intention—you have said so and I congratulate you on it—of going as far as the Elbe and the Spree, as far as Berlin and Hamburg, in order to carry out a kind of thrusting guerrilla operation, your argument means nothing more than to say that it is on the Ruhr and in the direction of Essen that you will take your securities.[85]

Above all, such actions seemed designed to provide France with a new defensive position and to give it the means, Fabry claimed, to establish its resistance on the Rhine so solidly that the German command would find that river impossible to cross.[86] And behind the protection offered by this barrier, national mobilization could proceed safely. If France suffered the misfortune, Poincaré argued, to be attacked once again, it should proceed to the mobilization and concentration of its forces under the shelter of a covering position

84. JO Sen. *Déb.*, March 2, 1923, p. 466.
85. JOC *Déb.*, March 14, 1922, p. 776.
86. *Ibid.*, March 10, 1922, p. 741.

on the Rhine so secure that the national territory would not be threatened until the process had been completed.[87]

Indeed when Maginot described the wartime deployment of French forces, even the notion of an advance by the six divisions stationed in the Rhineland and the six standing by as reinforcement seemed to evaporate. Arguing for the necessity of thirty-two divisions, the war minister maintained that they were essential because of the extent of the frontiers that the army would have to guard in the event of war.

> From Basel to Cologne . . . the distance is approximately five hundred kilometers. It is moreover about the same distance, or more exactly, the same extent of front that we will have to cover when, having evacuated the Left Bank of the Rhine, we will be back within . . . our political frontiers, with this difference, however, that this new front, being more exposed, will be much more difficult to protect than our present line along the Rhine. For fronts of such an extent—and with two divisions remaining in the interior in any case—to have thirty divisions at our disposal is not excessive. It is these thirty divisions that really constitute our covering force in the event of war.
>
> If we leave five of these thirty divisions in reserve . . . twenty-five divisions remain for a front . . . extending about five hundred kilometers.
>
> In other words, each of these divisions will have a front of twenty kilometers to protect, which corresponds fairly closely to the normal covering capability of a division.[88]

With such deceptively specific assurances for safeguarding French mobilization and concentration, the issue of operations to be undertaken at the beginning of hostilities was allowed to drop. What had emerged, however, from the ambiguous and, in the end, inconclusive discussion of initial

87. *Ibid.,* April 6, 1922, p. 1424.
88. JO Sen. *Déb.,* March 2, 1923, p. 466. Maginot made similar remarks to the Chamber, JOC *Déb.,* March 16, 1922, p. 861.

moves was the tacit understanding that the next war might be much like the last. Having admitted, at the very least, that operations undertaken at the outbreak of hostilities were unlikely to prove decisive, the government and its defenders were forced to consider the prospect of another war of stabilization and attrition. Much as the military implicitly recognized certain advantages in this kind of warfare,[89] if conducted at a minimal cost in French lives and matériel, so the deputies hoped that the next time the fighting would take place on German territory. France still held, Fabry claimed, such clear territorial advantages that in the event of a war of attrition that might "last four or five years," the conflict could be "definitively installed . . . on the enemy's soil."[90]

The debate was most accurately summarized by the Communist deputy Renaud Jean:

You tell us on the one hand: an army is necessary. On the other hand, you say you are renouncing offensive warfare. Thus you don't want any more victories. Consequently you are building your army to prevent defeat.[91]

Clearly he was correct: the discussion of the operations to be undertaken by the covering army indicated that the government was unwilling to start a war with offensive maneuvers of much scope. When indeed, or under what circumstances, other than a German attack, the country would feel obliged to go to war remained obscure: the necessity to avoid war rather than the imperative to defend certain national interests, with its accompanying risk of renewing hostilities, was the most common theme. "If there is one thing," Maginot

89. See above, "The Legacy of the First World War," in Chapter 2.
90. JOC *Déb.*, March 10, 1922, p. 741.
91. *Ibid.*, March 15, 1922, p. 835.

declared, "that has been proved about modern warfare—whose means of destruction can only get worse—it is that even victory does not compensate for the disaster of an invasion."[91] Victory itself, at the price of another conflict like that of 1914-1918, was considered almost the equivalent of defeat. When the president of the Chamber objected to Renaud Jean's remarks, he unconsciously underlined this equivalence: the concern of the Chamber, he declared, was "not to avoid defeat, but to avoid war and invasion."[93]

Yet the governmental majority felt satisfied that they had adequately provided for their country's security. And it was true that as long as Germany remained militarily weakened, an eighteen-month term of service would not jeopardize France's safety. Indeed Maginot described voting for the legislation as an act of "clairvoyance," one which carefully balanced the need for security with the desire to reduce the time spent under the colors.[94] Moreover, the mere fact that they had staved off the more drastic demands of the Left enhanced the majority's self-esteem. For it was only after strenuous efforts by Poincaré to keep his coalition together, including posing the question of confidence on a few key points, that the recruitment legislation was passed by the Chamber—though with a substantial Radical defection—in June 1922. The Senate voted the legislation in April of the following year, after a much briefer debate, but one that covered essentially the same ground. The accompanying proposals concerning the technicalities of organization and the status of cadres and effectives were not passed by the Chamber until March 1924. The Senate, however, had no chance to

92. Senate Army Commission, Procès-verbal, October 13, 1922.
93. JOC *Déb.*, March 10, 1922, p. 835; see also Maginot's remarks, March 16, 1922, p. 860.
94. *Ibid.*, March 16, 1922, p. 867.

consider this supplementary legislation before parliament was dissovled prior to the election held in May of that year. The reorganization of the army was thus incomplete, and the work of the Bloc National would have to be reviewed by the Left majority that triumphed at the polls.

4 | From the Ruhr to Locarno via Morocco

The Election of 1924 and the
Liquidation of the Ruhr Occupation

The years following the election of 1924 and the end of the Ruhr occupation have often been described as a new era in international relations. Even at the time, the Locarno agreements of late 1925 were interpreted as signaling the pacification of Europe, or at least the strong possibility that such could be accomplished: the legacy of the war, it seemed, might be amicably settled, with the continent no longer divided into hostile camps of former belligerents. These were the hopes of the participants in the diplomatic drama of the mid-decade, and the illusions with which they were taxed after the catastrophe of 1940.[1]

To the French and more particularly to Aristide Briand, their foreign minister throughout most of this period, went

1. See, for example, Viscount D'Abernon, *The Diary of an Ambassador,* III: *Dawes to Locarno 1924-1926* (New York, 1931); André François-Poncet, *De Versailles à Potsdam: La France et le problème allemand contemporain 1919-1945* (Paris, 1948), chap. 6; Jacques Chastenet, *Histoire de la Troisième République,* V: *Les années d'illusion 1918-1931* (Paris, 1960), chaps. 6 and 7; Bertrand de Jouvenel, *D'une guerre à l'autre,* I: *De Versailles à Locarno* (Paris, 1940), part 5.

the initial approbation and the subsequent reproof for what came to be called "the spirit of Locarno." Although French statesmen in fact contributed to the altered language of international affairs, the doctrinaire and often dogmatic pronouncements of some figures on the Left should not lead one to conclude that such an ideology was the mainspring of French policy. Quasi-pacifist and internationalist rhetoric never obscured the prime objective—to provide for France's security by cementing ties with former and potential allies. While this policy now came clothed in the garb of collective security arrangements, French leaders were rarely fooled or misled by the disguise. They applied more traditional standards to these new offerings and accepted them only when they understood that nothing else was available.

It is the years before 1924 that now seem to be full of illusions—the years when the weakness of France's international position was obscured by attempts to collect reparations and the hopes that such efforts encouraged. Though implicit in the costly victory of 1918 and the precarious peace that followed, this fragility stood clearly revealed only with the end of the Ruhr occupation. Indeed France after 1924 had little opportunity for major initiatives and small chance for directing European diplomacy; the nation's foreign policy leaders were forced to adapt, with as good grace as possible, to the pressures exerted by other powers.

The victors of the election of 1924 took great pride in asserting that their triumph at the polls marked a decisive turning point in French politics, and more particularly in foreign policy.[2] Yet the disparate nature of the electoral alli-

2. See, for example, the editorial in *Le Progrès Civique,* May 17, 1924.

ance, consisting of Radicals, Republican-Socialists, and Socialists, and campaigning under the banner of the Cartel des
Gauches, belied these claims. Though such symbolic gestures
as the eviction of Millerand from the Elysée, and the trans-
ferral of the ashes of Jaurès to the Panthéon might appear as
quasi-revolutionary acts, the major thrust of Cartel policy
was considerably more moderate. The new parliamentary majority did not represent a substantial shift in the distribution
of popular votes; it owed its existence, in large measure, to
the complicated system of proportional representation that
had been enacted in 1919. Reaping the benefits that this law
bestowed upon electoral coalitions and that had originally
worked to the advantage of the Bloc National, the Cartel now
gained almost fifty seats more than it would have received
under a strict system of proportional representation. Moreover, the Chamber majority was dependent upon the amor-
phous Center-Left, comprising the nationalist splinter of the
Radicals and the *Républicains de gauche.* Without the support of these deputies, the Cartel, reduced to its original
sponsors, would have fallen just short of a majority.[3]

A sharp conflict between two alternative foreign policies
was not central to the electoral campaign. It was the financial
crisis of late 1923 and early 1924 that, more than anything
else, led to a new constellation of political forces. Domestic
concerns moved to the forefront as the cost of living soared
and the value of the franc declined on foreign exchanges.
Although the franc had been temporarily rescued by the time
the nation went to the polls, the wrangling over the tax legislation, deemed mandatory for stabilizing the currency, had

3. André Siegfried, *Tableau des partis en France* (Paris, 1930), pp. 123-141;
Georges Lachapelle, *Elections législatives du 11 Mai 1924* (Paris, 1924), pp. 5-55
(for a breakdown of popular vote see the table on pp. 26-27).

left its mark. The parliamentary battles, while ending in the passage of the *double décime,* had so split the Center that Poincaré's strategy of a union of moderate groups proved impossible. When the Radicals injected into the electoral campaign such seemingly outworn issues as clericalism and educational policy, Poincaré, unwilling to repudiate his traditional laic views, refused to ally himself with the more conservative supporters of his foreign policy. He watched, almost from the sidelines, as the Cartel triumphed, suspecting that the victors' success at the polls would entail no drastic change in policy.[4]

Moreover, despite the fact that the executive committee of the Radical party in January 1923 had ordered its parliamentary members to abstain from voting the occupation of the Ruhr, only a minority of the deputies and none of the senators had obeyed this injunction. Thereafter the Radical group in the Chamber supported the government.[5] As Edouard Herriot, the leader of the party, explained repeatedly: while he had reservations about the initial move, once French troops and prestige were engaged, success became the prime national interest.[6] This stance was typical of the parliamentary Radicals; seldom innovators in foreign policy, content with vague, even incompatible, pronouncements upholding the Versailles Treaty and favoring international cooperation, they bowed to the pressures exerted upon them. Diplomacy had never been their strong point, and their whole cast of mind, concentrated on provincial politics and parlia-

4. For changes in public opinion see surveys made for the minister of the interior, AN F⁷ 12967: Rapports mensuels, 1923-1924.
5. Jean Carrère and Georges Bourgin, *Manuel des partis politiques en France* (Paris, 1924), pp. 128-129.
6. JO Sen. *Déb.,* July 11, 1924, p. 1050.

mentary supremacy, militated against its becoming their central focus.[7]

Nor was Edouard Herriot, the man designated as the next president of the Council, likely to reorder the mental universe of his followers. Having acquired an extensive literary culture and having developed an extraordinary forensic talent, he took great pleasure in exhibiting these skills while paying homage to the credos of Radical orthodoxy. His obvious humanity and good will, confirmed by his physical appearance—his sloppy dress, his vast girth, and his ever present pipe—made him appealing, if not always reassuring, to those beyond the confines of his own party. Nevertheless, for all his sincerity and real devotion to France's interests, Herriot had little preparation for the tasks he was about to undertake. He had held a cabinet post only briefly, serving as minister of supply in charge of coal distribution during the winter of 1916-1917. His tenure in office had coincided with a particularly brutal season, and he had proved unable to alleviate the suffering of his shivering countrymen. As longtime mayor of Lyon, a position he continued to occupy even while president of the Council, he was notably more successful. A novice in diplomacy, often overwhelmed by the unfamiliar complexities of foreign affairs, Herriot was sustained by the hope that he could rise to the greatness thrust upon him.[8]

7. For an excellent discussion of Radical ideology, see Peter J. Larmour, *The French Radical Party in the 1930's* (Stanford, Calif., 1964), chap. 2.

8. On Herriot see his own memoirs, *Jadis,* II: *D'une guerre à l'autre 1914-1936* (Paris, 1952); Michel Soulié, *La vie politique d'Edouard Herriot* (Paris, 1962); J.-L. Antériou and J.-J. Baron, *Edouard Herriot au service de la République* (Paris, 1957); for shorter descriptions see, Larmour, *The French Radical Party,* pp. 50-51; Joseph Paul-Boncour, *Entre deux guerres: Souvenirs sur la IIIe République,* II (Paris, 1945), pp. 87-88; Albert Thibaudet, *La République des professeurs* (Paris, 1927), pp. 33-35, 101, 209-211.

Aware of both the difficult problems he faced and his own relative lack of expertise, Herriot was prepared to proceed with caution and to be accommodating to those defeated in the election. Such moderation, however, ran contrary to the programmatic views of the other major element in the Cartel, the Socialist party. The Socialists, unlike the Radicals, had staked out independent positions on all major foreign policy questions. Unalterably opposed to the occupation of the Ruhr, they had long ago devised a scheme for scaling down reparations, commercializing international indebtedness, and linking these plans to a reduction in interallied war debts— this last resting on an unrealistic faith in the generosity of France's former allies. Nor did the Socialists accept what had been the cornerstone of French foreign policy, the sanctity of the Versailles Treaty. But here, as an alternative to the strict legalism that had characterized Poincaré's conduct of French diplomacy, the Socialists offered only professions of faith in international justice and morality. Such a juxtaposition of appeals to international good will with concrete proposals and, even more frequently, with accurate criticisms of the weakness of France's diplomatic position, was typical of the Socialists' public rhetoric. And while their moral appeals might express an abiding faith in the noblest sentiments and ideals, in the eyes of moderate and conservative deputies they rendered the Socialists unfit to play a commanding role in shaping French policy.[9]

Indeed Léon Blum, who had emerged as the leader of the democratically minded rump of the old Socialist party after the Communists split off in 1920, had adopted a most ambig-

9. For the Socialists' program and analysis, see speech by Léon Blum, JOC *Déb.*, August 22, 1924, pp. 3010-3021; correspondence between Albert Thomas and Vincent Auriol, early 1924, AN, 94 AP 387, Albert Thomas Papers.

uous stance vis-à-vis the French political system. Trying to reconcile the revolutionary and reformist wings of his own party, Blum rejected Socialist participation in the Cartel government, while pledging to support the new ministry. He later formalized the principles of Socialist nonparticipation in the almost obscurantist distinction he drew between "exercise of power" and "seizure of power." His devotion to the party and to the task of rebuilding its shattered organization—with its growth in the 1920's bearing eloquent testimony to his abilities—as well as his profound attachment to the humane principles it espoused, produced a disturbing intellectual deformation. A man with great analytical talents, having had a successful career both as lawyer and as literary critic before entering politics, Blum became a prisoner of his party's unquestioning internationalism and pacifism and of its doctrinaire lack of concern with problems of military policy.[10]

It was only among the reformist wing of the party that there was any serious consideration of military problems. Joseph Paul-Boncour, less urbane and cosmopolitan than Blum, but no less at home in respectable legal and administrative circles, became the party spokesman on military affairs. Owing his initial political experience to his work as assistant to Waldeck-Rousseau, he had been a Socialist in principle long before becoming one by party affiliation. A parliamentary leader without an organizational base, Paul-Boncour chafed under the party's ban on ministerial participation and its parochial refusal to assume responsibility for

10. On Léon Blum, see Gilbert Ziebura, *Léon Blum: Theorie und Praxis einer sozialistischen Politik,* I (Berlin, 1963), chaps. 6-12; Joel Colton, *Léon Blum: Humanist in Politics* (New York, 1966); James Joll, *Three Intellectuals in Politics* (New York, 1960), part 1.

France's national defense. In 1931, when the party reverted to its obstinate prewar stand of voting against defense credits, Paul-Boncour left its ranks. But throughout the 1920's he tried to reconcile the Socialist orientation on military policy with the imperatives of national defense. It was a difficult task and not without its inconsistencies. While aligned with Pierre Renaudel, the other major figure on the reformist side of the Socialist party, in advocating a reorganization of the army that would permit a reduction in the length of military service to nine months, Paul-Boncour also worked tirelessly, in his capacity as newly appointed director of the study commission of the Conseil Supérieur de la Défense Nationale, to obtain the enactment of legislation regulating the use of France's resources in case of war.[11]

Paul-Boncour's ambiguous stance—a refusal to accept constant military tension as a condition of life, along with a profound concern for the nation's safety—functioned as the common denominator for the Cartel. What had previously been confined to military debates now moved to center stage in foreign policy: the magnitude of the war losses and the passionate desire to avoid another such blood-letting. As Herriot put it: "Before finding out whether we live rich or poor, we must find out whether we are going to be alive at all."[12] And though no Frenchman would disagree with so poignant a formulation, it was the leaders of the Cartel who were forced to face up to the consequences of France's attempt to live beyond its means.

No pacifist sentiments, no Cartel rhetoric expressing deep

11. On Joseph Paul-Boncour see his memoirs, *Entre deux guerres: Souvenirs sur la IIIe République,* 3 vols. (Paris, 1945-46).
12. JO Sen. *Déb.,* July 11, 1924, p. 1059.

emotional responses to the tragedies of war, determined the end of France's efforts to collect reparations through coercive actions. Earlier Herriot had promised that he would not relinquish the Ruhr occupation until new guarantees for payments had gone into effect.[13] But at the London Conference, which met in July and August 1924, he proved unable to carry out this pledge; and in failing to do so, Herriot and the Cartel took upon themselves the onus of having abandoned strict enforcement of the Versailles Treaty. At the same time it was not fully appreciated to what extent Herriot's hands had been tied and the settlement he agreed to had evolved from Poincaré's policy. While Poincaré's reputation was spared and he subsequently emerged to save the franc, the Left's image suffered at the hands of those who sought a scapegoat for their country's weakness.[14]

Although it had been clear from the debates over the eighteen-month law that coercive actions were something of a luxury, in the sense that they were nonmilitary in conception and must proceed without recourse to mobilization, the moderate and conservative deputies who had voted this legislation did not anticipate that a little more than a year after its passage, these operations would be abandoned with such finality. Having implicitly decided that coercive actions must be a limited liability, they did not foresee their potential cost, nor the still higher price France would have to pay in liquidating the most important undertaking for which the military legislation had provided, the occupation of the Ruhr.

In the fall of 1923 Poincaré had clearly demarcated the boundaries of his policy. After the end of German passive

13. Herriot, *Jadis,* II, 138.
14. See, for example, Pertinax's article, *Echo de Paris,* August 25, 1924.

resistance, when the guarantees France had seized had finally become productive, Poincaré had taken no initiative toward a permanent and unilateral settlement of the reparations question. He had attempted neither to restructure German industry nor to encourage the possibilities of Rhenish separatism. Either move would have led to a rupture with Britain, a price he was not willing to pay. Financial considerations had also weighed heavily. In the winter of 1923-24, French financial difficulties had mounted in a new crescendo, in part the legacy of years of fiscal and monetary mismanagement, in part the result of foreign speculation on the franc. In order to save the exchange value of the currency, Poincaré had negotiated a credit from the Morgan bank. The precarious stability of the franc and its dependence on the confidence of Anglo-American financial markets thus further limited the risks that France could afford.[15]

Unable to settle unilaterally the outstanding diplomatic problems with Germany, Poincaré had been led to accept an international solution to the reparations question. And once having acquiesced in the broad scope of the Experts Committee proposed by Britain and the United States, he found it impossible to reject their report—the Dawes Plan. While no power, and certainly not France, could have turned down their unanimous recommendations, Poincaré still hoped to rescue something of France's position. In the forthcoming negotiations to implement the Dawes Plan he counted on tenacious bargaining, on resisting any infringement on the rights of the French-dominated Reparations Commission to declare default in the future, and on clinging at the very least

15. See Poincaré's defense of his behavior, JO Sen. *Déb.*, August 26, 1924, pp. 1295ff.; Stephen A. Schuker, "The French Financial Crisis and the Adoption of the Dawes Plan" (Ph.D. diss., Harvard University, 1968), chaps. 3 and 4.

to a skeletal military occupation of the Ruhr until other guarantees had become operative. No longer president of the Council in charge of French diplomacy, Poincaré elaborated these points for Herriot's benefit in a marathon speech delivered in the Senate shortly before the London Conference opened. Like a stern school-master, the former prime minister indicated the pitfalls and complexities that lay ahead, only occasionally allowing a hint of superciliousness to appear.[16]

After a month of extremely difficult and often tense negotiations, a month that Herriot described as "the most painful of his life," the new president of the Council was forced to concede the points that his predecessor had indicated as crucial.[17] But it was far from clear how Poincaré would have been able to resist the combined pressure of intransigent British diplomats and Anglo-American bankers. For these latter were determined to deny the French the legal basis for coercive operations and thus prevent them from again acting unilaterally to collect reparations. To that end they were insistent on restricting the authority of the Reparations Commission to declare default. Only then would the bankers be willing to undertake floating the loan that was essential for the implementation of the Dawes Plan. The complicated formula by which the Reparations Commission was shorn of its power is of little importance here. Suffice it to say that Herriot was left with the painful choice of either agreeing to the Anglo-American demands or allowing the conference to break up. Having accepted the Dawes Plan, France's diplo-

16. JO Sen. *Déb.*, July 10, 1924, pp. 1019-1038; on the Dawes Plan, see Rufus C. Dawes, *The Dawes Plan in the Making* (Indianapolis, 1925).
17. JO Sen. *Déb.*, August 26, 1924, p. 1314.

mats could not reject the conditions on which its success depended.[18]

Similarly, although Poincaré, free from Herriot's ideological predisposition toward an early evacuation of the Ruhr, had been intent on bargaining over this point, he would have soon found that the question of military withdrawal offered little opportunity for skillful maneuvering. In fact the legal basis on which he had justified the occupation would have acted to tie his hands. For French diplomats had consistently maintained that the presence of their country's troops in the Ruhr was simply an instrument for assuring reparations payments and that it was not vital for France's security. Once new methods that would guarantee these payments were worked out, once direct economic exploitation was terminated, it became exceedingly difficult to justify prolonging the military occupation. In addition, this juridical position doomed to failure the attempts of General Charles Nollet, former chief of the Interallied Military Control Commission and now minister of war in the Cartel government, to link military withdrawal with France's security problems, and more particularly with the still unresolved question of German disarmament. In the event, France's diplomats proved unable to exploit the occupation to force Germany's compliance on disarmament. They reaped no advantage from their presence in the Ruhr, and Herriot finally agreed to evacuate with a year's delay.[19]

18. This discussion of the London Conference rests heavily on Schuker, "The French Financial Crisis and the Adoption of the Dawes Plan," part 2; see also Jacques Bardoux, *Le socialisme au pouvoir: L'expérience de 1924* (Paris, 1930).

19. The Belgian foreign minister, Paul Hymans, thought that Poincaré would also have been forced to evacuate the Ruhr; see his *Mémoires,* II (Brussels, 1958), p. 576.

Moreover, despite Poincaré's belief that delaying the withdrawal would be France's trump in the negotiations, Herriot found that the British prime minister, Ramsay MacDonald, held the aces. MacDonald made it very clear that unless a satisfactory settlement was reached regarding the Ruhr, his government would not promise to keep its troops in the Cologne zone of the Rhineland after January 1925—the date stipulated for evacuation, but conditional upon Germany's fulfillment of its obligations.[20] Although withdrawal from this—the first zone of occupation—was theoretically a separate question, discussion of the issue was unavoidable. Both MacDonald and Herriot were interested in raising the subject, the former to exert pressure on the French, the latter to get some agreement on a matter so vital to his own country's security.[21] As it turned out, a minor British concession disguised what was in fact a cruel blow to France: while MacDonald and his colleagues, who had wanted to withdraw from the Cologne zone as early as possible, were induced to remain there temporarily by the Reich's continued and flagrant violations of the disarmament clauses, they made it clear that their interest in these matters was fleeting at best.

Indeed the real significance of the London Conference for the French lay in the fact that the continued occupation of the Rhineland, the basis of their nation's defense, was called into question. It had always been their claim that because of Germany's failure to fulfill its obligations, the delays stipulated by the treaty for evacuation had not yet begun to run. Herriot had reiterated this interpretation before departing for London.[22] But in the course of the conference he had aban-

20. *Echo de Paris,* July 28, 1924; August 10, 1924; August 11, 1924.
21. On the military importance of the Cologne zone, see *ibid.,* September 22, 1924; December 1, 1924.
22. JO Sen. *Déb.,* July 11, 1924, p. 1059.

doned the traditional formula. The importance of this change should not, however, be exaggerated. For the twin bases—reparations and disarmament—on which France's juridical position had rested had already been undermined. When the French lost their ability to obtain a declaration of default, nonpayment of reparations ceased to figure not only as the basis for coercive operations but as a possible justification for extending the Rhineland occupation.[23] Similarly the fact that Herriot had obtained British consent to delay the evacuation of the Cologne zone only by agreeing that such withdrawal would not be indefinitely postponed, made it clear that German failure to comply with the disarmament clauses of the treaty would offer no more than a short-lived justification for prolonging the French presence on the Rhine.

If the disarmament clauses could not serve that purpose, then their value was minimal indeed. For no one, least of all military authorities, had ever thought that control over Germany's military potential would be effective. As Brigadier-General J. H. Morgan, who had served as legal officer of the Control Commission noted: "The truth is that . . . the real security of Europe is not to be found in the results achieved, or likely to be achieved, by the Control Commission, or any Committee organized by the League of Nations."[24] Foch had continually underlined the chimerical quality of German arms limitation; Nollet made a similarly bleak assessment after serving five years as chief of the Control Commission.[25]

23. Poincaré himself had contemplated withdrawal, even ahead of schedule, if a modus vivendi on reparations could be established. For new evidence on this question, see Schuker, "The French Financial Crisis and the Adoption of the Dawes Plan," p. 397n.

24. Brigadier-General J. H. Morgan, "The Disarmament of Germany and After," *Quarterly Review,* 242 (October, 1924), 451; see also by the same author, *Assize of Arms: The Disarmament of Germany and Her Rearmament 1919-1939* (New York, 1946).

25. Foch Cahiers, Dossier F, October 14, 1921; Dossier G, November 15, 1923;

General Debeney, the French chief of staff, even accepted as inevitable the reintroduction of universal military service in Germany. As he warned the Senate Army Commission: "When Germany returns to universal military service, which is its aim, the danger will be much more grave."[26]

With no way to put pressure on MacDonald the most dramatic aspect of the London Conference was the determination of the British to assert their dominance over the French—Herriot stood by helplessly as the Versailles Treaty was dismantled. For with France no longer in a position to decide whether Germany had fulfilled its reparations obligations, and with the disarmament clauses undermined, the French had lost the two chief levers for prolonging the occupation of the Rhineland. During the conference one alternative had existed: if the British had carried out their threat to withdraw unilaterally from the Cologne zone, French troops could have advanced and taken over from their erstwhile allies. The lapsing of this option epitomized France's dilemma after the London Conference: simply to maintain the level of security that had prevailed before 1924 would require greater military exertion than the country, up to then, had been prepared to make. If such an effort was not forthcoming, new solutions to France's defense problems, both military and diplomatic, would have to be found.

and General Charles Nollet, *Une expérience de désarmement: Cinq ans de contrôle militaire en Allemagne* (Paris, 1932).

26. Senate Army Commission, Procès-verbal, July 7, 1927. On German rearmament, see Hans Wilhelm Gatzke, *Stresemann and the Rearmament of Germany* (Baltimore, 1954); Michael Salewski, *Entwaffnung und Militärkontrolle in Deutschland 1919-1927* (Bonn, 1966); John W. Wheeler-Bennett, *Nemesis of Power* (London, 1953); General Friedrich von Rabenau, *Seeckt: Aus seinem Leben 1918-1936* (Leipzig, 1940); Francis Ludwig Carsten, *The Reichswehr and Politics 1918-1933* (Oxford, 1966). For evidence that French intelligence remained accurate long after the withdrawal of the Control Commission, see Georges Castellan, *Le réarmement clandestin du Reich 1930-1935* (Paris, 1954).

Toward A Redefinition of the Military Role

When the time came for the Cologne zone to be evacuated—in fact British troops did not leave until January 1926—Allied concentration on the Left Bank of the Rhine would be entirely disrupted. Foch noted the military significance: additional troops would be necessary to guard the new Roer-Düren front.[27] Yet instead of increasing its level of military preparedness, France in the late 1920's shortened its length of service and decreased the number of its active divisions. At the very time that it became clear that Allied troops would soon leave the first zone of the Rhineland, the French were elaborating legislation that apparently weakened its military establishment. As the breathing space provided by the Versailles Treaty seemed to be coming to an end, France reduced its military burdens.

The High Command, moreover, instead of demanding an increase in the level of armed preparedness agreed to legislation that epitomized the country's war weariness and disinclination to shoulder heavy military burdens. General Nollet's behavior—as Herriot's minister of war—was typical of the military's peculiar blend of foreboding and political accommodation. At the London Conference he had advocated evacuating the Ruhr only in exchange for better security guarantees. Just before it had opened he had told the Senate Finance and Foreign Affairs Commissions to accustom themselves to perpetual tension with Germany: "We must become used," he had warned, "to living with the thought that things have always been like that along the Rhine."[28] Yet after the

27. Foch Cahiers, Dossier G, January 2, 1925; see also the interview with General Bourgeois, president of the Senate Army Commission, *Echo de Paris,* September 15, 1924.

28. Joint meeting of the Senate Finance and Foreign Affairs Commissions: Senate Finance Commission, Procès-verbal, July 2, 1924.

conclusion of the conference—when coercive actions had received their deathblow—he had proposed a first version of one-year military training. While it was true that the abandonment of these operations undercut the principal justification advanced by the advocates of eighteen-month service, this fact might well have been used to underline the diplomatic gains that Germany was making. Such was to be the assessment of Foch's protégé, General Weygand, when he came to write his memoirs. At the time, however, Weygand too, as a member of the Conseil Supérieur de la Guerre, voted in favor of a one-year service.[29]

Why then did France's army chiefs behave in a fashion that seemed to contradict their professional ethos of constant vigilance? For a more thorough understanding of the military's acquiescence one must turn to the impact of the difficulties confronting the army at mid-decade. The conflicts overseas which erupted during that period, together with the complex of problems commonly called *le malaise militaire,* dislocated France's military establishment. Inadequate for an active defensive policy based on the Rhineland, not to speak of French replacements for British troops in the Cologne zone, the system of thirty-two divisions, to be fully viable, would have required lengthening the term of military training. This conjunction crystallized the choice French leaders had to make: either increase the number of effectives on active duty by extending the time spent under the colors or create a new organization that, as a by-product, might permit the reduction in the term of service, which was almost universally desired. At the same time these interlocking problems reinforced the military's awareness of the limits to their

29. General Maxime Weygand, *Mémoires,* II: *Mirages et réalité* (Paris, 1957), pp. 319-321.

country's resources. Rather than leading the High Command to put additional pressure on their civilian counterparts, the difficulties of the mid-decade had the paradoxical effect of restricting and narrowing the scope of the military's demands. With an increasing sense of being engaged in a multi-front holding operation, France's army leaders became psychologically prepared to accept a reduction in the length of military service, provided only that the army itself remain a functioning organization.

Service in the colonies had bulked large in the formation of many First World War commanders. After the war the colonial attachment continued. Though actual duty in North Africa often provoked complaints, it remained an ideal or an inspiration to the military imagination. A few dashing officers chose to act upon it. While younger men at home suffered the monotony of garrison life and led a penurious existence, some of the most talented, such as the future Marshal Jean de Lattre de Tassigny, who served in Morocco in the mid-1920's, sought adventure in France's overseas holdings. For there Lyautey's notion of the officer's social role still had meaning; the military not only served as guardians of their country's growing empire, but brought with them French civilization and enlightenment.[30] With the war in Morocco against the Rif tribesmen and the Druse insurrection in Syria, this chapter of French imperial history was closed. Although former commitments were reaffirmed and the

---

30. Among the First World War commanders who had served in France's overseas possessions were Joffre, Galliéni, Franchet d'Esperey, and Mangin. On the officer's social role, see Anon. [Lyautey], "Le rôle social de l'officier," *Revue des deux mondes,* 3e période, 104 (March 15, 1891), 443-459; General Tanant, *L'officier de France* (Paris, 1927), part 6.

fundamental desiderata of French dominance remained un-changed, the military discovered that they were no longer the vanguard of an expanding imperial power.

At the beginning of 1925 the Rif leader, Abd-el-Krim, be-gan to attack French outposts in Morocco. Until then he had limited his endeavors to the Spanish zone, where he had met with remarkable success; except for the area around Melilla, the Spanish had lost the ground they had gained in the fif-teen previous years. The French in turn found themselves hard pressed to withstand the incursions; Marshal Lyautey, French resident-general since 1912 and now ailing, was shaken in his belief that he could pacify Morocco practically unaided. Throughout the spring he repeatedly appealed to Paris for reinforcements. Almost simultaneously an insur-rection broke out in Syria among the Djebel Druse. A French column sent to extinguish the rebellion was itself annihilated. The revolt spread; an insurrectionary government was estab-lished in Damascus. In order to restore French rule, the Cartel-appointed high commissioner, General Sarrail, resorted to the extreme measure of bombarding the city.

The ensuing parliamentary debates brought into clear focus the fact that France's drive for colonial conquest had spent its force. In countering the criticisms of the Socialists, Paul Painlevé—who in April 1925 had succeeded Herriot as prime minister—made it clear that the limits of French dominion had been reached. While he defended the initiative that Lyautey had taken in 1924—a movement of troops north of the Ouergha river in order to protect Fez—he denied the Socialist allegation that this action had provoked Abd-el-Krim, adding that his own government's aim was simply to re-establish peace and thus allow France's work overseas to continue. With this objective both Socialists and conservatives agreed.[31] From all sides came applause when Aristide Briand, now serving as foreign minister, proclaimed:

I reiterate that we will not go beyond our zone and that we are possessed by no spirit of conquest. We have our zone in Morocco; we have our colonial domain; we manage it in terms of a broad effort at civilization. It is amply sufficient for this effort, and we should be acting in a criminal fashion if we entertained the least *arrière-pensée* of dragging our country into bloody adventures in pursuit of a conquest that we couldn't even digest.[32]

Though only the Communists talked of liquidating the Empire and recognizing Abd-el-Krim as an independent sovereign, politicians of all persuasions were aware that France's position, particularly in North Africa, had become vastly different from what it had been before the war. Even those military most reluctant to relinquish their special role in their country's overseas possessions, realized that incipient Moslem nationalism had radically altered the political aspects of colonial rule.[33] The difficulties in Morocco and Syria—where rebel leaders had begun to use the language of self-determination—presaged the new concerns of colonial policy; while self-rule or some form of autonomy might not yet be imminent, it was clearly what the future would bring. Thus it was not only the loss of appetite for colonial expansion, but ferment, actual and potential, in the overseas territories

31. JOC *Déb.*, May 27, 1925, pp. 2444-2463; May 28, 1925, pp. 2472-2481; May 29, 1925, pp. 2515-2517; see also report of speech given by Painlevé in Grenoble, *Echo de Paris*, May 22, 1925. Despite general accord, the Socialists subsequently abstained in a number of important votes on Moroccan policy: Edouard Bonnefous, *Histoire politique de la Troisième République,* IV: *Cartel des Gauches et Union Nationale* (Paris, 1960), pp. 83-86.

32. JOC *Déb.*, May 29, 1925, p. 2517.

33. See, for example, Foch Cahiers, Dossier E, January 3, 1920; January 16, 1920.

themselves that turned the French Empire into a holding operation.

It was a holding operation that even to military planners constituted a burden that no longer justified its cost. Despite the talk of an empire of one hundred million, of utilizing North Africans, black Africans, and Indo-Chinese to replace or supplement France's depleted manpower reserves, such schemes never proved feasible.[34] The same difficulties that plagued the French army at home—the shortage of cadres and the desire to reduce the length of military service—seriously handicapped the colonial army overseas. Indeed it was generally agreed that to train native troops the proportion of cadres to recruits had to be much higher than was the case with French solders.[35] Yet France could ill afford to send additional noncommissioned officers abroad when the army was already seriously understaffed. Moreover it took considerably longer to train a native than his French counterpart. At the same time it was again generally recognized that political conditions, and more particularly incipient demands for equality among the *indigènes,* did not permit imposing a term of service that was substantially out of line with the obligations of French nationals. Fearful of the danger of training potentially hostile colonials, French leaders were cautious in applying conscription as well as skeptical of what might be expected of native reservists once their period of service was over.[36] Even if the problems of recruitment and training could have been solved, transportation to France in an emer-

34. General Charles Mangin was the chief advocate of using colonial troops; for an example of his propaganda, see AN, 149 AP 12: "Nos colonies aux secours de la France" (typed manuscript), General Charles Mangin Papers.

35. General Serrigny, "La grande pitié de nos effectifs de guerre," *Revue des deux mondes,* 7e période, 23 (October 1, 1924), 636.

36. "Note sur le service militaire des indigènes," June 29, 1922, Millerand Papers.

gency—since no one suggested stationing large numbers of colonial troops on French soil in peacetime—would have posed insuperable logistic difficulties.[37] In the end the colonial army (and the comparable troops in Morocco and Syria) functioned mainly as a police force in their own domain.

No longer the realm of untrammeled adventure and exercise in military virtue, the territories overseas were to be retained long after their costs had become disproportionate to their worth. Yet for people who saw any loss of colonial position as a prelude to France's decline and even to the eventual disintegration of the national territory, there could be no question of reducing the imperial commitment.[38] To have done so would have been to destroy their cherished image of their country's mission overseas.

At the same time as the revolts in Morocco and Syria set France's imperial position in a defensive mold, this posture aggravated the military's correspondingly defensive attitude about their mission and role in society. Their complaints formed a grab-bag of contradictory laments, suggesting both a desire for security and a yearning for glory. Shipped to North Africa and exposed to danger, many officers and enlisted men resented the low esteem in which their efforts were held. Expecting deferential treatment for the sacrifices their profession required of them, they nevertheless made constant comparisons between their lot and that of civilian state servants. While reacting bitterly to Communist anti-

37. Serrigny, "La grande pitié de nos effectifs de guerre," p. 638; for a further discussion of the colonial army, see Shelby Cullom Davis, *The French War Machine* (London, 1937), chap. 8; and by the same author, *Reservoirs of Men: A History of the Black Troops of French West Africa* (Chambéry, 1934).

38. For examples of this kind of rhetoric, see *Echo de Paris,* June 16, 1925; July 6, 1925.

militarism, to the party's propaganda in favor of the rebels in Morocco and Syria,[39] the army itself seemed reluctant to serve overseas and envious of the security that civilian functionaries enjoyed. Particularly angered when civilian employees received a salary raise and they themselves got only temporary subsidies, they continued to harbor a grudge about a change in protocol already nearly twenty years old that gave precedence to administrative officials over army chiefs in state ceremonies. Unsure themselves what their mission was—after Alsace and Lorraine had been returned to France the glamor had departed from their profession—they resented the inability of politicians to devise a glorious role for them to play.[40]

To these discontents, many of them long-standing, was now added the conviction that army leaders overseas had been badly treated. Most officers joined the Right in accusing the Cartel of having undermined competent military authority at critical points. In both of the imperial crises, a commander of rightist political persuasion, who epitomized the independent and effective military proconsul, had been replaced initially by a general with more acceptable political attitudes and subsequently by a civilian. Certainly there had been ground for complaint when in December 1924 General Weygand was summarily replaced in Syria by General Sarrail.[41] Without any diplomatic finesse, disdainful of local traditions and reli-

39. See, for example, *ibid.,* November 29, 1924; July 19, 1925; October 7, 1925; May 13, 1926.
40. Senate Army Commission, Procès-verbal, March 12, 1924; General Debeney's testimony to the Senate Army Commission, *ibid.,* July 7, 1927; War Minister Painlevé's testimony to the Senate Finance Commission, Procès-verbal, December 3, 1926; Letter from Marshal Pétain to General Nollet, July 18, 1924, published in the *Echo de Paris,* April 18, 1926; Lt. Col. Reboul, "Le malaise de l'armée," *Revue des deux mondes,* 7e période, 26 (March 15, 1925), 378-398; General Lavigne-Delville, *Inquiétudes militaires: officiers et fonctionnaires* (Paris, 1924); Tanant, *L'officier de France*; Lucien Souchon, *Feue l'armée française* (Paris, 1929).
41. On Weygand's work in Syria, see his *Mirages et réalité,* part 4.

gious sects, Sarrail managed in short order to provoke an angry coalition of disparate elements.[42] In the end the incompetence of the leftist general appalled even the moderate Cartel leaders, and he was replaced by a civilian in the person of Henry de Jouvenel.

Similarly the Right charged their political opponents with delay in sending to Morocco the reinforcements that Lyautey had requested and then with politics-as-usual in removing him when his prestige was most crucial to quashing the Rif. Initially the Cartel had been surprised by the grave turn of events in Morocco. When the Herriot ministry took office, Lyautey, perhaps fearful for his own position, had reassured the new leaders that the situation was well under control.[43] Though Herriot and his successor Painlevé claimed that they had fulfilled all of Lyautey's demands, when the crisis came it was to Pétain that Painlevé turned. His association with the marshal went back to 1917, when as president of the Council he had brought in Pétain as Nivelle's successor. In August 1925 Painlevé sent his esteemed military collaborator to Morocco with instructions to supervise operations there. Humiliated, with his military power drastically diminished, Lyautey returned to France in late 1925. Theodore Steeg, a moderate politician and longtime friend of Alexandre Millerand, was appointed the new resident-general.[44]

42. The Senate Army Commission made a detailed study of Sarrail's mismanagement and discussed its findings, Procès-verbal, February 16, 1927.

43. Lucien Lamoureux, "Souvenirs politiques 1919-1940" (microfilm of unpublished manuscript, Bibliothèque de Documentation Internationale Contemporaine), pp. 774-775; Colonel Noguès, adjoint to Lyautey, to Alexandre Millerand, early 1924, Millerand Papers.

44. On Pétain's work in Morocco, see Lt. Col. A. M. E. Laure, *La victoire franco-espagnole dans le Rif* (Paris, 1927); for Lyautey's account, see Pierre Lyautey, ed., *Lyautey l'Africain: Textes et lettres du Maréchal Lyautey,* IV (Paris, 1957), chap. 4; for the most recent work dealing with the entire Rif campaign, see David S. Woolman, *Rebels in the Rif: Abd-el-Krim and the Rif Rebellion* (Stanford, Calif., 1968).

The military also had reason to feel that their position had been undercut by the way in which hostilities came to an end. Instead of granting authority to the French commanders in Morocco to conclude peace, thus permitting them to make local arrangements in the field, Painlevé and Briand undertook to negotiate with Abd-el-Krim themselves. Although both of them clearly stated that discussions could not begin until the military situation had been stabilized, the rightist defenders of the army took a poor view of any kind of diplomatic conversations with the rebel chieftain. When in the following year, after a large infusion of French troops and joint planning with Spanish leaders had made a military victory feasible, the French and Spanish governments in fact began talks with Abd-el-Krim, the conservatives were duly and predictably incensed.[45]

Such cavalier treatment of revered military figures, coupled with the antimilitary and anti-imperial propaganda of the Communists, heightened the army's sense of vulnerability. This reaction is merely the natural response of men in a profession that on all fronts seemed scarcely able to hold its own. Indeed at the root of the malaise militaire lay the steady erosion of their material position, exacerbated by the acute inflation of 1925-26. The press carried stories of officers whose wives were forced to work, who themselves were compelled to find a second job, or who were separated from their families because they could not afford the expense of moving the household.[46] There were similar reports of offi-

45. Painlevé's testimony to a joint meeting of the Senate Finance, Foreign Affairs, Colonies, Army, and Navy Commissions: Senate Finance Commission, Procès-verbal, June 24, 1925; for the views of the Right, see *Echo de Paris,* June 27, 1925; May 13, 1926.

46. *Ibid.,* December 21, 1923; February 15, 1924; May 28, 1924; June 25, 1924; May 27, 1925; June 17, 1925; September 23, 1925.

cers who could not bear the cost of settling in Paris for the two years necessary to follow the course at the Ecole Supérieure de Guerre. As a result of such straitened circumstances the number of applications fell off, both for advanced military study and for entrance into Saint-Cyr, as did the proportion of graduates from the Ecole Polytechnique to choose a military career.[47] Moreover, even for those who entered or remained in the profession, promotion was slow.[48] Jean de Lattre de Tassigny became a captain at the age of twenty-six and remained one until he was forty. Thereafter his promotions were more rapid, and just as he was turning fifty he became the youngest general in the army![49]

While the malaise militaire, combined with the crises overseas, was accentuating the military's sense of being engaged in a defensive operation on many fronts, the army at home was desperately struggling to maintain itself as a fighting force. For Morocco and Syria did not fall within the jurisdiction of the colonial army. North Africa and the mandates in the Middle East were considered theaters of "external operations" that might draw on the main body of French forces at home and in Germany. Although regular army (as opposed to colonial) contingents on duty in North Africa itself bore a

47. In 1923 the Ecole Supérieure de Guerre had planned to admit ninety to one hundred officers, but the quality and quantity of the applicants were such that only fifty-nine were taken: *ibid.*, November 25, 1923, p. 4; for concern about Saint-Cyr, see *Le Temps,* June 14, 1927; and for the Ecole Polytechnique, see Senate Army Commission, Procès-verbal, June 10, 1925.

48. In part this was due to the still unresolved problem of excess officers. The situation in the infantry was particularly severe, while other arms, notably the artillery and engineer corps, suffered from a shortage of trained personnel at all ranks.

49. Interviews with Madame la Maréchale de Lattre de Tassigny, October 25, 1966, and November 10, 1966. See also the collection of essays entitled *Jean de Lattre, Maréchal de France: Le soldat—l'homme—le politique* (Paris, 1953).

large share of the burden of garrisoning that area, in a time of crisis reinforcements were sent from France and the Rhineland. When the troop requirements soared—during the Rif campaign they passed the 150,000 mark—the additional forces had to be transferred from the French divisions stationed in Germany.[50] Still more, the withdrawal of units from the Rhineland for service in Morocco and Syria completely upset the order of French mobilization. The troop transfers disorganized France's cover and plans for concentration, both of which depended upon the Rhineland divisions.[51]

At the same time the units stationed in France were incapable of action.[52] Although the Senate had never voted the organization legislation passed by the Chamber in early 1924, the number of divisions had in fact been reduced to the specified figure of thirty-two by the device of inserting provisions in finance bills.[53] Yet even this proved an unsatisfactory solution. As early as December 1924, Jean Fabry had argued that with the effectives available, the thirty-two divisions deemed necessary by the High Command were actually too many. By late 1925 their perennial shortage of manpower was being aggravated by constant drains on their personnel. The units, understaffed and undermanned, remained merely skeletal; as a result training was disrupted, creating general demoralization among officers, enlisted men, and recruits.[54]

Moreover, at mid-decade France's army chiefs found them-

50. Senate Finance Commission, Procès-verbal, April 8, 1926.
51. See speech by Jean Fabry, JOC *Déb.*, December 19, 1925, p. 4479.
52. Senate Finance Commission, Procès-verbal, March 11, 1925.
53. Statement issued by André Maginot, *Echo de Paris,* June 17, 1924.
54. JOC *Déb.*, December 9, 1924, pp. 4293-4296; December 19, 1925, p. 4479.

selves confronted by a chronic shortage of *militaires de carrière*. These professional soldiers, noncoms and long-term enlisted men, were in fact the keystone of French military preparation. They were the life of the active units in which recruits were trained, and they would provide the backbone for mobilizing France's manpower reserves. Originally the military's acceptance of eighteen-month service had been based on the understanding that 100,000 professional soldiers, excluding officers, would be recruited. In fact the figure never got much above 70,000.[55] Pay was so low and conditions of work, both material and psychological, so unattractive that the number of re-enlistments failed to reach the level anticipated. Financial difficulties still appeared to the High Command, at least, a legitimate cause for the government's inability to fulfill this commitment. As General Debeney, the army chief of staff, remarked rather delicately, when the War Ministry made attempts to reach the desired number: "By a singular misfortune events rushed across our path: the risings in Morocco and Syria necessitated supplementary credits at the very moment when the uninterrupted fall of the franc was endangering public finance."[56]

Had the government succeeded in recruiting the specified number of trained personnel, there would have been far less reason for the military to abandon eighteen-month service, and General Debeney would not have testified as he did before the Senate Finance Commission. Had the government been able to fulfill its earlier promise, Debeney would not have concluded that under two-year service—let alone eighteen months—there was insufficient trained personnel avail-

55. Senate Army Commission, Procès-verbal, July 5, 1927.
56. General Debeney, "Armée nationale ou armée de métier?" *Revue des deux mondes,* 7e période, 53 (September 15, 1929), 256.

able for the double function of troop training and maintaining in good condition a quantity of matériel that had been enormously increased as a result of the war.[57] If the length of service should be significantly lengthened, such functions might be performed by the conscripts themselves; on the eve of the First World War, after the three-year law had been passed, it was hoped that soldiers with two years of training would, in their last year of duty, help provide the *encadrement* for reserve divisions and serve as instructors for new recruits. In the vastly altered circumstances of the mid-1920's Debeney underlined his dilemma by describing himself as obliged to choose between three-year service and "the creation of permanent specialized personnel for whom funds would be found by reducing the length of active service."[58]

To be sure the choice was not a real one. Yet this kind of reasoning paved the way for acceptance of the one-year term. The High Command was willing to compromise on the length of service in return for an increase in the number of militaires de carrière. Anxious to create a stable organization as a solid bulwark for and as psychological encouragement to the military profession, army leaders reconciled themselves to the almost universal demand for shortening the time spent under the colors. The interlocking crises in finance, the colonies, morale, and recruitment had both heightened the military's sense of urgency about establishing a functioning army organization and forced them to fashion the new military machine under severely straitened circumstances.

Although the actual reorganization legislation was not enacted until 1927-28, the outlines of the army's new structure

57. Senate Finance Commission, Procès-verbal, July 11, 1927.
58. Debeney, "Armée nationale ou armée de métier?" p. 257.

became clear during 1925. Throughout the interwar period the chief concern of French military planners was to assure the utilization of their country's entire resources, and particularly its manpower reserves. The organization plans of 1922-23 had attempted to provide for this mobilization while supplying the troops necessary for coercive actions. In 1925, with the inadequacies of the earlier legislation apparent and with coercive operations abandoned, military leaders focused strictly on France's mobilization needs. Yet in emphasizing the necessity for a smooth and complete mobilization, guaranteed this time by an adequate cadre of professional soldiers, military planners did not neglect the role of the covering forces. In fact by stressing the importance of mobilization, with its unavoidable delays, French army chiefs could not fail to underline the crucial tasks assigned to those troops. Caught between the one imperative of assuring mobilization and the competing imperative of providing adequate cover, army leaders carefully apportioned their resources between the two. In the end the manpower available for both was stretched extremely thin.

The first reorganization proposal was drawn up in late 1924 by General Nollet. His appointment as Herriot's minister of war had been well received in conservative circles, where he was spoken of as a bulwark against dangerous Cartel experiments in military policy. Even his announcement that army reorganization would permit a reduction in the length of military service to one year found a cordial response. When, however, his actual proposals became generally known, the conservatives were outraged. For Nollet, the esteemed military chief, had proceeded in disregard of his former colleagues. Without allowing the Conseil Supérieur de la Guerre sufficient time to give his proposals full consideration, he transmitted them forthwith to the Chamber Army Commission.[59] His entire work showed signs of haste. First Nollet recommended a complete redistribution of peacetime troops: the bulk of French forces would henceforth be stationed on the frontier for immediate action. And to cope with the grave problems of mobilization and training, he offered only a sketchy outline of new solutions.[60] The Conseil Supérieur de la Guerre refused to rush into untried experiments. Pressed to approve the proposals, they unanimously declared them to be "dangerous and inopportune."[61]

Shortly thereafter a compromise was hammered out. Paul Painlevé, who succeeded Nollet as minister of war in April 1925, won the consent of the Conseil Supérieur de la Guerre to the one-year term of service by agreeing to certain clear stipulations.[62] These included increasing the total of militaires de carrière to 106,000, recruiting 15,000 *agents militaires* (police), and raising the number of civilian employees to 30,000—all of which were written into the recruitment legislation itself under the heading of *conditions préalables.* Unlike the legislation of 1922-23, which had reduced the term of military service without legally binding the government to take the measures deemed necessary by the High Command, the further reduction to one year now became conditional upon obtaining the designated number of professional men.[63] Indeed the conditions préalables figured as

59. *Echo de Paris,* June 15, 1924; June 16, 1924; October 18, 1924; February 14, 1925; February 18, 1925; February 25, 1925, March 9, 1925; March 16, 1925; March 30, 1925; April 2, 1925; April 3, 1925; April 7, 1925.

60. Even in his apologia Nollet was far from clear; see his "Ce que j'ai voulu faire," *Revue de Paris,* 32, no. 12 (June 15, 1925), 738-764.

61. *Echo de Paris,* April 14, 1925; see also *ibid.,* April 12, 1925.

62. *Ibid.,* September 19, 1925; October 16, 1925; January 13, 1926; January 18, 1926.

63. JOC *Doc,* 1927, annexe no. 4659, pp. 1052-1055.

the major issue in the ensuing debates. The left wing of the Radical party under the leadership of Edouard Daladier, as well as the Socialists who followed the guidance of Pierre Renaudel, drafted separate counterprojects that had as their touchstone an *immediate* reduction in military service, i.e., without prior conditions. When the issue finally came to a head in 1927-28 (though the proposals had been ready since early 1926), Painlevé stood firm. With the solid backing of Poincaré, who had in the meantime formed a government of National Union and who made the matter a question of confidence, Painlevé stuck to his agreement with France's army chiefs.[64]

Similarly Painlevé, on the insistence of the military, was adamant in rejecting training centers detached from active units, an idea that had figured in Nollet's projects and which was dear to the Socialists.[65] Training would continue, as before, to take place within the regiments themselves. But the system of mobilization by regiments would be abandoned. The function of mobilization was now considered too great a burden for the reduced number of standing regiments. Instead Painlevé borrowed from his predecessor a proposal for establishing mobilization centers. Staffed by officers, yet independent of the troop command, these centers would supervise the maintenance and distribution of matériel, as well as assign reservists to their units at the time of mobilization.[66]

To provide adequate cover, the military maintained that a

64. Simon Robert, "Revue des questions militaires," *Revue politique et parlementaire,* 130 (January 1927), 129; *Le Temps,* March 19, 1927; JOC *Déb.,* June 28, 1927, pp. 2130ff.; January 19, 1928, pp. 156ff.
65. Richard D. Challener, *The French Theory of the Nation in Arms 1866-1939* (New York, 1955), p. 171.
66. General Brindel, "La nouvelle organisation militaire," *Revue des deux mondes,* 7e période, 51 (June 1, 1929), 481-501.

standing army of twenty divisions was essential. Just as thirty-two divisions had been the sacrosanct counterpart of eighteen-month service, so now twenty divisions took on that relationship to a one-year term. Yet according to the government's proposals only six would be up to full strength in peacetime. In time of danger, the High Command planned on filling out the remaining fourteen as well as mobilizing an additional twenty.[67] Faced with the prospect of fourteen undermanned divisions, the chief conservative spokesman for the army's interests, Jean Fabry, drew up a counterproposal calling for only fourteen active divisions in all. He argued that these units, which would be fully manned, could themselves immediately mobilize another fourteen and proceed to act with great rapidity. While Fabry's plan may have had the advantage of speed, it failed to provide a link between the active divisions and the mass of manpower reserves. For once the initial fourteen had doubled, how other divisions would be mobilized remained unclear. In the end Fabry dropped his counterproposal, through fear that by dividing the government's supporters, it might open the floodgates to a more drastic solution.[68]

To compensate for the reduction of France's active army, and to provide the troops necessary for the initial doubling of the standing divisions, the government's plan as well as Fabry's relied on a special category called the *disponibilité*—a half-way station between active and reserve service. The re-

67. Debeney's testimony to the Senate Army Commission, Procès-verbal, July 7, 1927.

68. *Echo de Paris*, July 7, 1926; September 1, 1926; September 15, 1926; November 24, 1926; see also Jean Fabry, "Où va notre armée?" *Revue de Paris*, 32, no. 18 (September 15, 1925), 241-268; General Duval, "La crise de notre organisation militaire," *Revue de Paris*, 33, no. 8 (April 15, 1926), 756-796. For implicit criticism of Fabry's proposal, see General Antoine Targe, *La garde de nos frontières* (Paris, 1930), pp. 91ff.

cruitment legislation stipulated that every conscript, on the completion of his twelve-month tour of duty, would be assigned to the disponibilité for the next three years. Although this notion had figured in André Lefèvre's original recruitment proposals, it did not become central to French military plans until the one-year law was passed.[69] Now as former War Minister Maginot argued in support of the government, and after admitting that cover was "not perhaps in normal times as solidly constituted as it should be," France had available "the possibility of reinforcing it in case of need by recalling the disponibles."[70] The legislation, moreover, empowered the government to recall these men without consulting parliament, and made it clear that such action should not be considered as equivalent to mobilization. In the words of the Senate *rapporteur* General Hirshauer:

The executive power can, then, take a rapid, instantaneous decision, at the moment danger appears, with only the need to go before the Chambers later on to justify its act . . . In these matters . . . the government should have a free hand. It bears a heavy responsibility; it must not suffer from any restraint involving a loss of time; such a delay might cost us dear.[71]

This was a far cry from the kind of protection France had enjoyed before the First World War. Then plans had called for three classes *under arms,* while now it was officially recognized that the active army could not perform its covering mission without the immediate calling up of the three youngest *reserve classes* (i.e., the disponibilité). This mission, moreover, was considered much more difficult than it had

69. Challener, *The French Theory of the Nation in Arms,* pp. 166-167.
70. JOC *Déb.,* May 19, 1927, p. 1523.
71. JO Sen. *Déb.,* July 11, 1927, p. 970.

been in the past. Michel Missoffe, a conservative deputy, simply reaffirmed the military's understanding of the crucial and arduous role of the covering troops when he commented: France's armed forces now needed "to defend the frontier . . . in an efficient fashion, for three or four months, and to give the country time to attain its full potential, both at home and in the colonies, of men, of armaments, and of provisions."[72] Such were the imperatives that the 1920's had produced. Having held the line against an immediate and unconditional reduction in the length of military service, France's military leaders were now obliged to proceed to the incomparably more difficult task of similarly holding off an enemy whose ultimate military potential was far greater than theirs.

Locarno: The Internationalization of Security Problems

As long as French troops remained in the Rhineland, the defects of France's new military organization would not seriously jeopardize the country's security. For the divisions kept at full strength would be stationed on the enemy's territory, and their presence, Frenchmen confidently assumed, would deter the Reich from aggression. Yet after August 1924 France's leaders were well aware that their country's position on German soil was only a temporary solution to its security problems.[73] The weakness of France's military forces combined with a sense of time running out to make more urgent and precise what until then had been merely a general necessity to gain international aid and support.

72. JOC *Déb.,* May 19, 1927, p. 1525.
73. See Briand's passionate remarks on this point, *ibid.,* March 1, 1926, p. 1091.

The London Conference had left the question of the evacuation of the Cologne zone still undecided. The withdrawal of British troops had subsequently been delayed, and had been made contingent upon German compliance with demands set forth in a joint note delivered in December 1924. Yet the evacuation would clearly not be postponed indefinitely. Throughout 1925 the imminent departure from the Cologne zone relentlessly prodded France's diplomats to arrange some security system before the inevitable agreement to withdraw was reached.[74] In the face of this impending reality, the Versailles Treaty, France's sole compensation for 1,400,000 dead, appeared hollow indeed. Only the articles relating to the demilitarization of the left bank now seemed to offer a way to safeguard the nation's security. To preserve these clauses and to cement international guarantees of the Rhine as Germany's effective military frontier thus became the imperatives for French foreign policy.

The fifth session of the League of Nations, which met in September 1924 shortly after the close of the London Conference, marked the beginning of new attempts to regulate security questions. Throughout that meeting, which witnessed the drafting of the Geneva Protocol, and into the early part of the following year, the main thrust of such efforts was in the direction of international arbitration and adjudication. In February 1925, however, the German foreign minister, Gustav Stresemann, working in concert with Lord D'Abernon, the British ambassador in Berlin, put forth proposals for a security pact considerably more limited in scope.

74. On the negotiations leading to the evacuation of the Cologne zone, see C. A. Macartney *et al., Survey of International Affairs 1925,* II (London, Oxford University Press, 1928), pp. 172-193.

When the Conservatives regained power in Britain in late 1924, and when Austen Chamberlain, the new foreign secretary, subsequently made it clear that the Geneva Protocol was unacceptable, Stresemann's project became the basis of further negotiations. The main item the Germans offered was a pledge to respect the demilitarization of the Rhineland; by thus assuaging French (and Belgian) security fears, they hoped to hasten the evacuation of the left bank. The French response was cautious. Both Herriot and Briand, who took over the Foreign Ministry with the formation of the Painlevé government in April 1925, proceeded carefully, anxious to safeguard the juridical basis for French action in the Rhineland.[75]

The original German proposals, although referring to arbitration with Poland and Czechoslovakia, had said nothing about the eastern borders of the Reich. And throughout the spring and summer of 1925, this was the issue over which Briand waged diplomatic battle, not with the Germans but rather with the British. While Chamberlain was willing to have his country act as guarantor to a Rhineland pact offering protection to France and Belgium, he refused to depart from Britain's traditional stance of disregard for eastern Europe. Initially the French government seemed prepared to reject

75. Great Britain, *Cmd. 2435: Papers Respecting the Proposals for a Pact of Security made by the German Government on 9th February 1925* (London, 1925) (henceforth cited as *Cmd. 2435*); France, Ministère des Affaires Etrangères, *Pacte de sécurité: Neuf pièces relatives à la proposition faite le 9 février 1925 par le gouvernement allemand et à la réponse du gouvernement français, 9 février-16 juin 1925* (Paris, 1925); France, Ministère des Affaires Etrangères, *Pacte de sécurité*, II: *Documents signés ou paraphés à Locarno le 16 Octobre 1925, précédés de six pièces relatives aux négotiations préliminaires, 20 juillet 1925-16 octobre 1925* (Paris, 1925); D'Abernon, *The Diary of an Ambassador*, III; Arnold J. Toynbee, *Survey of International Affairs 1924* (London, 1926), pp. 36-64; Macartney et al., *Survey of International Affairs 1925*, II, 1-66; Herriot, *Jadis*, II, 168-195.

the German proposal unless the British extended their proffered guarantee to the East. Briand, in fact, drafted a reply to Stresemann's note that called for a "single homogeneous pact covering all disputes between Germany and any of her neighbors, all alike being covered by an unlimited guarantee from Great Britain."[76] Only when Chamberlain made it crystal clear that the British would make no commitments to Poland and Czechoslovakia, did Briand modify his position. His subsequent versions, while leaving Britain free to withhold its guarantee, were so worded that France retained the liberty to act in case of a violation by Germany of its arbitration treaties with Poland and Czechoslovakia.[77]

In the course of the parliamentary debates over the ratification of the accords signed at Locarno in October 1925—the Rhineland pact, the arbitration treaties, and French agreements to guarantee the latter—Briand noted in poignant tones that one could judge them properly only if one posed two preliminary questions: "Before Locarno, what did we have? And if there had been no Locarno, what would we have now?"[78] He admonished his critics to keep clearly before them the current diplomatic situation and to refrain from using as their reference point a mythical past in which all options had been open to French statesmen. In sum he pointed out that it would be unrealistic to expect that France's diplomats could produce single-handedly an airtight and automatic solution to the nation's security problems.

Briand's exchange with Louis Marin offered the best example of his attempts to focus the discussion on the alternatives actually available to his country. While Marin pointed

76. Macartney *et al., Survey of International Affairs 1925,* II, 34.
77. *Ibid.,* p. 37; see also *Cmd. 2435,* pp. 28, 44.
78. JOC *Déb.,* February 26, 1926, p. 1017.

out the limited scope of the Locarno agreements, his own suggestions smacked of fantasy:

One day or another, a pact will be made which will reunite all the victors of the war on the European continent, France, Belgium, Italy, Poland, Czechoslovakia, Yugoslavia, Rumania ... The bloc of these continental victors constitutes a population three times as great and a force infinitely more powerful than that of Germany, even from the military point of view—despite the latter's economic organization, despite the generally recognized warlike qualities of that race.

Briand's response was directly to the point:

In order to make alliances there must be several parties. At the time when there arose the question of the negotiations that led to Locarno, I guarantee that you would not have found a single one of the nations of which you were speaking a moment ago ready to sign a pact of the kind you are dreaming of.

Marin: It can't be done in six months.

Briand: It can perhaps be done in seven, eight, or ten years. But in the interim, we might encounter grave events that would suddenly place us face to face with war. . . .
The country must not be led to believe that there was a choice between two political systems, one of which would have given us the advantage of an alliance which would have made us much stronger. The reality is completely otherwise: we had none of the elements of such an alliance, and we could not have counted on it without exposing ourselves to disappointment.[79]

Even the hopes France's planners had entertained of military alliances with the new nations of eastern Europe had proved vain. Indeed by mid-decade the close relations be-

79. *Ibid.,* March 1, 1926, pp. 1085-1086, 1088-1090.

tween France and Germany's eastern neighbors that had characterized the immediate postwar period had been considerably loosened. The initial phase of strong French influence in organizing the new armies of Poland and Czechoslovakia had come to an end.[80] In the case of Poland, the military convention of 1921 had been limited in scope, and by 1924 Poland was considered a weak ally. In addition, the Czechoslovaks, who had relied heavily on French military advice, had subsequently been reluctant to sign a specific agreement with their mentors, fearing that they might thus be committing themselves to support French attempts to collect reparations. According to Lord D'Abernon's account of his conversation with the Czech minister in Berlin, it was only because the French brought great financial pressure to bear that Foreign Minister Beneš had consented to sign a treaty in January 1924. Yet the crucial element was missing. Although Beneš had agreed to continued staff consultations, he had been successful in rejecting a military convention.[81]

In similar vein Briand forced his colleagues to confront the realities of their situation vis-à-vis Britain. While conservative deputies, both those who abstained and those who joined the overwhelming majority that ratified the Locarno accords, emphasized the fact that the British, whose guarantee applied to Germany as well as to France, would be merely spectators until the outbreak of hostilities,[82] Briand repeated over and over again that a limited guarantee was better than none at all. What did it matter that the British would thus be unable

80. Piotr S. Wandycz, *France and Her Eastern Allies 1919-1925* (Minneapolis, Minn., 1962), pp. 279-281.
81. D'Abernon, *Diary of an Ambassador*, III, 3; see also Wandycz, *France and Her Eastern Allies*, chap. 11.
82. See, for example, speech by General Bourgeois, JO Sen. *Déb.*, June 4, 1926, p. 1133.

to engage in joint staff planning, in view of the fact that they had consistently refused to enter into such conversations? Since 1919 French diplomats had attempted to cement a meaningful alliance with Great Britain, and the repeated failure of their efforts had left a gaping hole in the structure of the Versailles Treaty. France's role had always been that of a suppliant, though a proud one; in early 1922 Poincaré had declined to make the diplomatic concessions in other areas on which Lloyd George had insisted as a basis for further consideration of a tentative and limited alliance offer. The London Conference had subsequently underlined the weakness of France's position, leaving the victor of 1918 more uncertain than ever of what might be expected from its erstwhile ally.

Now—on the morrow of Locarno—Briand could claim that the British had taken the first step toward a continental commitment. Even though the Locarno agreements made complicated distinctions between doubtful and flagrant violations of the Rhineland's neutrality—which in turn placed different obligations on the two guarantors, Great Britain and Italy—and despite the fact that the British government reserved to itself the right to determine whether a flagrant act of aggression had occurred,[83] it seemed perfectly clear to France's leaders that the march of substantial German forces into the Rhineland would fall into the flagrant category and that Britain would be required to declare war on the aggressor. While the French had always maintained that the Versailles Treaty made German violation of the military neutrality of the Left Bank an act of war, the British had heretofore proved reluctant to accept this interpretation. Even Jean

83. Macartney *et al., Survey of International Affairs 1925,* II, 43.

Fabry, who was skeptical about many aspects of the accords, pointed out in their favor: "They have simply allowed Britain to state precisely and publicly—something which in itself is sufficiently important—that it interpreted articles 42 and 43 in the way we interpreted them ourselves. They now read: if Germany violates these articles ipso facto it creates the casus belli."[84]

In this context, moreover, the insufficiency of standing forces that the proposals for one-year military service would entail had to be taken into account.[85] According to the proposed reorganization plans, whose outlines were already clear in 1925, any operation by France's covering forces in the direction of the Rhineland would require resorting to the youngest reserve classes. At the same time such a recall of the disponibles—a partial mobilization that was not to be considered a mobilization at all—might cause grave diplomatic repercussions. Unless there was a prior understanding on the legitimacy of such a move, France might find itself isolated and engaged in a major conflict. Even Franklin-Bouillon, who had voted against the Versailles Treaty because it failed to guarantee a permanent occupation of the Rhineland, now recognized this imperative and spoke on behalf of the Locarno accords:

We cannot forget that our weak birthrate governs and governs more strongly every day our general policy. It must be conducted in such a manner that on the day of danger we shall be assured of finding again

84. JOC *Déb.*, February 25, 1926, p. 974. See also remarks in JOC *Déb.* by Paul-Boncour, February 25, 1926, pp. 963-964; by Marcel Plaisant, February 26, 1926, p. 1009; and in JO Sen. *Déb.*, by Briand, June 4, 1926, p. 1137.

85. Indeed it was reported to the Senate Finance Commission that Briand had declared before another commission that "sa politique était conditionnée par l'état de notre armée," Procès-verbal, November 8, 1927.

all those whom the evident justice of our cause so recently grouped around us.[86]

In the end the Rhineland pact signed at Locarno did not amount to much; in 1936 German troops marched into the Rhineland, while France and Britain responded with no more than verbal protests. In retrospect Briand has often been depicted as having been duped by the wily Stresemann amidst the pastoral charms of Italian Switzerland. Yet in such a picture the perspective is askew. Germany gained nothing more than had already been conceded at the London Conference: a tacit recognition that coercive operations would be abandoned and an unspoken understanding that the Cologne zone of the Rhineland would shortly be freed of allied troops. Briand was not entirely disingenuous when he insisted, after being taxed with having consented to the Cologne evacuation, that this should be regarded as separate from the Locarno accords.[87] For when shortly after the meeting in Switzerland, the Conference of Ambassadors finally agreed to the withdrawal, even though Germany had not fulfilled all its disarmament obligations, the decision figured simply as a postscript to the London Conference. Meantime the French had attained their limited diplomatic objectives: they not only had safeguarded the juridical basis for a possible future advance into the Rhineland, but had obtained guarantees that if such action became necessary, they would not find themselves deserted and alone. It was not Briand's fault that his countrymen subsequently failed to make use of the legal weapon with which he had provided them.

86. JOC *Déb.*, March 2, 1926, p. 1134.
87. *Ibid.*, February 25, 1926, p. 976; March 1, 1926, pp. 1082, 1090.

5 | To the Maginot Line

France Uncovered

The moderate and conservative deputies who acquiesced in or more actively supported the ratification of the Locarno accords did not do so without misgivings. With rhetorical fervor they cautioned their fellow citizens to beware lest an atmosphere of détente engender a false sense of security. [1] While the guardians of their country's interests addressed their arguments to the internationalists and the supporters of the League of the Nations in their midst, they failed to see the applicability of their remarks to themselves and their close colleagues. For despite their resolute pronouncements on matters of foreign policy, conservative deputies were at that very time agreeing to the reduction of the length of military service to one year. Paradoxically enough, the presence of French troops in the Rhineland had already produced what these spokesmen now warned against; the reassurance it

---

1. See speeches by Jean Fabry, JOC *Déb.*, February 25, 1926, pp. 975-977; March 1, 1926, p. 1100. See also remarks by Joseph Barthélemy, February 26, 1926, p. 1016; and Louis Madelin, March 2, 1926, pp. 1140-1141.

provided had disarmed the critics of the one-year law and had facilitated its passage. No wonder then, that the Center and Right should have insisted on maintaining the shield that protected their country not only from its traditional enemy, but from the consequences of their own unwillingness to make greater military sacrifices. And when at length their admonitions to vigilance and resistance once again modulated into acquiescence, this time in the early evacuation of the Rhineland, when the crucial buttress of France's security was withdrawn, they came face to face with their own fears and failures.

Regardless of the defects in France's military machine, the country's position remained unimpaired so long as French troops were stationed on German soil. Even though the number of soldiers had been reduced to 50,000 and allied forces had been withdrawn from the Cologne zone, the French presence in the Rhineland was of the utmost importance. If the Germans should once again attempt an offensive through Belgium along the line from Cologne to the rivers Meuse and Sambre, aiming at the Oise, they would find a French army in their rear. To assure their advance, the Germans might of course first turn on the French troops stationed in the Koblenz and Mainz zones of the Rhineland. But such an attack would be hindered by geographical obstacles; between the Mosel and the Rhine the country is hilly and broken. A small number of French troops could delay a German advance long enough to permit the concentration of substantial reinforcements. And thus the initial battle, the one that might once more produce a stabilized front, would be fought on German territory. Under these conditions, most Frenchmen reasoned, the Reich would be highly unlikely to start another war.[2]

After the signature of the Locarno agreements, however, most observers had foreseen the possibility of an accelerated evacution of the Rhineland. With the declaration of the Conference of Ambassadors in December 1926 that Germany had disarmed and the consequent withdrawal of the Interallied Control Commission, a major justification for the occupation of the left bank was at length explicitly abandoned. Now that disarmament and security questions had apparently been resolved, and the reparations problem removed from international dispute, Germany argued that the stipulations of the Versailles Treaty had been fulfilled. Invoking Article 431 of the treaty, which provided for the early evacuation of the Left Bank in the event of Germany's compliance in its treaty obligations, the government of the Reich called for the withdrawal of foreign troops. France's Anglo-American partners were susceptible to this kind of reasoning. In contrast, it was only by stressing the link between the Rhineland occupation and actual reparations payments, as opposed to mere promises of such, that France could justify prolonging the stationing of its troops on German soil.

So it was not unexpected that negotiations for evacuation and for the revision of the reparations agreement should converge. The Dawes Plan had, in fact, left open the possibility of further adjustments and changes. From the outset that document's complicated mechanisms for assuring payment, including a direct lien on German revenues, and its failure to fix the total debt gave the plan an impermanent quality.

2. See articles by André Pironneau in the *Echo de Paris,* January 5, 1927; August 22, 1928. See also speech by Georges Mandel, JOC *Déb.,* December 24, 1929, p. 4647.

Although rumors of possible revisions circulated in late 1927 and early the following year, no decisive action was taken until September 1928. The agreement reached at the time to constitute another Committee of Experts in effect called into question the occupation of the Rhineland. After months of discussion, the issue in the end became whether the last zone would be evacuated before or after the revised plan for reparations, the Young Plan, went into effect. The French succeeded at least in maintaining the latter interpretation.[3]

When during 1929, it became clear that the troops in the Rhineland would leave ahead of schedule, few Frenchmen had reason to be surprised. Indeed those who had renounced as impractical, dangerous, or possibly immoral, the use of the left bank for French military operations, were unshaken by the prospect of early evacuation. The Socialists, true to their internationalist faith, regarded Germany's acceptance of the Dawes Plan and its signature of the Locarno agreements as grounds for an immediate withdrawal from the two remaining zones.[4] Although the Radicals were less doctrinaire, their basic position that the army should perform its defensive mission without budging from France's frontier—a view that was clearly enunciated in debates on military questions throughout the decade—meant that they found little reason to be alarmed by their country's evacuation of German territory. Moreover, after the Radicals left the Poincaré ministry in late 1928, they once again focused their attention on domestic affairs. Although the subsequent Poincaré and Briand governments appeared to be executing the foreign policy of

3. For a summary of the reparations question from the Dawes Plan to the Young Plan, and of the negotiations leading to the evacuation of the Rhineland, see Arnold J. Toynbee, *Survey of International Affairs, 1929* (London, 1930), pp. 91-189.

4. See speech by Charles Spinasse, JOC *Déb.*, March 1, 1926, pp. 1099ff.

the Left, the advocates of international détente withheld support from both of them.[5]

It was moderate and conversative deputies, rather, who formed the majority on which Poincaré and Briand depended. Unhappy supporters of a foreign policy that was not their own, they could find no leverage for offering resistance. Little by little their objections to withdrawal became reduced to platonic and fruitless demurrals. André Maginot, who had earlier declared that the evacuation of the Left Bank would be an act of treason, in late 1929 justified this very step, arguing that since withdrawal was inevitable, the move should be made while Germany was still prepared to make concessions in return.[6] When Briand dramatically offered his detractors an opportunity to force his resignation, by turning a vote on a small item of his ministry's budget into a question of personal confidence, his opponents implicitly retracted their blanket condemnation of his foreign policy, concentrated their ire on matters of detail, and either abstained or voted in favor of the point in question.[7] Thus despite Georges Mandel's pronouncements that the men who had occupied the Ruhr would never consent to evacuate the Rhineland, he in fact found himself virtually isolated in this attitude.[8]

5. For a detailed account of the Left's parliamentary maneuvering in the late 1920's, see Edouard Bonnefous, *Histoire politique de la Troisième République,* IV: *Cartel des Gauches et Union Nationale* (Paris, 1960), part 2.

6. See reports of speeches given by Maginot in the *Echo de Paris,* November 1, 1926; October 1, 1929.

7. JOC *Déb.,* December 26, 1929, pp. 4683ff. The debates on the Foreign Affairs budget, which provoked discussion of a wide range of diplomatic problems, extended over a number of days: December 23, 1929, pp. 4610ff.; December 24, 1929, pp. 4639ff.; December 26, 1929, pp. 4673ff.; December 27, 1929, pp. 4707ff.

8. See interview Mandel gave to the *Echo de Paris,* January 12, 1927; and his speech, JOC *Déb.,* December 24, 1929, pp. 4647ff.

For people who since 1919 had resolutely demanded the strict enforcement of the Versailles Treaty, who had considered the occupation of the Rhineland the only automatic barrier against the holocaust of another war, the prospect of relinquishing that bulwark was a stunning blow. Moreover, with the last French positions on German soil about to be evacuated, the weakness of France's military establishment at home stood clearly revealed. What should have been remarked on and warned against in 1927, when one-year military service and the corresponding army organization were debated, only now fully emerged. In the earlier debates Maginot had based his argument in favor of the government's proposals on the very ground that two and a half years later gave way beneath him. In mid-1927 he had persuaded his auditors, and perhaps himself most of all, that France's cover would be adequately provided by the recall of the three youngest reserve classes, the *disponibles*.[9] By late 1929 he had discovered this scheme to be dangerously insufficient. Gone were his factitious and specious assurances; in their place was a forthright and undoubtedly painful recognition that at the outbreak of another war France's protection would depend upon men comfortably enmeshed in civilian life.[10] In their own eyes Maginot and people like him now stood guilty as accomplices in jeopardizing the safety of their country.

With each successive revision of French mobilization plans, the scope of offensive operations from the Rhineland base had progressively diminished. Plan P, which was in effect from June 1921 to March 1923, had projected French advances

9. JOC *Déb.*, May 19, 1927, p. 1523.
10. *Ibid.*, December 28, 1929, p. 4774.

from the Left Bank aimed at Germany's two closest industrial centers, the valleys of the Ruhr and the Main. In 1924 a
new plan, Plan A, drawn up in the wake of the Ruhr occupation and on the basis of eighteen-month service, had called
for mobilizing a slightly greater number of divisions whose
aim would still have been a multiple crossing of the Rhine.
But when scarcely more than a year had elapsed, this plan
was already outdated. Even before one-year military service
had been voted, France's colonial difficulties had necessitated
a significant change in the mission of its army. With more
than 200,000 effectives serving outside Europe, the remaining forces were directed to adopt a "protective posture for
the defense of the national territory."[11] In thus revising Plan
A, France's military chiefs had quietly eliminated the firm
and immediate offensive originally envisaged. When, finally,
in 1929, one-year military service became the basis of a new
mobilization plan, Plan B, the assignment of the troops in the
Rhineland at the outbreak of hostilities was reduced to "beat-
ing a retreat on successive lines of withdrawal."[12]

As French plans lost their dynamism and as the evacuation
of the Rhineland became imminent, the fear of a German
attaque brusquée began to figure prominently in military discussions. Such an assault should not be confused with the
strategy Germany eventually adopted. Although mobility was
the major element in the attack French planners now feared,
they did not, at this point, consider that a lightning blow
could be backed up immediately by masses of well-trained
and fully equipped reserves, as in fact happened in 1940.

11. General P.-E. Tournoux, *Défense des frontières: Haut Commandement-
Gouvernement 1919-1939* (Paris, Nouvelles éditions latines, 1960), p. 335.
12. *Ibid.,* pp. 335-336. Tournoux, who was in fact granted access to the War
Ministry's archives, gives the only complete summary of French mobilization
plans (pp. 332-341).

Rather such spokesmen for a strong French military establishment as Jean Fabry and André Maginot speculated that
Germany would rely solely on its existing military machine.
Estimating that their country's eastern neighbor had 300,000
to 400,000 highly trained men, they contended that these
forces could in a few days or even a few hours create irrepara-
ble havoc in France's frontier regions.[13] In similar vein, General Targe, a member of the Conseil Supérieur de la Guerre,
while envisaging the actual attack the way the others did,
wrote of the assault as a means to secure the integrity of
German soil and to assure the time necessary for general
mobilization. General von Seeckt, the major architect of the
Reichswehr, had outlined operations of this very sort, and his
ideas found a place in all French discussions.[14] To the
pointed objection that Germany's army was poorly equipped,
Fabry and those who thought like him replied that the moment the German General Staff came to the conclusion that
such an attack had a chance of success, it was ipso facto a
clear and present danger.[15]

Yet did not such warnings ascribe to the Reich a daring
bordering on the foolhardy, or at least an audacity that
France's leaders had seldom contemplated? For the outlines

13. They arrived at this figure by adding the 150,000-man Schutzpolizei to the
100,000 soldiers of the Reichswehr. In addition they calculated that every year
each organization released 5,000 men and replaced them with new recruits. The
discharged troops, better trained than the French, could be easily reincorporated.
See speeches by Jean Fabry, JOC *Déb.,* November 28, 1928, p. 2974; December
10, 1929, p. 4224.

14. General Antoine Targe, *La garde de nos frontières* (Paris, 1930), pp. 82-84;
see also General Debeney, *Sur la sécurité militaire de la France* (Paris, Payot,
1930), pp. 10-11.

15. See speeches by Jean Fabry, JOC *Déb.,* December 10, 1929, pp. 4224-
4225; December 28, 1929, pp. 4770-4771. See also remarks by André Maginot,
ibid., December 28, 1929, p. 4774; by General Hirschauer, Senate Army Commission, Procès-verbal, November 14, 1928; February 27, 1929.

of French mobilization plans should be read against the background of hesitation and timidity so clearly evident in discussions of defense policy. Although French military writers in the early 1920's had described operations designed to hinder German mobilization and concentration, they had simultaneously suggested that such an advance was unlikely to prove decisive. Even in the immediate postwar period France's army chiefs had seemed uncertain how to bring to bear their country's military superiority. Civilian political leaders, in the course of parliamentary debates, had further underlined this hesitancy, exposing their apprehensiveness about taking any initiative at all.[16] Now as the defects of France's own army organization stood clearly revealed, the country's leaders magnified their enemy's capabilities. Indeed it was their sense of their own vulnerability that led French politicians and military chiefs to attribute so emphatically to their foe rash designs that they themselves would never have acted upon.

As a result, politicians who regarded themselves as the defenders of France's security urged the military to expedite plans for the fortification of Alsace and Lorraine. The outcome was tragically ironic. In order to guard against a small but sudden danger, France's political leaders—at the one time during the interwar period when the country was enjoying a budgetary surplus—appropriated large sums of money for building a bulwark out of proportion to the menace that then existed. When less than a decade later, a far greater danger began to materialize, they found themselves with inadequate means to parry the coming blow.

16. See above, "The Legacy of the First World War," in Chapter 2; and "Apprehensiveness Unmasked," in Chapter 3.

On the Defensive in the Northeast

The occupation of the Rhineland, no matter how reduced, assured far more than France's own defense; by leaving German soil in French hands, it made unlikely a German attempt to revise, by force, the territorial clauses of the Versailles Treaty. It thereby safeguarded—with a minimum of French effort—the integrity of Poland, Czechoslovakia, and Austria. This point was stressed again and again by those who campaigned against an early French withdrawal from the Rhineland. Yet in the course of arguing for a delay in the final evacuation of French troops, they failed to envisage any substitute that could fulfill the role of these forces as automatic guardians of European peace. At most they considered—and here Marshal Foch joined in the chorus—that a postponement of the evacuation date would give the new nations of eastern Europe additional time to put their own defenses in order.[17]

In fact the predominant theme in the debates over the withdrawal from the Rhineland was the need for France itself to buy time. As the polemics continued, it became increasingly clear why additional time was now necessary: until France's fortification system was operational, the evacuation would jeopardize the nation's security. This increasingly narrow focus on creating a defensive organization to replace the bulwark of the occupied Rhineland foreshadowed the psychological effect that fortifications would actually have.

17. Anon. [Foch], "Un crime de lèse-patrie, l'évacuation anticipée de la Rhénanie," *Revue de France,* 6, no. 6 (November 1, 1926), 5-12. The *Echo de Paris* waged a vigorous campaign against the early evacuation of the Rhineland, during which the editors interviewed important political figures. See the following issues: November 1, 1926; November 6, 1926; January 5, 1927, January 6, 1927; January 7, 1927; January 8, 1927; January 9, 1927; January 10, 1927; January 18, 1927; January 24, 1927, July 11, 1927; June 11, 1928; August 22, 1928; August 24, 1928; August 30, 1928; November 6, 1928; March 1, 1929; July 6, 1929; July 24, 1929; August 17, 1929; August 19, 1929.

In coming to depend upon such works France would tacitly relinquish its option to reoccupy German soil and would simultaneously abandon its interests in eastern Europe. And in thus implicitly renouncing the one substantial provision of the Locarno agreements, the French would feel a still greater need to buy time, in this case, in order to avoid a war they could not win.

When invasion actually came in 1940, the permanent fortifications built in Alsace and Lorraine proved to be far removed from the main theaters of combat. Even at the time they were conceived, in the late 1920's, France's army chiefs were aware that in concentrating on their northeastern frontier and leaving their northern border unprotected, they were inviting attack from the latter direction. Indeed, if a massive assault comparable in scale to the one launched by Germany in 1914 had been their only concern, they might not have focused so intensely on the northeast. The fact that military and civilians alike were also worrying about an attaque brusquée—whose very quality of surprise precluded the Germans giving a warning signal by an initial march through Belgium—naturally led French planners to assign top priority to Alsace and Lorraine, the regions in which their country had a common border with the Reich.[18]

Yet such anxieties cannot entirely account for the scale of the fortifications actually built. The particular diplomatic configuration produced by the Versailles Treaty both heightened the fear of an attaque brusquée and prevented French army leaders from assuming a totally defensive posture. While

18. For evidence of these concerns, see General F. Culmann, *La fortification permanente aux frontières* (Paris, 1931), p. 112. This book is particularly important because the author served in the secretariat of the commission charged with drawing up the actual plans.

the definite time limit set on the occupation of the Rhine-land and the existence of a powerful German professional army increased their sense of vulnerability, the fact that the Rhineland was to remain militarily neutral after the evacuation of Allied troops meant that military planners could not abandon forthwith the notion of a French advance into that area. Paradoxically enough, it was because France's army chiefs were less exclusively defense-minded than has commonly been thought that such large works were constructed.

Had Pétain exercised controlling influence in military planning, had the High Command accepted as dogma his belief in the virtues of a linear and continuous front, cement might have been poured at a less prodigious rate. For Pétain was not the guiding force behind the initial plans for permanent fortifications. Subsequent studies have made too much of the laudatory preface he wrote in 1939 for a volume by General Narcisse Chauvineau entitled *Une invasion est-elle encore possible?*[19] This book was published after the fortifications had been built and after their original function had been substantially altered. It would be a mistake to infer the original intentions of France's military chiefs from the statements of the elderly marshal more than a decade after the event. In the late 1920's optimism about establishing a continuous front and a preference for a static defense had not in fact been the dominant attitudes. The reasoning behind the construction of permanent fortifications offers ample evidence to that effect.

Almost as soon as the guns of the First World War fell

19. Chauvineau had been a professor at the Ecole Supérieure de Guerre in the late 1920's and had given the course on fortifications. For comments on the preface and the book see, for example, Philip Charles Farwell Bankwitz, *Maxime Weygand and Civil-Military Relations in Modern France* (Cambridge, Mass., 1967), p. 123; Pertinax, *Les fossoyeurs,* I (New York, 1943), p. 22; Donald J. Harvey, "French Concepts of Military Strategy 1919-1939" (Ph.D. diss., Columbia University, 1953).

silent, defensive works became a topic for discussion within the High Command. The ink on the peace treaty was barely dry before the issues and protagonists of a new struggle appeared. When the Conseil Supérieur de la Guerre first assembled in May 1920 to consider the problem, polemical positions were already staked out. Even before this meeting opened, Pétain and Buat, the chief of staff, had issued directions for the defense of the country in which their joint conceptions had been clearly outlined. Relying heavily on methods employed in stemming the final German attacks of 1918, they based their plans on a series of well-prepared battlefields that would form a continuous line of light defensive works designed to assure the inviolability of the nation's territory. At the general meeting of the High Command, these views did not go unchallenged. General Guillaumat warned against attempting to create a barrier analogous to the unbroken front of trenches during the First World War, and insisted that fortifications must be used to facilitate the offensive actions of the army. Foch even more resolutely affirmed this position. The battle appeared joined between those advocating a static defense and those favoring a war of maneuver that would link fortifications to operational plans.[20]

For the next five years the debate continued. The Conseil Supérieur de la Guerre reviewed the problem again in May 1922. After its collective efforts had once more proved fruitless, a special commission was appointed, chaired initially by Joffre and then by Guillaumat, to study the question. This commission in turn became the locus of continuing contro-

20. Tournoux, *Défense des frontières,* pp. 13-27; see also by the same author, "Les origines de la ligne Maginot," *Revue d'histoire de la Deuxième Guerre Mondiale,* 9, no. 33 (January 1959), 3-15.

versy. The majority, under Guillaumat's leadership, adopted his views and recommended building permanent fortifications. General Buat, however, along with General Hergault, the *sous-chef* of the General Staff, dissented from their final report; as Pétain's surrogates they advocated copying the marshal's First World War methods of defense.[21] This was the situation when at the end of 1923 Buat suddenly died, and General Debeney was appointed his successor as chief of staff. In him Guillaumat found an important ally.[22] Although no decisions were actually made during the next two years—with the Ruhr occupation monopolizing the government's attention, the commission's mandate was in effect allowed to lapse—the balance was clearly shifting in favor of Guillaumat and those who thought like him.

It was not until Paul Painlevé returned to the Ministry of War in November 1925 that work was resumed in earnest and the decision to build permanent fortifications finally took shape. Despite his close ties to Pétain, Painlevé made it clear that he preferred concrete to barbed wire. He accepted Guillaumat's assessment that field works hastily built at the time of mobilization would lack solidity and might be practically useless. Having achieved a facsimile of consensus within the Conseil Supérieur de la Guerre on this question, Painlevé assigned to the newly formed Commission de Défense des Frontières the task of specifying the structure of the fortifications themselves.[23] And in the following year, as the

21. Tournoux, *Défense des frontières,* chap. 2.
22. See Debeney's testimony to a joint meeting of the Senate Finance and Army Commissions in which he declared that the experience of 1918 had been a misleading guide in discussions of fortifications: Senate Finance Commission, Procès-verbal, December 16, 1927.
23. Tournoux, *Défense des frontières,* pp. 40ff. Even Pétain's views were being modified; for this evolution, see General A. M. E. Laure, *Pétain* (Paris, 1941), pp. 277ff.

commission began its work, with Guillaumat again serving as chairman, the cherished notions of Pétain and his supporters—a continuous and linear front—were firmly brushed aside. Both Guillaumat and Debeney pointed out that continuous defensive positions, even in concrete, could serve only as preparation for precisely the kind of engagement France should avoid. For a battle of frontal defense would be prohibitively expensive in terms of the manpower and matériel it would require.[24] Only the army's ability to maneuver would assure an effective defense; no fixed line could serve as a substitute for that capacity.

With such arguments Guillaumat pressed with success for the construction of fortified regions. In the end the commission's report specified those regions very much as its chairman had defined them in 1923:

not as a simple slice of a battlefield on the frontier, but as a real instrument of maneuver at the disposition of the commander-in-chief. Extending along a front of a minimum of 60 kilometers, or better of 80, supported by systematic devastations or, depending on the nature of the terrain, by a deep flank similarly fortified, [such a region] would be equipped, at a distance of 30 kilometers in its rear, with a stop-gap barrier capable at the beginning of a conflict of halting cavalry . . . or tank . . . raids, and should be able to hold out, even if it were temporarily outflanked. . . . Even in the event of an army's withdrawal behind the front, the commander would still retain the possibility of giving battle in depth without losing the support of this fortification.[25]

Once it was decided to build fortified regions, the question of their geographical location was comparatively easy to

24. For a summary of the arguments made against a continuous front, see Culmann, *La fortification permanente*, pp. 138ff.; see also General Debeney, *La guerre et les hommes* (Paris, 1937), p. 205.

25. Tournoux, *Défense des frontières*, p. 54; see also Culmann, *La fortification permanente*, pp. 142ff.

solve. The military considered it practically impossible to defend the northern frontier with permanent works. Geography alone offered a compelling argument to the contrary. The flat, muddy terrain did not permit fortifying the actual border; the best possible defensive positions within France, at some distance from the frontier, would have covered neither Lille and its adjoining industrial zone nor important railroad networks. In fact there was general agreement that the nation's best defense in the north would be an advance into Belgian territory—a view that was acted upon in 1940. In addition, France's relations with Belgium made fortifications diplomatically unsuitable; for the French to construct such works along their common border would constitute an invitation to the Belgians to return to their pre-1914 status of neutrality. If the Belgians thought that they could avoid involvement in another European conflict, they might see little reason to continue their alliance with the French.[26]

Further, the fact that Guillaumat and his colleagues envisaged the role of fortified regions as something more than ancillary to defensive operations led them to focus their efforts on Alsace and Lorraine. France's army leaders in 1926 and 1927 were still thinking of the northeast as an area for their own forward movements. And it was with attack as well as defense in mind that Guillaumat's commission chose the two particular northeastern zones to be treated in concrete: Metz-Thionville, and the area between the Lauter and the Lower Vosges. The latter region, in addition to its essential mission of covering Alsace, was envisaged as a buttress to a French attack in the direction of Pirmasens, Zweibrücken, Landsthul, and Kaiserslautern. The other major region, around Metz, was also conceived as having a multiple role.

26. *Ibid.*, pp. 73-74.

Besides facilitating a French move toward the Saar and Trier, it was intended to assure liaison between the armies of the north and those stationed in the northeast, in effect, to act as a hinge between these two zones of concentration.[27] In the early 1920's, with French troops occupying the Rhineland, the nation's army leaders had already sketched out similar plans for limited offensives. For when French forces should no longer be stationed on German soil, they anticipated that operations of this sort would alone be feasible. From this view even Marshal Foch did not dissent. Indeed throughout the discussions of defensive works, he sided with Guillaumat and consistently saw fortifications as offering support to the army's maneuvers. Although Foch proclaimed in lofty terms that attention should be concentrated on the dynamic partner in this strange marriage, he felt satisfied with the final proposals that emerged.[28] He had no opportunity to assess their implemention; he died in 1929, two years after his colleagues had reached their decision.

In the event, fortifications proved more a brake on army operations than a goad to action. Though Guillaumat had succeeded in convincing the High Command of the strategic advantages offered by the fortified regions, his victory proved insubstantial. Few heeded his warnings; few appreciated the danger of allowing the army and the public to believe that concrete alone could assure the integrity of French soil, when extended human effort was necessary to such a task. Even before actual construction started and Germany began to re-

27. Tournoux, *Défense des frontières,* pp. 56-58, 79. See also Debeney's comments on the strategic role of Metz in his article, "Nos fortifications du nord-est," *Revue des deux mondes,* 8e période, 23 (September 15, 1934), 255.

28. Foch Cahiers, Dossier F, August 21, 1921; January 26, 1922; May 31, 1922; June 15, 1922; Dossier G, February 1927. See also Tournoux, *Défense des frontières,* pp. 86-89.

arm, it became clear that French troops were unlikely to move out beyond the fortified regions into the adjacent areas of the Rhineland. For the role assigned to fortifications was as much a function of France's own military capability as it was of the works themselves. And the very reason—a lack of confidence in their own forces—that caused military and civilian leaders to fear a German attaque brusquée and to hasten the construction of fortifications in the northeast, led them to stress almost exclusively the defensive qualities of the proposed concrete bastions.

This lack of confidence had already been implicit in the appointment of the Commission de Défense des Frontières. For the decision to speed up work on fortifications was intimately connected with the reduction in the length of military service to one year. When General Nollet had first proposed a one-year term, he had planned to complement this measure with a reorganization of the army that would increase both its mobility and the number of its cadres. Trusting to advanced weaponry to counterbalance the decrease in conscripts on active duty, Nollet had advised against investing in a vast defensive program. His views, however, were not accepted by the majority of the Conseil Supérieur de la Guerre. Discouraged by the failure to raise the number of militaires de carrière, they considered Nollet's proposals for streamlining the army both risky and unrealistic. As compensation for the reduction in the length of military service, they opted for the sturdiness of permanent fortifications. Paul Painlevé, minister of war, shared this preference and simultaneously pushed ahead in reducing the strength of France's active army and erecting concrete works to protect its dimished forces.[29]

29. *Ibid.,* pp. 48-51.

Hence from the outset fortifications were a confirmation of the army's weakened state, a sign of the altered military balance between France and Germany. The French had relinquished the notion of maintaining on active service a superior military force, and while this shift in power justified and stimulated the construction of fortifications, concrete bastions could not re-establish the preponderance that had existed in the immediate postwar years. In fact the discussions of military policy in 1928 and 1929 were suffused with such an awareness. Even those who for a decade had been staunch advocates of safeguarding their country's armed strength now echoed the defensive commonplaces of their ideological opponents. It was surely no change in political philosophy that led Jean Fabry to declare that France must be resolutely prepared to receive the first blow.[30] As late as 1927 he had exhorted his colleagues to organize the army in such a fashion that its standing units would be capable of immediate action.[31] Less than two years later the terms of the discussion had changed. With one-year military service and the evacuation of the Rhineland impending realities, the point at issue for Fabry was no longer what the active army might initiate but rather how it should be equipped to withstand a German attack.

It was in this context that the dispute over fortified regions versus continuous front reappeared in late 1929 during the parliamentary debates on fortifications. Pierre Cot, who emerged as the Radical spokesman on military affairs, was the chief advocate of a policy that had also been Marshal

30. JOC *Déb.*, November 28, 1928, p. 2974, and December 10, 1929, p. 4223.
31. *Ibid.*, June 9, 1927, pp. 1786ff. In late 1925 he made a ringing statement about the importance of French operations in an unoccupied Rhineland and expressed skepticism about the value of fortifications: "Où va notre armée?" *Revue de Paris*, 32, no. 18 (September 15, 1925), 241-268.

Pétain's. Arguing that the range of the guns installed in the large bastions would be inadequate to provide protection along the entire frontier, Cot recommended spending money in building smaller defenses in an unbroken line.[32] Although War Minister Maginot refused to alter the official proposals, since any delay would have magnified the dangers France already faced, he conceded that the government had taken Cot's objections into account. Regardless of the forms of the permanent works themselves, he declared, "the first objective of a system of fortifications" was "to assure that the defenders of the terrain" would enjoy "the protection of a continuous line of fire."[33] Thus in answering the proponents of continuous, though lighter, works, Maginot implicitly accepted his antagonists' image of the first stages of a new war—a defensive battle on the frontier. What had originally seemed to be a sharp divergence of opinion now no longer represented differing strategic notions.

Since continuity of fire could not be guaranteed by permanent fortifications, the advocates of the official policy underlined the importance of equipping unfortified zones with at least rudimentary defensive works. Where Guillaumat had conceived the intervals between the fortified regions as providing space in which the army could maneuver, such possibilities now remained unmentioned. When General Debeney, who had been a staunch supporter of Guillaumat's views, appeared before a joint meeting of the Senate Finance and Army Commissions, he put his major stress on the measures that would be taken to protect the unfortified areas: "in these open spaces" he explained, there would be "everything necessary . . . , the troops and the corresponding matériel"

32. JOC *Déb.*, December 10, 1929, pp. 4218ff.
33. *Ibid.*, December 10, 1929, p. 4235; see also December 28, 1929, p. 4775.

that could fortify the battlefield at the very moment [of attack] and perhaps even earlier."[34] In brief, Debeney tried to reassure the senators that the unfortified gaps could be held.

Thus the whole conception of fortified regions had been substantially revised. Although their actual construction followed fairly closely the specifications laid down by the Commission de Défense des Frontières, civilians and military alike increasingly saw them as part of a defensive and continuous front.[35] Indeed there was a tone of homey reassurance in the descriptions of how the northeast would be protected. Two of the six fully manned divisions—all that were provided by the recently passed army reorganization law— would be assigned to the fortified regions themselves. The four remaining divisions would be deployed in the intervals.[36] According to Debeney, "at the first sound of alarm" these troops would "occupy sites" that they had already "reconnoitred" and where their place was "marked out in advance."[37] Subsequently, as Maginot remarked, they would "cling to the ground, in order to hold on and await the recall of the disponibles and the beginning of . . . mobilization."[38] Similarly, while Fabry reiterated his demands for a reduction in the total of skeleton divisions and for the redeployment of a smaller number of fully manned units along France's fron-

34. Senate Finance Commission, Procès-verbal, December 16, 1927.
35. On the construction, see Tournoux, *Défense des frontières,* chap. 7. Debeney, however, did point out that the tendency to sacrifice the flanks of the fortified regions in an attempt to increase linear continuity marked an important modification of the original proposals: Debeney, "Nos fortifications du nord-est," p. 254. As for Guillaumat, although he recognized the value of the actual fortifications, he objected to the strategic role they were assigned: Léon Noël, *Témoignage d'un chef: le Général Guillaumat* (Paris, 1949), pp. 127-128.
36. Tournoux, *Défense des frontières,* p. 112.
37. Senate Finance Commission, Procès-verbal, December 16, 1927.
38. JOC *Déb.,* December 28, 1929, p. 4774.

tiers, he made it clear that these troops were not to engage in immediate action but were to occupy positions that had been partially prepared in advance.[39]

What measures might be taken once mobilization had been completed or once the disponibles, at least, had been recalled, was not discussed in the public forum. Yet this silence was as much a sign of common understanding as it was of military prudence. No one doubted that the initial stance of the mobilized army would be purely defensive. For the same defects in training and cohesion that required prepared positions as compensation for one-year military service obliged the French army as a whole to assume such a posture.[40]

A defense policy is a function of particular fears. It was the heightened fear of an attaque brusquée, crystallizing in the late 1920's, that moved fortifications from the realm of theory to the drafting boards and finally implanted them in the ground. Yet this anxiety, though acting as a catalyst, did not displace long-standing concerns. For a full decade the possibility of another holocaust on the scale of the First World War had dominated French debates on military questions as well as discussions of foreign policy. In drafting legislation for army organization and in revising mobilization plans, France's military leaders had been preoccupied with preparing the nation for total war. It was this overriding concern for general mobilization that had led them to accept one-year military service and subsequently to resign themselves to what an army built on that foundation could offer—a defensive posture in the northeast.[41]

39. *Ibid.*, December 28, 1929, pp. 4768-4771.
40. See, for example, Targe, *La garde de nos frontières*, pp. 78-79.
41. See Debeney, *Sur la sécurité militaire de la France*, pp. 44-45; Targe, *La garde de nos frontières*, p. 88.

Had an attaque brusquée been the only fear, had French military chiefs and politicians firmly believed that Germany would definitely act in a way in which they themselves had never planned to behave, that is, without resort to general mobilization, launch an attack aiming at victory in a conveniently limited war, they might have found a professional army (*armée de métier*) more appealing. Although General de Gaulle was to popularize this idea in the mid-1930's, the conception was by no means original with him. Throughout the 1920's there had been muted suggestions of creating a small, well-armed, and highly mobile striking force as a substitute for a national army. Until the stabilization of the franc, however, the financial difficulties that hampered the recruitment of militaires de carrière would have proved an insuperable obstacle—a problem De Gaulle sidestepped by depicting in rhapsodic tones the congruence between a military career and the spirit of the age.[42] In the late 1920's, when order had finally been restored to France's finances, such difficulties, in theory at least, might have been overcome.

But a mere improvement in the French treasury could not change preconceptions about the nature of the next war. No matter how the conflict should begin, nearly everyone was in agreement that it would eventually be total. De Gaulle's proposals were based on assumptions that simply were not shared by the overwhelming majority of France's military and political leaders. Dismissing the preoccupations of his fellow citizens with his usual ease, if not arrogance, De Gaulle argued that total war was no longer a grave danger.

As we know, ever since armed nations began destroying each other, the facade of principles has apparently remained intact, because the mass of

42. Charles De Gaulle, *Vers l'armée de métier,* translated as *The Army of the Future* (Philadelphia, Lippincott, 1941), p. 107.

people are reluctant to relinquish ideas once they have acquired them, and most specialists cling to recognized ideas. This does not prevent the conditions from which "total war" grew from gradually disappearing and making way for others. There are good reasons for believing that a war starting tomorrow would be only remotely connected, at the beginning, with the premature attack of mobilized masses.

Surrounded by disapproving neutrals, flanked by suspicious allies, it is doubtful whether the aggressors would want frankly to wage unrestricted warfare for the sake of seizing a province or a colony.[43]

Even the more moderate proposal of establishing professional élite formations whose ranks would be filled out with conscripts was unacceptable to France's military chiefs. Although such a force could be constituted only with the greatest difficulty on the basis of one-year military service, it was not this obstacle that loomed largest. It was rather, as General Debeney argued, that the creation of an élite force would ineluctably lead to a divorce between those units and the rest of the army. The special army would inevitably become the prime beneficiary of military credits and advanced weaponry; the national army, poorly trained, staffed, and equipped, would eventually sink into impotence. Recalling the French defeat of 1870, Debeney reminded his readers of the price his country had once paid for such a military system.[44]

Moreover, the fact that the élite forces would be ready for instant action was not necessarily an argument in their favor, since the need for caution at the beginning of a new war had become a staple of French military thinking. Already in the immediate postwar years, France's army chiefs had tacitly agreed that their country's survival in another conflict with a rearmed Germany would depend upon husbanding its active

43. *Ibid.*, pp. 73-74, 76-77. I have altered the translation.
44. Debeney, *Sur la sécurité militaire de la France,* pp. 21ff.

forces in such a way as to allow time for complete mobilization and for the arrival of allied reinforcements.[45] To risk everything in the first moments, through concentrating efforts on an attack by the professional forces, would be to court disaster. As Debeney remarked, it would be "dangerous to put all the eggs in one basket," and "the thesis of a short war," having as its logical conclusion a plea for a "professional army followed by a mediocre second army," would necessitate "playing a game of poker, with the country itself at stake."[46]

Debeney did not foresee, however, what the French military establishment as constituted in the late 1920's would eventually cost the nation. In building immobile concrete works without at the same time providing an army that might use these bastions as a base for its own offensive operations, France's military and civilian leaders signaled their unwillingness to enforce the Locarno agreements and to secure the neutrality of the Rhineland. Instead, by transforming fortified regions into symbols of armed protection, they made it clear that military initiatives no longer figured as an adjunct to French diplomacy and that the prospect of an invasion alone would goad them into action. In thus assuaging their fear of a German attaque brusquée, France's army chiefs gave reality to the still more pervasive nightmare of another total war. Having coped with their immediate anxiety, they would find future problems far more intractable.

The Dilemmas of the North

In the ten years that had passed since the signing of the Versailles Treaty, French diplomats had failed to find a

45. See above, "The International Desiderata for Military Planning," in Chapter 2.
46. Debeney, *Sur la sécurité militaire de la France,* pp. 50-51.

permanent and effective safeguard against Germany. Whatever slim hopes the army chiefs may have entertained that diplomatic bargaining might insure France's security had been continually disappointed. Nor in that time had they created an armed instrument that could forestall the military recovery of their nation's traditional enemy. Where diplomacy had been unable to provide a solution, they had failed to manufacture one themselves. Now, in 1930, with the Rhineland about to be evacuated, French military leaders were faced with difficulties they had long anticipated. Yet being on familiar ground offered cold comfort indeed. While they had always assumed that they must prepare their country for total war with a potentially more powerful enemy, they were as eager as their fellow citizens to postpone the day of reckoning.

In coming face to face with the prospect of total conflict, French military planners were once more confronted by the disquieting legacy of the First World War. The staggering losses of the years 1914-1918 had underlined France's demographic weakness, and the postwar diplomatic configuration gave little guarantee that the nation's numerical inferiority could be redressed at the outbreak of hostilities. For the potential—though by no means certain—aid offered by the new nations of eastern Europe was never considered an adequate substitute for the pre-1914 Russian alliance, which in any case had proved to be overvalued. Nor did France's army chiefs make the kinds of plans that might facilitate possible joint action with these eastern allies. Indeed their desire to have Polish and Czech soldiers march in step with French *poilus* against Germany necessarily took second place to their more urgent wish to protect their own territory against invasion. Instead of concentrating the bulk of French forces in

Alsace and Lorraine and aiming at a major move into the Rhineland, French military planners devised concrete defensive bastions. In thus foreclosing an offensive in the northeast, they were simply repeating the primitive (and perfectly valid) reasoning that past experience had taught: "To defeat the enemy in Alsace is not a success unless at the same time one is not defeated at Charleroi" on the Belgian frontier.[47]

The problem of guarding France's northern frontier against a German invasion was not a new one. Moreover the likelihood of Germany concentrating its troops for an attack in that area became much greater after the construction of concrete works in the northeast. It did not take extensive historical knowledge to recall that France's prewar investment in fortifications—which had been much less pretentious than those of the late 1920's—had been a major factor in Schlieffen's decision to march through Belgium. Clearly, as Painlevé pointed out in praise of the government's proposals, the necessity of bringing up heavy equipment for a frontal assault on the fortifications subsequently called the Maginot Line would dissuade France's enemy from attempting an attaque brusquée.[48] Similarly it took little imagination to realize that if the Germans should decide instead for total war, they would prefer the Belgian route. The Commission de Défense des Frontières recognized this danger at the outset: "The fortified regions might possibly, or even probably, divert the attack toward Belgium."[49]

Thus it was not surprising that at the same time as French parliamentarians voted appropriations for fortifications in

47. Colonel Chauvineau, "L'organisation du terrain et ses conséquences," *Revue militaire française,* no. 104 (February 1930), 273n.
48. JOC *Déb.,* November 28, 1928, p. 2972.
49. Tournoux, *Défense des frontières,* p. 55.

Alsace and Lorraine, they should voice concern about the northern frontier. Indeed the risks involved in concentrating heavy works solely in the northeast had been urged as an argument against the fortified regions themselves. As the Radical spokesman Edouard Daladier pointed out: "it would be . . . dangerous . . . to become hypnotized . . . by . . . Lorraine" while leaving "open the route from the north to Paris."[50] Even those who backed the government's final proposals were made more than a little uneasy by the delays in planning the defensive organization of the north. Nor in this instance did the reassurances offered by General Debeney produce their usual calming effect. Senator Berger accurately summed up the feelings of his colleagues on the Army Commission: "The declarations of General Debeney, despite the sympathy he expressed for the population of the north, do not seem adequate to me. They were garbled and sometimes imprecise. I fear that in reality the government is not resolved to fortify our northern frontiers."[51]

The senators' response was entirely appropriate. Although the government had decided to trace out in advance a line of defense along the Franco-Belgian border, it had specified that this line would be guarded by the mass of the French army rather than by concrete bastions. These positions were to be strengthened by the construction of light works at the time of mobilization. To supply the equipment for such hasty field-works the government accepted the recommendations of the Commission de Défense des Frontières and proposed the creation of so-called *parcs mobiles de fortification*. These provisions for the rapid building of defensive works were

50. JOC *Déb.*, November 28, 1928, p. 2972.
51. Senate Army Commission, Procès-verbal, February 27, 1929.

already well known. Identical measures had been prescribed for filling the intervals between the fortified regions in the northeast. To such "transitory fortifications" would now be assigned the far more crucial role of facilitating the army's deployment in the north. According to Debeney's account they would consist of "field defenses reinforced by certain concrete works," plus stocks of matériel placed "at determined points . . . so that the troops might instantaneously establish this fortification."[52] Maginot's description went even farther in attempting to allay possible fears:

In truth, these *parcs mobiles* are reserves of matériel and gear stocked close to the sites whose defense in time of war they will be responsible for organizing, or close to railroad intersections which will enable them to be transported rapidly to where their intervention is called for.

Thus . . . you will have extremely mobile defensive organizations . . . a kind of fortification on wheels . . . susceptible of being rapidly carried from one point to another and capable in a few days, at points predetermined by the command or imposed by circumstances, of organizing a line of defense sufficient to permit the troops occupying the terrain to cling to it and to hold on.[53]

With these measures the senators were quite rightly dissatisfied. Nor could the military derive much comfort from such cumbersome and imprecise provisions. Indeed to depend on them was to contradict the logic behind the establishment of the fortified regions. Debeney and Guillaumat had both argued that new fronts hastily organized at the outbreak of the war could be easily broken, and with this argument they had finally convinced even Pétain that France must build permanent fortifications. Why, then, the senators reasoned, should

52. Senate Finance Commission, Procès-verbal, December 16, 1929; see also Tournoux, *Défense des frontières,* pp. 114-125.
53. JOC *Déb.,* December 28, 1929, p. 4775.

organizing the defense of the north be postponed until the last moment? With the military thus condemned out of their own mouths, it was natural that the Senate Army Commission should continue to urge the War Ministry to push ahead with fortifications on the Belgian frontier.

Throughout the following decade, however, the fortification of the front between Montmédy and Dunkirk was given low priority in allocating financial resources—which became increasingly scarce as the Depression made itself felt. In the early 1930's, at the insistence of the Senate Army Commission, recommendations for the construction of two fortified regions in that area were drawn up. These proposals were shelved by the Conseil Supérieur de la Guerre in 1932. Instead, the High Command urged that the available money be appropriated for tanks and other armaments—and the sum was small in comparison to what had been spent and was being spent on the northeast. Two years later more modest plans to create a bridgehead at Montmédy and to improve the defenses at Maubeuge were acted upon. But subsequent attempts to fortify the north were slighted, since such proposals vied for funds with efforts to modernize the older fortified regions. General Gamelin, who in 1932 as chief of staff had advocated permanent works on the Franco-Belgian frontier, after 1935, when he became generalissimo-designate, placed his major emphasis on increasing the defensive capabilities of the Maginot Line. As a consequence the light works constructed between Mezières and Dunkirk, except for those at Maubeuge, constituted nothing more than a prearranged battlefield. And between Mezières and Montmédy—where the Germans in fact broke through in 1940—the rugged terrain of the Ardennes offered an excuse for leaving that zone without substantial defensive positions.[54]

Yet the paltry efforts made to fortify the north were not simply the result of an unwise allocation of resources. Behind this low priority lay an uncertainty about the strategic role of the area. Even those who with Gamelin favored, if finances permitted, constructing permanent works were unsure where the initial battle would be fought. In contrast, the older fortified regions had acquired a clear strategic significance. With the evacuation of the Rhineland and the loss of overwhelming French military preponderance, they had become the bulwark for a defensive battle on the frontier; the earlier conceptions of an advance into the Rhineland to secure better positions for defense and counteroffense had been virtually abandoned. What had been a dominant feature of French military thinking about the northeast in the early 1920's, what had now been implicitly given up, again came into prominence in the discussions about the north. For there the French army, with only friendly or neutral forces before it, was in a position to make an initial advance in order to gain both time and space.

Indeed, the idea of marching into Belgian territory had been central to the decision to concentrate permanent fortifications in Alsace and Lorraine. Debeney and Guillaumat considered it axiomatic that only an advance across the northern frontier offered France a chance to defend its own territory. Moreover, Pétain, the advocate of a continuous front and the notorious architect of a defensive army, consistently upheld this view. Instead of concentrating France's

54. General Maurice Gamelin, *Servir*, I: *Les armées françaises de 1940* (Paris, Plon, 1946), pp. 102, 303-308; II: *Le prologue du drame* (Paris, Plon, 1946), pp. 66ff., 127ff. See also Tournoux, *Défense des frontières*, chap. 8.

forces along the border and equipping them with permanent fortifications, he insisted that they must be prepared to move into Belgium. Even Weygand, who did not fully accept the orthodoxies of the 1920's and who sided with Gamelin in the discussion of 1932, couched his defense of permanent fortifications in terms of providing a backstop for a French advance across the Belgian border.[55]

In the event Gamelin had eight months—from September 1939 to May 1940—in which to strengthen defensive positions along France's northern frontier. Despite this breathing space, he still calculated that lacking any natural obstacle on the Franco-Belgian border, without any solid rear position, the French army, if it remained on national soil, would almost surely be forced to abandon the major part of its country's northern industries and mines. Instead he chose the line Meuse-Namur-Antwerp, deep inside Belgium, as the destination of France's troops. This new front was seventy to eighty kilometers shorter than the Franco-Belgian border. Moreover, "the Meuse, with cliffs on both banks, the flooding of the Dyle and the Nete," offered defensive advantages that nature had failed to bestow on France itself.[56] But above all, as Gamelin candidly remarked, "the occupation of the front Namur-Antwerp diverted the war from our northern province . . . If one considers the devastation that a modern battle entails in the region where it takes place, isn't this argu-

55. *Ibid.*, pp. 148-161. On Weygand's attitude, see also *Documents diplomatiques belges,* II (Brussels, 1964), no. 231, pp. 675-678 (henceforth cited as *DDB,* II). For Gamelin's account see his *Servir,* II, 66ff. In 1931 Weygand had succeeded Pétain as vice-president of the Conseil Supérieur de la Guerre, and Gamelin in turn had taken Weygand's place as chief of staff. Although Pétain had at that time retired from the vice-presidency and from his post of inspector-general of the army, he remained a member of the Conseil Supérieur de la Guerre by virtue of his rank as Marshal of France, and in 1932 he played the crucial role in defeating plans for constructing additional fortified regions.

56. Gamelin, *Servir,* I, 94.

ment [for an advance into Belgium] even more convincing?"[57]

In the light of such a statement it is hard to believe—despite Gamelin's claims to the contrary [58]—that the construction of fortifications in the north would have altered France's battle plan. Against so determined a preference for fighting on Belgian soil, the existence of defensive works along the frontier could have offered scant restraint. With vivid memories of how the country's most productive departments had been laid waste in the First World War, it is not surprising that the French High Command should have directed its efforts toward avoiding a repetition of such a disaster. Nor can it be a cause for wonder that France's northern neighbor was motivated by a similar concern to divert military action from its own territory.

In the course of the 1930's an advance into Belgium became increasingly prominent in French mobilization plans. In Plan C, drawn up after the evacuation of the Rhineland, the High Command for the first time envisaged sending French armies north. This disposition was scarcely modified in the following plan—Plan D—which remained in effect from 1933 to 1935. Although both plans called for French troops to cross the Franco-Belgian border, the center of gravity had not yet shifted from the northeast. The decisive changes, embodied in Plans D-bis and E, occurred after 1935, when Germany began to rearm openly and reinstituted universal military service. Yet throughout the entire period the specific destination of French forces was never made precise. For their advance was contingent upon a Belgian invitation, and

57. *Ibid.*, p. 92.
58. *Ibid.*, pp. 85, 94, 105.

the exact line French troops might reach depended upon how early or late they were called to defend their northern neighbor.[59] Thus when two months after the outbreak of the Second World War, in November 1939, the French High Command drew up orders for such an advance, they refrained from carrying them out. They waited another seven months before giving the actual signal to march.[60]

Foch's hopes for Franco-Belgian military planning, for a joint defense against a former enemy, had long since proved illusory. Even in 1920, when the two countries had concluded an alliance, Foch had been disappointed by the vague and elusive defensive provisions that were to go into effect after the evacuation of the Rhineland. And as the last Allied troops withdrew from German soil, Belgian leaders, instead of pursuing joint staff talks, sought to disentangle themselves from the agreements that bound them to the French. In a speech before the Belgian Chamber of Deputies on March 4, 1931, Foreign Minister Paul Hymans spelled out his country's position. Declaring that in effect the Franco-Belgian military accord was a dead letter, that since the evacuation of the Rhineland most of its provisions no longer applied, and that in any event it had been superseded by the Locarno agreements, he reaffirmed Belgium's independence in matters of military policy.[61] Not until May 1940, when Germany actually invaded Belgian territory, did that country's leaders be-

59. Tournoux, *Défense des frontières,* pp. 336-341.

60. Gamelin, *Servir,* I, 81-83.

61. Hymans' speech was preceded by a series of diplomatic exchanges with the French in which Belgian negotiators outlined the substance of what would be said. For a résumé of the negotiations and Belgian views on the Franco-Belgian military accord, see *DDB,* II, no. 236, pp. 686-697; see also *Documents diplomatiques belges,* III (Brussels, Palais des Académies, 1964), no. 30, pp. 116-117; Paul Hymans, *Mémoires,* II (Brussels, 1958), pp. 601-636.

come convinced that their national interests were the same as those of France.[62]

Above all the Belgians were determined to resist possible French attempts to get them involved in another European conflict. It was this determination that lay behind their particular reading of the Rhineland pact signed at Locarno in 1925. To the French parliamentarians who had voted the accord, its provisions relating to a flagrant violation of the Rhineland's neutrality represented an unambiguous guarantee of Belgian as well as British action.[63] Not so to the Belgians. In the early 1930's, after Allied troops had withdrawn from the left bank and a German reoccupation of the area became less hypothetical, the Belgians carefully elaborated their own understanding. According to their interpretation each signatory to the pact would decide independently whether or not a violation had occurred and similarly whether immediate action was required. While they thus reserved their right to abstain from such action, they also insisted that no country could gain access to Belgian territory until the Belgian government itself had decided on the questions of legitimacy and necessity.[64]

Besides signaling Belgian reluctance to react to a German remilitarization of the left bank, this interpretation affirmed Belgium's intention to remain uninvolved in the event of a German assault against the new nations of eastern Europe.

---

62. For new information and documents on Franco-Belgian military relations, or rather the paucity of such, between 1936 and 1940, see the collaborative volume based on a conference of Belgian and French historians entitled *Les relations militaires franco-belges de mars 1936 au 10 mai 1940* (Paris, 1968).

63. See above, "Locarno: The Internationalization of Security Problems," in Chapter 4.

64. *DDB,* III, no. 6, pp. 39-46; and no. 89, pp. 253-254.

For at the time of Locarno it had been made clear that if the Reich should attack Poland or Czechoslovakia, the French would still be free to go to the aid of their eastern allies—and the Belgians wanted it understood that they would not lend their territory to any such effort at assistance. In explaining to the British ambassador in Paris in early 1933 why Belgium was so preoccupied with clarifying its interpretation of the Rhineland pact, the Belgian envoy spelled out these concerns. In the case of a German attack against Poland, he remarked, "Germany will not leave its frontier with France unprovided for; it will effect concentrations in the demilitarized zone. Would France be justified in marching its troops across Belgium without the latter's agreement . . . ? This claim seems to us inadmissible."[65]

The British ambassador tried to reassure his Belgian counterpart by pointing out that Belgium had no cause to fear involvement in another war as the result of French efforts to defend the Versailles Treaty. He accurately predicted France's subsequent inaction when he commented:

You reason . . . about a hypothetical case and a very improbable one at that. If Germany attacks Poland, France will let it go ahead; it will not move . . . They [the French] will react only if Germany violates their frontier. In my opinion they would refuse to consider a violation of Articles 42 and 43 as an act of aggression.[66]

Yet French passivity alone could not safeguard Belgium. While Belgian diplomats might raise obstacles to induce inaction, they recognized they could exercise no such influence over their far more powerful neighbor on the Rhine. And clearly it was from that direction that the real danger threatened. For if the Germans should decide to invade France

65. *Ibid.*, no. 12, p. 58; see also *DDB*, II, no. 215, pp. 616-618.
66. *DDB*, III, no. 12, p. 58.

itself, the British ambassador continued, they would feel obliged to pass through Belgium. Herewith the diplomat from across the Channel reached the bedrock of Belgian anxieties.

Nevertheless, even if their national soil should be endangered, the Belgians wanted it understood that French troops could not cross the border without their consent. When in January 1933 Pétain remarked that in the event of a German attack, his countrymen would immediately advance to lend assistance, failing to specify that such a maneuver would follow only upon the Belgians' request, the latter were indignant.[67] In place of the planned advance to the north, they urged that the French High Command equip their common border with permanent fortifications. The Belgian ambassador to Paris pointed out to France's leaders that they could not count on "Belgian bodies alone to oppose the march of Germany," concluding with a flatly stated warning that it would be "madly imprudent" for the French to leave their "northern door wide open."[68] For the Belgians viewed France's failure to construct concrete bastions in the north as primarily a danger to themselves; the unfortified frontier constituted an invitation to the Germans to repeat their strategy of 1914.

Knowing perfectly well that their own military effort could not stem a German invasion, they stubbornly refused to collaborate with the French. For aside from building light works along their border with the Reich, and heavier fortifications at Liège and Namur on the Meuse, they did little in the 1930's to protect their national soil.[69] To the majority of

67. *Ibid.*, no. 4, pp. 35-36.
68. *Ibid.*, no. 78, p. 231.
69. On Belgian military planning, see General van Overstraeten, *Albert I-Léopold III, vingt ans de politique militaire belge* (Bruges, 1946), especially pp. 11-54.

Belgians, disentanglement from France—epitomized in 1936 by their country's return to its traditional neutrality—seemed the best way to avoid another conflict and to spare their own land and people.

Belgian reluctance to make common defensive preparations in peacetime sharply aggravated the difficulties inherent in a French advance. Even in the late 1920's, when few military leaders dissented from the notion of safeguarding France by marching into Belgium, it had been apparent that to transport *parcs mobiles de fortification* north across the border was a poor substitute for well-established defensive positions. The Senate Army Commission's earlier criticism of such measures—that a hastily contrived front would be untenable— became no less apt because the locale had been shifted to Belgium. Moreover were not French military leaders overestimating the speed with which defensive positions might be constructed or underestimating the rate of a German advance? Even if the army of the Reich should follow the rhythm of 1914, even if it should first have to cross an unoccupied Rhineland, newly prepared lines would be difficult to hold.[70] In the event, for the French to advance northward might prove to be stumbling into a trap.

The French were not unaware of these difficulties. They hoped, nonetheless, that modern technology, more particularly motorized vehicles, would assure the arrival of their troops in time to parry a German assault. From the start, French experiments with motorized units had been conducted with an eye to their eventual use in Belgium. As Gamelin explained in 1933 to the Belgian military attaché:

It is out of the question to think of sending you troops on foot; they would arrive too late. Similarly if they should go by rail: the lines

70. Tournoux, *Défense des frontières*, p. 55.

follow disadvantageous routes, and there are not enough of them: besides, you will need your railroads yourselves . . . We shall count, then, from the very start on our large motorized units, set up, I reiterate, with this end in view.[71]

In similar vein, Debeney remarked, in discussing De Gaulle's proposal for a specialized armored corps, that the value of such units would be their ability to "leap to the aid of neighbors entreating our support."[72]

Facilitating an advance into Belgium, however, was not the mission De Gaulle and Paul Reynaud, his chief parliamentary spokesman, assigned to the specialized corps. Reynaud made it perfectly clear that he wanted a force capable of action in the Rhineland. Debeney firmly rejected such a plan, citing the insuperable difficulties armored units would encounter in that area. The hilly and wooded terrain, he argued, was unsuitable for their deployment and would sharply reduce their ability to maneuver. While initially some progress might be made, the Germans could easily improvise defenses to counter a further advance. In sum, the French forces would despatch "a glittering communiqué at the start, then there would be silence, and at the end of a few days, a futile S.O.S."[73] Behind this gloomy forecast, moreover, lay an attachment to plans already devised. For by March 1935, when the matter was fully aired in the Chamber, France's army leaders had abandoned the notion of a major attack in the northeast. From this point on, the troops stationed in France were destined simply to fend off a German onslaught, while those assigned to advance north would attempt a similar feat on Belgian territory.

71. *DDB,* III, no. 48, annexe I, p. 159.
72. General Debeney, "La motorisation des armées modernes," *Revue des deux mondes,* 8e période, 32 (March 15, 1936), 279.
73. General Debeney, "Encore l'armée de métier," *Revue des deux mondes,* 8e période, 28 (July 15, 1935), 283.

In May 1940, three of the four French light mechanized divisions (*divisions légères mécaniques,* or D. L. M.), accompanied by the bulk of France's motorized infantry and the British Expeditionary Force, advanced into Belgium. The fourth D. L. M. and three heavy armored divisions (*divisions cuirassées*)—all that France had at the outbreak of the war—were initially held in reserve on French soil, ready for a counteroffensive north.[74] The major part of France's tank forces, however, were broken down into forty battalions "assigned in groups of three or four to each army and distributed from the North Sea to Switzerland."[75] Where the German command welded together an attacking force of motorized and armored units, the French spread their resources thin in a vain attempt to break the momentum of the enemy's advance. Where the Germans had forged a "lightning" offensive weapon, their French counterparts had merely tried to adapt modern technology to their army's overall defensive mission.

This deployment of tank forces has been subject to much criticism. Indeed the failure of the French High Command to develop ground and aerial tactics equivalent to those employed by the Reich has often been cited as one of the prime causes of France's defeat.[76] Without going into the question of tank and aviation technology—problems that should be studied in the context of the nation's poor industrial and

74. A fourth armored division, under the command of General de Gaulle, was constituted only after the fighting had begun. For a detailed account of the deployment of France's forces in May 1940, see Gamelin, *Servir,* I, 309-334.

75. Colonel Georges Ferré, *Le défaut de l'armure* (Paris, Charles-Lavauzelle, 1948), p. 184.

76. See, for example, Alvin D. Coox, "French Military Doctrine 1919-1939: Concepts of Ground and Aerial Warfare" (Ph.D. diss., Harvard University, 1951); Lt. Col. de Cossé-Brissac, "Combien de chars français contre combien de chars allemands le 10 mai 1940?" *Revue de défense nationale,* new series, 3 (July 1947), 75-92.

economic performance during the 1930's[77] —one can point out the cruel dilemma that faced the High Command. In essence France's military chiefs were forced to choose between husbanding their tank formations for later use in massive counterattacks or giving support to infantry units that might bear the brunt of the enemy assault.[78] Only by stripping the infantry of its tank battalions could a substantial increase in reserve armored divisions have been accomplished. Such was the retrospective advice offered by one commentator after the defeat:

If they had abandoned our infantry divisions in part and provisionally, our tanks would perhaps have supported them better, by slowing down, no doubt more effectively the progress of hostile vehicles that in May 1940 were, along with aviation, the most dangerous enemies of our foot-soldiers.[79]

In suggesting that French military leaders should have prepared to mount massive counterattacks, critics have too often overlooked the locale of their hypothetical maneuvers. A strategy that depended upon counteroffensive operations by heavy armored divisions would have designated northern France as the major battlefield. For such attacks would have been launched only after a defeat in Belgium or a breach of

77. The obvious starting places for such a study are: Commission d'Enquête parlementaire sur les événements survenus en France de 1933 à 1945, *Rapport de M. Charles Serre, député, au nom de la Commission d'Enquête parlementaire*, 2 vols. (Paris, 1951-1952), and the accompanying *Témoignages et documents recueillis par la Commission d'Enquête parlementaire*, 9 vols. (Paris, 1952); Robert Jacomet, *L'armement de la France 1936-1939* (Paris, 1945); Gamelin, *Servir*, I, 149-193; Pierre Cot, *Le procès de la République*, 2 vols. (New York, 1944). For the most recent work on French aviation during the interwar period, see "Numéro spécial sur l'aviation française (1919-1940)," *Revue d'histoire de la Deuxième Guerre Mondiale*, 19, no. 73 (January 1969).

78. Gamelin, *Servir*, I, 251ff.

79. Ferré, *Le défaut de l'armure*, p. 201.

France's own defensive system had already occurred. Yet no French commander could have in advance consigned those heavily populated and industrially crucial departments to that fate. Although the battle of France has been replayed ad infinitum, the problem of how the north could have been safeguarded from devastation remains unsolved.

The French High Command, like Sisyphus, ceaselessly labored to prevent their defenses from being overrun. Faced with a potentially more powerful enemy, France's military leaders had long ago concluded that they would be unable to launch a major attack at the outbreak of hostilities. While they did not deny the obvious, that a short and victorious war was devoutly to be wished, they tacitly admitted that a speedy and favorable conclusion to a new conflict was beyond their capabilities.[80] They could not envisage Germany's defeat until their enemy had exhausted its reserves and resources. (And this in fact was what happened in 1945.) Hence the French could contemplate undertaking an offensive aimed at victory only late in the conflict and with allied support. In the interim military and civilian alike agreed that the primary mission of the army was to prevent defeat.

Although modern weaponry and new combat procedures threatened to disrupt the notions of battle inherited from the First World War—something that the French were slow to realize—France's army chiefs still hoped that a new conflict would follow the sequence of the last. While declaring that an active defense alone could stem a German assault, they nevertheless tacitly assumed that such operations would recreate some kind of stabilized situation. A continuous line of trenches might never reappear—and certainly not at the out-

---

80. See, for example, Debeney, *Sur la sécurité militaire de la France*, pp. 45-46.

break of a new war—yet the French expected that allied rein-forcements would again play the crucial role. No other form of salvation seemed possible. The First World War had bled the country white and had exposed the nation's vulnerability; but France had finally emerged victorious. The prospect of reliving that experience—even without a series of costly offensives—cast a dark spell on all French efforts to resist German aggression.

6 | Epilogue, 1930-1940

With the decision to construct the Maginot Line, the account of French military preparations in the 1920's reaches its end. Such a terminus is dictated not simply by a coincidence of dates but rather by the fact that this decision set the framework for future French military planning and thinking. Yet even the most incurious reader would like to know the sequel: what was the effect of the steps taken in the 1920's on the far better chronicled military—diplomatic events of the 1930's down to the outbreak of war in 1939 and France's defeat the following year?

A selective treatment alone is possible. Against the familiar background of endemic social and economic crisis, a few key episodes starkly reveal the legacy of the policy evolved in the 1920's. France's ineffective maneuvers in diplomacy and its halfhearted response to new military threats at mid-decade suggest that the nation's chiefs, political and military alike, had fewer options than has been commonly imagined. Still more, the sluggishness of France's traditional leaders, their increasing reluctance to assume responsibility for their nation's defense, brings into clear focus the undercurrent of depression and hopelessness that pervaded the late 1930's. With a military situation grown desperate, the rational incentive to heroic effort—the belief that circumstances could be altered by such measures—slowly withered away.

Mise en Scène

Six months before Adolf Hitler came to power in the Reich, the circumstances of international diplomacy underwent a radical change. When in July 1932 Germany's representatives issued an ultimatum demanding equality of rights in matters of armaments and withdrew from the Disarmament Conference then underway, they signaled their intention to scrap the military clauses of the Versailles Treaty and to re-establish their country's armed strength. The German declaration in fact bore the marks of a fait accompli: it did not constitute a basis for further bargaining and compromise.[1] The significance of the event was fully apparent to Edouard Herriot, who had become once more president of the Council after the Left's electoral victory in May 1932:

We are thus at a turning point in history. Up to now Germany had practiced a policy of submission, not one of resignation . . . , but a negative policy; now it is inaugurating a positive policy. Tomorrow it will have a policy of territorial demands backed by a formidable means of intimidation: its army. Therein lies the drama for the French government.[2]

1. On the proceedings of the Disarmament Conference, see Arnold J. Toynbee, *Survey of International Affairs 1932* (London, 1933), part 3; Arnold J. Toynbee, *Survey of International Affairs 1933* (London, 1934), pp. 224-318. On preparations prior to the opening of the conference, see John W. Wheeler-Bennett, *Disarmament and Security since Locarno 1925-1931* (London, 1932).

2. *Documents diplomatiques français,* first series, I (Paris, Imprimerie nationale, 1964), no. 250, p. 479 (henceforth cited as *DDF,* I:I).

That Germany should strive to regain its position as a dominant continental military power came as no surprise to its former enemy. Since 1919 French observers had predicted and warned of such an eventuality. The more prescient among them had recognized that armaments control was a chimera, that short of permanent occupation of German soil no means existed to prevent the Reich's military resurgence. Limited coercive operations—which in theory seemed an appealing solution—had been designed primarily to deal with German recalcitrance about paying reparations. In any event, such actions had been attractive only so long as their cost, in diplomatic, financial, and military terms, had remained low. Even before German armed strength increased, even before the likelihood vanished that resistance would no longer be merely passive, limited military operations had ceased to figure in public discussions. By 1932 the category of coercive actions had lost its meaning; henceforth military power would be resorted to only in the event of a major national emergency.

Although the German demand for equality in armaments was not unexpected, France's diplomats were nevertheless correct in viewing the ultimatum as signifying a crisis of the first order. The new German declaration threatened to undermine the careful equilibrium established in the mid-1920's. From that point on protracted diplomatic discussions had acted as a buffer, muting the dangers to France's international position. The French had made concessions with a view to trading secondary or nonenforceable parts of the Versailles Treaty, such as disarmament control and reparations, in return for German acceptance of more limited and more basic obligations, notably the military neutrality of the Rhineland. At the same time France's diplomats had always kept a keen eye on London; every reluctant gesture of leniency toward their traditional enemy had been accompanied by the hope that the British would thereby be induced to guarantee French security in a meaningful fashion. Thus Germany had freely accepted a demilitarized Rhineland, and, what was more important, Great Britain had assumed the role of guarantor to this agreement. In short, the discussions leading to the acceptance of the Dawes Plan in mid-1924 and the Locarno agreements in late 1925 had delineated the major problems and had demarcated the areas of diplomatic bargaining. Subsequent negotiations on reparations, the Interallied Control Commission, and the evacuation of the Rhineland can be viewed as the resolution of the issues that had dominated the years 1924 and 1925.

Now there seemed no way to soften the blow. Unless the French government could counterbalance agreement to Germany's ultimatum by obtaining a substantive British guarantee—which was most unlikely—it would be unable to disguise a concession as grave as the abandonment of the Versailles Treaty's military clauses. Face to face with a situation that left no room for maneuver, it would be obliged to acquiesce in whatever demands Germany might make. With no acceptable *quid pro quo* in sight, France's leaders found themselves in uncharted seas. The era of French appeasement was at an end; the period of capitulation was beginning.

The bankruptcy of France's diplomacy should have become apparent as the government labored to forestall German rearmament. The futility of the enterprise was matched only by the grandiosity of the plans drawn up. One might conclude that the French government's feverish activity had the quality of a farce; the results, however, were far from comic.

Indeed the tragic possibilities were never distant from the thoughts of France's leaders, and acted as a goad to continued efforts. While such endeavors failed to prevent German rearmament, the importance of the activity itself delayed conscious recognition that French diplomacy had reached a dead end.

From the beginning of the crisis it was clear that it was impossible to reject the German note out of hand.[3] Such a response, tantamount to accepting the failure of the Disarmament Conference, would have provided Germany with the legal justification it sought. For Part V of the Versailles Treaty, which defined the Reich's military status, had cast German obligations in the framework of a first step toward general disarmament. Germany's spokesmen had repeatedly pointed out that if other powers refused to fulfill this general imperative, they would themselves be freed from the necessity of further compliance.

The implications of this juridical complexity were appalling. Failure to reach a general agreement would open the way for a new armaments race in which France was bound to be the loser. Herriot was candid in underlining the horror of such an eventuality. To the special commission constituted to work out France's position, he declared that if his country should say no, Germany would "free itself," and that if Germany should rearm, "the French army would be unable to fulfill its mission."[4] Before the Chamber of Deputies he was equally forthright:

Let us suppose that the Disarmament Conference, having arrived . . . at a critical point, fails . . .

3. See *ibid.,* no. 250, pp. 479-480.
4. *Ibid.,* no. 250, pp. 485-486.

There would be only one recourse left— . . . an armaments race . . .

The question . . . is to determine . . . Germany's chances, with its dense population, with its heavy industry, how very heavy! and . . . how dangerous—*schwer* in every sense of the word.

Imagine what this armaments race would become . . .

Imagine what the relative situation of the two countries would become.

And lest his listeners accuse him of being melodramatic, Herriot remarked that he was not introducing "from the outside any elements of pathos"; there was "enough of it in the subject itself."[5]

If France's leaders were in no position simply to leave Germany's armaments claims unanswered, they were equally unable to assent to an agreement that would guarantee the Reich a right to limited rearmament. In August André François-Poncet, the French ambassador in Berlin, suggested that his country's diplomats attempt to reach an agreement along just such lines. At the same time he recognized that "even should this accord be concluded, it would doubtless be vain to hope that Germany would cut off the list of its claims at that point."[6] Yet if the Reich did not cease its demands, what good would such an agreement be? How could it remain valid for ten or twenty years, as François-Poncet, in a rather contradictory fashion, imagined? Nor would such an accord improve France's position for resisting further German claims. While Germany might violate its part of the bargain, France, ever susceptible to the pressure of ex-allies, might feel compelled to fulfill its own side of the agreement. In

5. JOC *Déb.*, October 28, 1932, p. 2919.
6. *DDF*, I:I, no. 125, p. 224.

view of these considerations, Herriot's marginal comment was altogether appropriate: while finding François-Poncet's note "very intelligent," he insisted that his country should "stick to the ground of Germany's non-rearmament" and that such had been the opinion of his cabinet.[7] No French ministry, Herriot realized, could officially condone German rearmament.

Thus the government was naturally led to make new efforts in the direction of a general disarmament agreement—to revise and go beyond the French plan presented in February 1932 by Herriot's predecessor, André Tardieu. Yet the proposals drawn up were so far-reaching that there was little chance of obtaining Germany's agreement to them. The military section of the so-called maximum plan envisaged the disappearance of the Reichswehr and its replacement by a militia. In return for the liquidation of Germany's armée de métier, France would alter its own military organization to bring it into line with the Reich's hypothetical new army. For France, with an army already organized on the basis of one-year military service, the proposed changes would be relatively slight. Germany, on the contrary, would be deprived of its greatest asset, the ability to launch a surprise attack. Moreover, it was no secret that the Reich's real aim was to supplement its existing professional troops with short-term recruits and that it had not the slightest intention of abandoning the forces on which its military planning and power rested.[8] While France's proposal thus reflected both fear of a German attaque brusquée and an appreciation of the

7. *Ibid.*, no. 125, p. 224n.
8. For the military and security aspects of the French plan, see *DDF*, I:I, no. 244, pp. 439-462; no. 250, pp. 476-491; no. 255, pp. 499-503; no. 260, pp. 509-525; no. 268, pp. 543-553; no. 272, pp. 560-571; no. 286, pp. 614-641; no. 331, pp. 710-718.

limited capacities of its own forces, it was simply fantastic to suppose that such an offer could be the basis of fruitful negotiations.

The security pacts outlined in the maximum plan were almost equally far-fetched. While the degree of commitment of different countries would vary in relation to their involvement in continental Europe, and was described in terms of concentric circles, the scope of the proposed accords went far beyond those concluded at Locarno. Where the agreements reached in 1925 had limited obligations of mutual assistance to countering a flagrant violation of the Rhineland's neutral status, now the security of all members comprising the innermost circle (including Germany) would in effect be given similar guarantees. Although Great Britain was not asked to be a guarantor of this restricted circle, the pact in question nevertheless approximated an eastern Locarno. Realizing that "if Locarno were to be redrawn," it was "not certain that the London government would adhere to it," France's diplomats took care not to offend the sensibilities of their British friends.[9] They seemed less concerned with the obstinate refusal of their former enemy to recognize as definitive its own eastern frontier. Yet without German assent to this aspect of the proposed agreements, such a pact would be meaningless.

By now it must be quite clear that these proposals were not seriously intended, in the sense of constituting a realistic basis for a new military equilibrium. Had Germany agreed to the maximum plan, France's diplomats would have been surprised indeed. Although the government considered the technical aspects of the proposals, rather hastily to be sure, it did so merely as a precaution.[10] General Weygand, then vice-

9. See note by René Massigli, *ibid.,* no. 255, p. 499.
10. See the statement by War Minister Paul-Boncour, *ibid.,* no. 250, p. 478.

president of the Conseil Supérieur de la Guerre, was rather shocked by this cavalier attitude. In view of the unfavorable international situation, he questioned whether "the presentation of this plan might be only a tactic." If so, he continued, it was "contrary to our dignity. A great country as cruelly tried as ours," which defended "its security without any hidden motive, should not resort to such procedures." They were "unworthy of it."[11]

In fact this feverish activity was directed far more toward France's former allies than toward its traditional enemy. At one and the same time its diplomats were hoping to undercut pressure for its own disarmament and cement resistance to the Reich's demands. For it had always been the French contention that security and disarmament must be linked together and that until new security arrangements went into effect, France would not substantially reduce its own military establishment. Having made a magnanimous gesture toward a general agreement and having been rebuffed, the French would be absolved from whatever disarmament obligations might exist. By simultaneously establishing its own innocence in the eyes of the rest of the world, France could avoid responsibility for the failure of the Disarmament Conference. The solidity of his government's juridical position, Herriot claimed, would enable his country to escape the danger of facing alone its powerful enemy, now so clearly intent on rearming.[12] In private discussions as well as in the public forum, France's political leaders repeated this refrain, which as early as 1919 had appeared their only alternative.[13]

11. *Ibid.*, no. 250, p. 481. For a discerning analysis of Weygand's attitude toward disarmament, see Philip Charles Farwell Bankwitz, *Maxime Weygand and Civil-Military Relations in Modern France* (Cambridge, Mass., 1967), chap. 2.

12. *DDF,* I:I, no. 250, p. 489.

13. See JOC *Déb.,* October 28, 1932, pp. 2919-2920.

It soon became clear, however, that proving the justice of France's cause could not by itself create a united front. If the French proposals marked an attempt to gain primarily British, but also American and Italian, support for a policy of firmness toward Germany, the effort was notably unsuccessful. When the French plan was made public in November 1932, it was scarcely considered by the diplomats from across the Channel. The British instead concentrated their attention on finding a way to induce Germany to return to the Disarmament Conference.[14] In December 1932 intensive negotiations among France and its former allies, expanded shortly to include German representatives, got under way with this end in view. While the French insisted that equality of rights could be only the final goal of general disarmament and security arrangements, the British tacitly accepted the German claim that this principle should be the starting point of further discussion. From the records of these conversations it is quite clear that Prime Minister Ramsay MacDonald was prepared to see the disarmament talks transformed into a conference on the modalities of German rearmament. And although the final text seemed to give comfort to the French position, it was apparent that Germany had just begun to practice the fine art of blackmail.[15] Seven weeks later, Hitler came to power, and the following autumn the Reich withdrew from both the Disarmament Conference and the League of Nations.

14. *Documents diplomatiques français,* first series, II (Paris, 1966), no. 25, pp. 43-44.
15. *Ibid.,* no. 59, pp. 116-120; no. 60, pp. 120-126; no. 67, pp. 148-151; no. 68, pp. 151-156; no. 71, pp. 160-163; no. 72, pp. 164-172; no. 76, pp. 181-183; no. 80, pp. 201-205; no. 81, pp. 205-206; no. 82, pp. 206-207; no. 83, pp. 208-209; no. 84, pp. 209-211; no. 88, pp. 216-220; no. 89, pp. 221-225; no. 92, pp. 231-232; no. 93, pp. 233-240; no. 94, p. 241.

Since France's former allies had no intention of resisting Germany's demands, the precept to avoid diplomatic isolation seemed to have little bearing on the matter at hand. Yet independent action without the use of substantial military force had long since ceased to be an option, and the resort to military force without allied support was equally out of the question. As long as Great Britain was prepared to make concessions of considerable scope, France was reduced to the role of spectator. For accepting German faits accomplis could hardly be dignified by the name of foreign policy. Until the moment when France finally declared war on Germany, and even then by simply tagging after Great Britain, its diplomacy could only drift, with no fixed point as a guide.

Point of No Return

From the end of 1932 until the spring of 1938 the course of French history seemed to be out of step with international events. For France the decisive dates refer to domestic happenings, to abrupt shifts in internal politics that were only tangentially connected to the aggressive rumbles from across the Rhine. The disturbances of February 1934 and the Popular Front election of May 1936 overshadowed what in retrospect appeared the more fateful watersheds: Hitler's assumption of power in January 1933, his reinstitution of conscription in March 1935, and the remilitarization of the Rhineland that came almost exactly a year later. That the French failed to make these dates turning points in their own history by responding to Germany in decisive terms has caused them to be severely judged.

Such indictments, however, show little comprehension of the cruel dilemmas of French military and foreign policy.

What should be viewed as an understandable and altogether anticipated failure of nerve has too often become the subject of endless "if only's." The crux of the matter was that France's moderate leaders were unwilling to assume the responsibility for leading their country into war. Faced with a German menace no longer conveniently remote in time, unable to defend themselves against a devastating recognition of ever increasing danger, they were slowly forced to admit that short of war no means to redress the military and diplomatic balance were at hand. Fully aware of the significance of Hitler's moves, they could find no acceptable way of countering them.

In the spring of 1935, military problems briefly occupied the political limelight. For France now faced the onset of the *années creuses,* the "hollow years"; owing to the low birthrate during the First World War, the number of young men available annually for military service in the years 1936-1940 would be only about half what it had been before. This manpower shortage, coupled with the fact that German rearmament, though still unannounced, was gaining momentum, made an extension of military service seem unavoidable.

In response to this situation the government took a modest step and prolonged the time spent under the colors to two years. The increase, however, was not to go into effect immediately. The "demi-contingent" to be inducted in April 1935 would remain in uniform for eighteen months, and only the remaining portion of that class, to be conscripted in October 1935, would serve the full two years. Parenthetically this meant that in March 1936, when German troops moved into the Rhineland, the French army was still under the regime of one-year military service. Moreover the government had been careful not to abrogate the legislation of 1927. Basing its action on Article 40 of that law, it had simply decreed the extension of military service.[16] In so doing it had distorted the clear intent of that clause; while Article 40 provided for the possibility of retaining a specified class under the colors, it had been understood at the time it was voted that such a decision would be made when the troops in question were to be discharged, presumably in the context of a national emergency, and not before their induction as recruits.[17] Rather than engage in a lengthy parliamentary battle, the government had preferred an undisguised sleight of hand.

Such tact in dealing with political sensibilities was not new in matters of military legislation. Pierre-Etienne Flandin, leader of the Alliance Démocratique and heir to the government of national union that Gaston Doumergue had formed in February 1934, was merely imitating the cautious approach of his immediate and more distant political forebears. In 1934, Marshal Pétain, called upon to take over the War Ministry despite his advanced age, had been fully aware of the need to extend the length of military service.[18] Yet fearful that such a proposal would stir up political passions just as the government was attempting to restore calm, he had refrained from making any public move.[19] Throughout the 1920's successive moderate governments had been careful to

16. See speech by Flandin, JOC *Déb.*, March 15, 1935, p. 1021.

17. See speech by Fabry, *ibid.*, March 15, 1935, p. 1030.

18. General Maxime Weygand, *Mémoires*, II: *Mirages et réalité* (Paris, 1957), p. 424.

19. It was not until the following year, when he was no longer war minister, that Pétain overcame his scruples and wrote an article in favor of two-year military service, "La sécurité française pendant les années creuses," *Revue des deux mondes,* 8e période, 26 (March 1, 1935), i-xx.

tailor their proposals to public sentiment, thereby reflecting the war-weariness of a nation profoundly marked by the ordeal it had gone through.

Political trimming of this sort—though never called by that name—had been accepted in good conscience by the Center-Right majority that invariably insured the passage of military legislation, in large part because the long range issue, the danger of a potentially more powerful Germany, could be postponed. In fact, to minimize dissent within the governmental coalition, to quiet the Cassandras who belonged to it, successive ministries had avoided posing military questions in their starkest terms.[20] Still more, the short-term goals behind proposals for army recruitment and organization were clearly understood and widely accepted, and hence to narrow the focus of discussion did not seem altogether inappropriate. Indeed such aims bulked large when military legislation came to the floor of the Chamber, and when moderate deputies had to defend the government against the Left's counterproposals.[21] But by 1935 compelling short-term goals had disappeared, and the solution of an immediate problem no longer served to camouflage the dangers France faced. Thus despite the fact that the Chamber debate of March 15, 1935, produced the familiar political alignments, and Flandin's action was supported by a large margin, moderate and conservative spokesmen were far from soothed by the government's measures. What deputies of the Center and Right would earlier have applauded in a self-righteous fashion they now branded as irresponsibility.

Yet victory had never before been so easy. Few deputies could dissent from Flandin's assessment that "the mere de-

20. See above, "Fixing the Limits of Disagreement and Debate," in Chapter 3.
21. See above, "Apprehensiveness Unmasked," in Chapter 3.

fense of the fortifications protecting the country against invasion as well as experience with and the maintenance of modern matériel" required "the minimum of effectives assured by the one-year law." And these needs could not have been met during the années creuses if the government had not acted. Even Léon Blum, who initiated the debate by interpellating the ministry on the decree that had been issued, made only a halfhearted attempt to dispute Flandin's technical argument. Limiting himself to an unsubstantiated affirmation that a defensive posture required few forces, he remarked that if it were "a question only of covering the process of mobilization and subsequently confronting a possible aggressor with an organized, continuous, and impenetrable line, . . . the effectives of 1936 massed in the East and supported by a fortified system" could suffice. Edouard Herriot, who was still a member of the government, made a flowery speech defending the decree and suggesting that to back Flandin was to show loyalty to the one-year service law. This argument was not altogether convincing, and former Prime Minister Edouard Daladier and Jean Sénac, both frequent Radical spokesmen on military affairs, tried to avoid the embarrassment of supporting an extension in the length of military service by proposing other measures to alleviate the manpower shortage. All in all in comparison with past performances the Left opposition played its usual role in a most subdued manner.[22]

It was far from clear, however, that merely compensating for the troop shortages caused by the années creuses, that simply providing the effectives that would permit the military organization agreed upon in 1927 and the fortifications constructed in the early 1930's to remain operational, was

22. JOC *Déb.,* March 15, 1935, pp. 1022, 1024, 1046-1048, 1049-1050.

sufficient to safeguard France against an invasion. The legislation of the late 1920's had been designed primarily to cope with a German attaque brusquée launched by the Reich's limited professional army.[23] While this term was still used in the mid-1930's, its meaning had changed. It now referred to any lightning attack regardless of the numbers involved. In the interim Germany's armed forces had been substantially enlarged, and although Hitler did not proclaim the Reich's return to universal military service until the day following the Chamber debate, the fact of the Reichswehr's growing strength dominated that discussion. According to Flandin, at the beginning of 1935 Germany had 480,000 men ready, whereas his own country had only 270,000 troops "available at all times in France itself."[24] Jean Fabry recited similar figures and quite logically wondered whether the French army constructed in 1927 could "face up to the German army of 1935-36."[25] It was a rhetorical question. Unequal to the dangers that threatened France, the government's decree floated in a vacuum divorced from any military objective.

In short, with the proverbial menace from across the Rhine no longer willing to make its entrances and exits on cue, such palliatives as the government offered were bound to seem inadequate. Franklin-Bouillon, who had so often warned his fellow citizens, now merely echoed and underlined the sentiments of previous speakers.

What has seemed to me most shocking . . . is a double hypocrisy: first, what I shall call the hypocrisy of surprise at German rearmament,

---

23. See above, "France Uncovered," in Chapter 5. See also General Guillaumat, "L'armée française devant le réarmement allemand," *Revue politique et parlementaire,* 163 (May 1935), 209-222.

24. JOC *Déb.,* March 15, 1935, p. 1021.

25. *Ibid.,* March 15, 1935, p. 1028.

and second, hypocrisy with regard to the means proposed for dealing with it . . .

Those who are familiar with the situation know very well that it is infinitely more grave than our governments have admitted up to now. . . . Salvation can be found . . . only in a complete knowledge of the truth and in a hatred of illusion.[26]

It was in this context that De Gaulle's spokesmen made a public plea for the creation of an armored corps. The royalist deputy Jean Le Cour Grandmaison led off. While agreeing that France's fortifications must be manned by an adequate number of troops, he pointed out that quantity alone would not suffice. "The indispensable complement to the fortified system in the East," he argued, would be "a maneuvering force, mobile enough and powerful enough either to stem a breakthrough without delay, . . . or to exploit immediately in depth a halt in the enemy's offensive." Paul Reynaud, who followed him to the tribune, elaborated further on the value of such a corps:

Let us imagine that tomorrow there is a war and Belgium is invaded . . . If we do not have the means to go to its rescue at once and help it cover its eastern frontier, what will happen?[27]

Such a statement was in accord with the strategic reasoning of France's military leaders, though the High Command was rather slower in organizing armored divisions than these spokesmen would have liked.[28]

While Le Cour Grandmaison stressed the urgency of establishing a military force sufficient for his country's defensive

26. *Ibid.,* March 15, 1935, p. 1051.
27. *Ibid.,* March 15, 1935, pp. 1034, 1042.
28. See above, "The Dilemmas of the North," in Chapter 5.

needs, Reynaud underlined the necessity of creating an army equipped to carry out a wider mission. As he put it:

Have we, perhaps, abandoned our policy of assistance and of pacts? Do we conceive of assistance as running in only one direction, something that we can go to London to ask for, but that we would owe neither to Vienna, nor to Prague, nor to Brussels? . . .

Do we want to change our policy . . . and let Hitler march up and down Europe?[29]

If these questions were not to be answered in the affirmative—which was in fact the case, but which was not what Reynaud was after—he argued that his country needed a force ready for intervention. In 1922 somewhat similar considerations had dominated French military debates. Then the chief concern had been to provide enough troops to conduct coercive operations against a practically unarmed Germany. After the passage of thirteen years, the mere creation of an armored corps could not turn the clock back to that earlier time when French troops had been able to advance beyond their frontier unopposed.

Indeed Paul Reynaud's questions came a decade too late. The problem was no longer one of reorganizing France's army so that it would be an adjunct to a foreign policy of treaty enforcement—which since 1924 had effectively ceased to be the case—but rather one of whether and when to risk war. The crucial question was not simply what kind of armed force should be available but at what moment it would be employed. Léon Blum, although he frequently sounded naive

29. JOC *Déb.*, March 15, 1935, p. 1042. Reynaud's most extensive argument on this subject can be found in his *Le problème militaire français* (Paris, 1937). For Reynaud's subsequent account of his battle for an armored corps, see his *Mémoires,* I: *Venu de ma montagne* (Paris, 1960), pp. 420-443.

in discussing military matters, nonetheless showed his sure instinct for the political jugular when he commented: "If you are really convinced of the inevitability of war, if you are really convinced of the necessity of an arms race, . . . then . . . you should push this country into war while it still has an advantage."[30]

Blum scored a point but did no more than that. While leading moderate and conservative deputies could not fail to recognize that the government's decree was inadequate to counter the growing disparity between French and German forces, no one had ever considered waging preventive war. A forthright recognition of France's deteriorating situation did not make the moderates any more eager to assume a posture that might provoke a general conflagration. Not a single deputy, not even Paul Reynaud, challenged the statement of the war minister, General Maurin: "How can anyone believe that we are still thinking of an offensive, when we have spent billions on setting up a fortified barrier? Would we be so crazy as to march out in front of this barrier on the way to some kind of adventure?"[31]

When German forces moved into the Rhineland on March 7, 1936, in flagrant violation of the Locarno agreement, the French government was not taken unawares. From the beginning of the year, such a move had been considered likely, if not probable. In mid-January the war minister had predicted that the Reich would send troops into the demilitarized zone in the course of 1936.[32] For France's failure to take preven-

30. JOC *Déb.*, March 15, 1935, p. 1025. Whether France still had an advantage, or how much of one, is unclear; on this point, see Weygand's gloomy assessment in *Mirages et réalité*, pp. 422-423.
31. JOC *Déb.*, March 15, 1935, p. 1045.
32. *Documents diplomatiques français*, second series, I (Paris, Imprimerie nationale, 1963), No. 62, p. 90 (henceforth cited as *DDF*, II:I).

248

tive measures or to respond forcefully after the event, the nation's military chiefs have been severely criticized. Although the country as a whole accepted the new German fait accompli and only a minority of the government seemed prepared to react with firmness, the army leaders have been assigned a particularly heavy burden of guilt. On the basis of a close study of the recently published French documents, Jean-Baptiste Duroselle has commented: "The new fact brought out by the *Documents diplomatiques français* is the extent of the responsibility of the military chiefs, especially Maurin and Gamelin."[33] Certainly Maurin's declaration to the Chamber the previous year—and from late January to June 1936 he again held the post of war minister—had suggested that the army's leaders were disinclined to move beyond their own frontier. Indeed, as a simple statement of fact one can scarcely object to Duroselle's conclusion, echoing that of Charles Serre, *rapporteur* for the postwar commission studying the events from 1933 to 1945, that "for the High Command 'inaction had become the supreme wisdom.' "[34]

Yet such a verdict need not imply that France's military chiefs were mistaken. Though no one would suggest that they covered themselves with glory during the crisis, their behavior at least had the merit of consistency. Their country's defense system had been set in the late 1920's, and whatever new problems might arise they necessarily considered within the framework of that system. Their concentration on the Franco-Belgian frontier and their defensive attitude toward Alsace and Lorraine, where their country had a common border with Germany, intensified in direct relation to the

33. Jean-Baptiste Duroselle, "France and the Crisis of March 1936," trans. Nancy L. Roelker, in Evelyn M. Acomb and Marvin L. Brown, eds., *French Society and Culture Since the Old Regime* (New York, Holt, Rinehart and Winston, 1966), p. 257.
34. *Ibid.,* p. 258.

Reich's increasing military strength. In short the High Command's growing anxiety over Germany's aggressive intentions simply reinforced their sense that there was no alternative to the course they had already laid out. Thus, on January 18, three days after the War Ministry had predicted that Germany would soon march into the Rhineland, a meeting of the Haut Comité Militaire touched on this subject only glancingly.[35] Though generalissimo-designate Gamelin gave an accurate sketch of the Reich's future behavior—enumerating the sequence of remilitarization, construction of fortified positions, and assault on eastern Europe—he did not suggest that his country take action to thwart these designs.[36]

In theory, as late as 1935 France's mobilization plans had included the contingency of an advance into the Rhineland to aid its allies in eastern Europe—though only after considerable delay.[37] But by the beginning of the following year, when the country's leaders were faced with the prospect of a German move, the then War Minister Jean Fabry felt obliged to point out that "the plan of April 1935, which corresponded to a relatively favorable situation," was "no longer capable of coping with a singularly aggravated state of affairs." And the picture Fabry (who remained war minister only another four days) presented of the relative strengths of the two countries was sobering indeed:

To the one million men Germany can have under arms in time of peace from 1936 on, France can oppose effectives which are certainly

35. This committee, formed in 1932 and attached to the presidency of the Council, included the three service ministers as well as their respective chiefs of staff. It thus had primary responsibility for formulating military policy.

36. *DDF,* II:I, no. 83, pp. 121-124.

37. General P.-E. Tournoux, *Défense des frontières: Haut Commandement-Gouvernement 1919-1939* (Paris, 1960), p. 337.

substantial, but which, if no new measures are taken . . . , run the danger of an even clearer numerical inferiority. From the point of view of matériel, Germany is on the verge of surpassing us; thus our superiority rests . . . on our fortifications.[38]

What Fabry did not want to admit was that this situation had been a long time on the way.

When the question of how to respond to a German reoccupation of the Rhineland *was* directly posed, France's military authorities carefully refrained from suggesting an advance beyond their own frontier. On February 12, Fabry's successor, General Maurin, drew up a memorandum for Flandin, now installed at the Quai d'Orsay, making it clear that in the event of a German remilitarization of the Rhineland, France should assume a defensive posture; he limited himself to outlining precautionary measures to be taken by the commanders in the frontier regions. Fearful that a German move might be a preamble to an attack on French territory, Maurin planned to "reduce to a minimum the number of measures currently envisaged in the case of a threat of attaque brusquée, so as to avoid giving Germany any valid pretext" for going to war. Five days later, in response to a demand for greater precision, Maurin merely enumerated the means by which the French war machine might slowly come to life. He did no more than describe the various steps in marshalling France's forces short of mobilization; nowhere did he suggest that troops should actually move.[39]

Maurin's note ended with a plea for strengthening the army organization and speeding up production of war matériel. To counter the threat of an imminent German move, the new

38. *DDF,* II:I, no. 83, p. 122.
39. *Ibid.,* no. 170, p. 247; no. 186, pp. 277-278; no. 196, pp. 290-293.

war minister could find no single formula; he simply urged more troops, more armaments, and offered the prayer that his country would receive support from its allies. Such vague and discouraging prescriptions were considered most unsatisfactory by René Massigli, *directeur adjoint* for political affairs at the Quai d'Orsay. The war minister had obviously failed to specify what initiatives France might take "to intimidate the adversary or to make him retreat." Instead of answering Flandin's request for precise information on this matter, he had merely suggested "precautionary measures that could be taken immediately, and countermoves in the sphere of rearmament, with long-term deadlines," since a German re-occupation of the Rhineland evidently struck Maurin as "a favorable opportunity to obtain new credits."[40]

Massigli's criticisms were certainly appropriate, but he missed the real significance of the war minister's memorandum, which had been implicit in its opening statement on possible military moves. Maurin had prefaced his remarks by declaring:

It appears that there would be a danger of acting contrary to France's interest if we should make use of our right to occupy the demilitarized zone. In view of the measures an action of this sort would entail, we would risk appearing as the aggressor and of thus finding ourselves confronting Germany alone.[41]

Since the steps he subsequently outlined were insufficient to counter a German move, he must have meant by the phrase "the measures an action of this sort would entail," that if the government was determined to oppose the Reich, it must consider resorting to *les grands moyens,* that is, to general

40. *Ibid.,* no. 233, pp. 317-318.
41. *Ibid.,* no. 196, p. 291.

mobilization. Why, however, did he not spell this out? Indeed he laid this particular card on the table only after the event. In view of the rest of his statement, one might speculate that Maurin's vagueness concealed a lack of enthusiasm for undertaking action that could lead to a war at the wrong time and in the wrong place. It was a truism of French military policy that France could hope to prevail in a major conflict only when supported by an allied coalition. Moreover, the High Command considered the Rhineland unsuitable for major offensive operations. Rather than being trapped into concentrating its troops in the hilly and broken territory of its enemy, it preferred to fight in the flat terrain of Belgium—which four years later was itself to become the trap and graveyard of the French army.[42]

Even without dotting the i's and crossing the t's, France's political leaders should have been fully conscious of these considerations. Prominent government leaders, including Prime Minister Albert Sarraut, as well as Pierre-Etienne Flandin, Joseph Paul-Boncour, and Georges Mandel, who urged resistance to Germany after the event, had all sat for years in the Chamber of Deputies, had listened to debates on military questions, and presumably understood the legislation that had been passed.[43] Jean Fabry, that indefatigable advocate of military preparedness, as early as December 1932 had spelled out in the public forum what a French reoccupation of the Rhineland would entail:

It has been said that I favored reoccupying the Rhineland. No, I am not a partisan of such a measure, and I am going to tell you why . . .

42. For further evidence that the High Command reasoned in this fashion, see *ibid.*, no. 334, pp. 444-446.

43. Mandel's position during the crisis is not altogether clear. Paul-Boncour claimed he favored resistance, whereas Maurin denied that he did so. See Duroselle, "France and the Crisis of March 1936," p. 254.

When somebody recommends reoccupying the Rhineland, he must tell the country that he is leading it to war.[44]

Although there are no records to show that the ministers actually posed the question in these stark terms, by the end of February the government had in effect decided to do nothing. In a note handed to the Belgian ambassador on February 27, Flandin summarized the conclusions reached by the cabinet that very day.[45] In case of a German violation of Articles 42 and 43 of the Versailles Treaty relating to the demilitarized zone, the note read, "The French government" would "undertake no isolated action." It would "act only in agreement with the cosignatories of Locarno." When later in this same document possible French preparations were mentioned, such measures were put in the context of "collective action that might be decided on by the Council of the League of Nations and by the guarantors of Locarno."[46] According to Flandin a somewhat similar conclusion had been reached at a cabinet meeting early in the month. At that time he had urged that the government consult with France's military authorities before making a final decision.[47] After February 27, however, no further discussions seem to have taken place.[48] No evidence can be found that Flandin continued

44. JOC *Déb.*, December 22, 1932, p. 3618, quoted by Jean Fabry, *De la Place de la Concorde au Cours de l'Intendance* (Paris, Editions de France, 1942), p. 16.

45. Even then, it would appear that in discussing a possible offensive in the Rhineland, War Minister Maurin did not present candidly the prospect of general mobilization. See General Maurice Gamelin, *Servir,* II: *Le prologue du drame* (Paris, Plon, 1946), p. 199.

46. *DDF,* II:I, no. 241, p. 339.

47. Pierre-Etienne Flandin, *Politique française 1919-1940* (Paris, 1947), pp. 196-197.

48. The air minister did communicate with the navy and foreign affairs ministers on March 2. But the annexes to the document indicate that Air Minister Déat was merely tardy in responding to Flandin's inquiries of mid-February. See *DDF,* II:I, no. 269, 377-378.

his correspondence with War Minister Maurin.[49] Moreover, Gamelin's account skips entirely the eight days between February 27 and March 7.[50] Yet one thing at least is clear: on February 28, the government proceeded with the ratification of the Franco-Soviet accord, negotiated almost a year earlier, knowing full well that Hitler might use such a vote as a pretext for the remilitarization of the Rhineland.[51]

When on Saturday, March 7, German troops did move into the demilitarized zone, this tacit agreement threatened to come unstuck. Thrown into confusion by the decisiveness of Hitler's move, the government naturally turned again to France's military leaders. Yet according to Gamelin the discussion that day remained in the realm of generalities.[52] Nor was progress made at the cabinet meeting held the following day. Nevertheless that evening Prime Minister Sarraut addressed the nation and declared that he and his colleagues were "not disposed to leave Strasbourg exposed to German guns."[53]

Mock heroics? So it would seem in view of the conference of French military chiefs on the eighth and the cabinet's decision to refrain from action on the ninth. For at both sessions nothing had been left vague about what the use of military force would mean. Though there exists a *compte-rendu* for only the first of these meetings, it seems clear that War Minister Maurin subsequently communicated in no uncertain terms the substance of the earlier discussion to his cabinet colleagues.[54] In answer to the question whether

49. Duroselle, "France and the Crisis of March 1936," p. 251.
50. Gamelin, *Servir,* II, 200.
51. See *ibid.,* p. 200; *DDF,* II:I, No. 344, p. 444.
52. Gamelin, *Servir,* II, 201-202.
53. Quoted by Duroselle, "France and the Crisis of March 1936," p. 253.
54. See Joseph Paul-Boncour, *Entre deux guerres: Souvenirs sur la IIIe République,* III: *Sur les chemins de la défaite 1935-1940* (Paris, 1946), pp. 32-33;

France's military forces could "drive the Germans out of the zone," Gamelin had replied that "by the very fact of . . . entering the zone, war" would "be unleashed. Thus an action of this sort would necessitate general mobilization." And in such an event he had pointed out that if the conflict were limited "to the ground front of the Franco-German border, there would be on both sides effectives amply sufficient to achieve rapid saturation. The fronts" would "be stabilized."[55] From this he concluded that France could not hope for a favorable outcome without allied support.

It would appear, then, that by March 9, the possibility of France's taking unilateral action had been foreclosed. Such, however, does not seem to have been the case. It was just at this point that the government, desperately clutching at straws, first seriously considered the feasibility of limited measures.[56] Although Gamelin mentions instructing frontier commanders to study possible local actions as early as mid-February, it was not until March 9 that Foreign Minister Flandin officially asked the generalissimo-designate to look into the possibility of "taking a guarantee" on the Left Bank of the Saar.[57] On the evening of the tenth Prime Minister

---

Flandin, *Politique française,* p. 199; Duroselle, "France and the Crisis of March 1936," pp. 254-255.

55. *DDF,* II:I, no. 334, p. 444.

56. There existed a plan for an operation on the left bank of the Saar dating from 1932. Though this plan was drawn up at the time of Germany's demand for equality of armaments, it seems to have led a secret existence, since France's civilian leaders apparently never considered it, nor did it figure prominently in discussions among the military themselves. Moreover this plan, sketched out at a time when Germany had only begun to rearm, was more extensive than the one considered after March 7. See Commission d'Enquête parlementaire sur les événements survenus en France de 1933 à 1945, *Rapport de M. Charles Serre, député, au nom de la Commission d'Enquête parlementaire,* I (Paris, 1952), pp. 47ff.; Duroselle, "France and the Crisis of March 1936," pp. 255-256.

57. Gamelin, *Servir,* II, 197-198, 204.

Sarraut called together the three service ministers and their chiefs of staff to discuss this proposal. It soon became clear that reducing the scope of an advance did not necessarily reduce its difficulties. As Gamelin pointed out, if Germany yielded, "everything would be easy," but if the Reich resisted, it would be necessary "to proceed to general mobilization without delay."[58] Analogous inquiries directed to the Navy Ministry brought similar replies: a variant on the occupation of the Ruhr could not be repeated in 1936.[59]

Why, then, did Flandin go to London on the twelfth and solicit British cooperation for a French police action? According to his own account, he outlined this possibility to Prime Minister Stanley Baldwin, making it clear that it was moral rather than material support he was seeking from France's former ally. At the same time he misrepresented and minimized the dangers inherent in such an operation, disregarding the advice of his country's military chiefs as well as reports from the French ambassador in Berlin.[60] At first glance it would appear that Flandin was trying to lead the British into war by the back door. But in fact his démarche was an attempt to shift responsibility to Great Britain. [61]

58. *Ibid.*, pp. 205-206. See also *DDF,* II:I, no. 392, pp. 504-506, and no. 525, pp. 696-700; Tournoux, *Défense des frontières,* pp. 251-257.

59. *DDF,* II:I, no. 390, pp. 501-502; no. 391, pp. 502-503; no. 392, pp. 504-506; no. 406, pp. 522-524.

60. Flandin, *Politique française,* pp. 207-208. Although François-Poncet's reports were not crystal clear on Hitler's intentions, they did indicate that Germany was materially equipped to fight, which the French military considered to be the case: *DDF,* II:I, no. 384, p. 496, and no. 392, pp. 504-506. For convincing evidence that German commanders would have fought before withdrawing, see Donald Cameron Watt, "German Plans for the Reoccupation of the Rhineland: A Note," *Journal of Contemporary History,* 1, no. 4 (1966), 193-199.

61. For a perceptive account of the crisis, highlighting the attitudes of Britain's diplomats, see W. F. Knapp, "The Rhineland Crisis of March 1936," in James Joll, ed., *The Decline of the Third Republic* (New York, 1959), pp. 67-86.

While his scheme did not succeed in hoodwinking the British into believing that a limited operation against Germany was possible, it did persuade future commentators that his country might have found an intermediate course between war and acceptance of the German fait accompli.

Too often indictments of French behavior have rested on the assumption that it was within the capacity of France's army to settle the matter neatly, to force Hitler to recall his troops from the Rhineland with only a minimum show of force. And this interpretation has gained currency from the fact that it figured in the deliberations of the time. In the case of those like Paul-Boncour who both subscribed to such a view and urged resistance to the Reich, one can only speculate that it was an illusion of this sort that enabled them to maintain their attitude of firmness and to pass it on as a legacy to subsequent historians.[62]

Dead End

France's *défaillance* in March 1936 came as the culmination of more than a decade of military and diplomatic weakness, marking the end of one phase and the beginning of another. With German troops securely in control of the Rhineland, the

62. Paul-Boncour, *Entre deux guerres,* III, 34. The attitude of Alexis Saint-Léger Léger, general secretary at the Quai d'Orsay, was similar to that of Paul-Boncour. With the publication of new documents, it is now clear that Elizabeth R. Cameron's statement that Léger "recognized that heavy sacrifices would be called for to meet the risk of German resistance" is incorrect. The Belgian ambassador reported on March 14 that Léger was in fact convinced that Germany would offer no resistance. Moreover on the eleventh he had given the naval chief of staff an over-optimistic assessment of the possibilities of French action. See Elizabeth R. Cameron, "Alexis Saint-Léger Léger," in Gordon A. Craig and Felix Gilbert, eds., *The Diplomats 1919-1939* (Princeton, N.J., Princeton University Press, 1953), p. 389; *Documents diplomatiques belges,* IV (Brussels, 1965), no. 46, p. 150; *DDF,* II:I, no. 391, p. 503.

French army was doomed to watch passively while Hitler proceeded to revise the territorial clauses of the Versailles Treaty. As Gamelin noted, after March 7, "The Germans could . . . be confident of their military freedom of action against Austria, Czechoslovakia, and Poland."[63] The last theoretical possibility of a French response to insure the integrity of the new nations of eastern Europe had vanished. Little wonder, then, that until the moment three years later when France followed Great Britain in declaring war on the Reich, its record should have been one of impotence and capitulation.

And it was only in May 1940, more than four years after the remilitarization of the Rhineland, that France itself was at length forced to give battle. Had the end come more quickly, had France been attacked in 1936 or 1937, the nation might have been in better psychological shape to make a heroic stand. Although one would hesitate before saying the same of the country's military preparation—British policy and armaments production, as well as German and French, would have to be taken into account—clearly the four years of waiting helped undermine the nation's determination to resist. The many reprieves along the way, capped by the eight months of the *drôle de guerre,* were profoundly demoralizing.[64] It was a divided and uncertain France that finally faced the onslaught of the Reich. Even subgroups that had once commanded loyalty and devotion had been fragmented. By 1938 party unity both on the Right and on the Left was in ruins.[65] It was as though the approaching holocaust had

63. Gamelin, *Servir,* II, 213.

64. The best work on this subject is Marc Bloch's short evocative testimony, *Strange Defeat,* trans. Gerard Hopkins (London, 1949). On the military side, see General André Beaufre, *Le drame de 1940* (Paris, 1965).

65. See Stanley Hoffmann, "Paradoxes of the French Political Community," in Stanley Hoffmann *et al., In Search of France* (Cambridge, Mass., 1963), pp.

stripped away layers of political identification, leaving each individual to confront the deluge alone with his own human resources.

For almost exactly two years, from the spring of 1936 to the spring of 1938, the dominant tone on the Right was set by an impassioned rhetorical attack on communism. The attraction of Fascist Italy for France's conservative and moderate leaders, their perception of foreign policy through the distorting lens of ideological hatred, seem at first glance to suggest a heightening of political identity rather than its gradual disintegration.[66] Paradoxically, however, it was precisely because the anticommunism of the late 1930's went far beyond hostility to the economic program of the Popular Front, that it took on an apolitical quality. In comparison with the antisocialist and anti-Bolshevik rhetoric employed during the electoral campaign of 1920, the new attacks were both more widespread and less specific. In 1920 such polemics had helped to reaffirm faith in the French political and social order and to sustain a mood of resolution for enforcing the Versailles Treaty. After 1936 this ideological passion reflected neither coherent policy nor allegiance to a definite set of institutions. And while it could no longer provide much moral sustenance, it had acquired a new power to undermine the sense of responsibility for France's national defense.

Even before the Popular Front assumed power in June 1936, ideological recrimination was fast becoming the order

---

21-34; Peter J. Larmour, *The French Radical Party in the 1930's* (Stanford, Calif., 1964), chaps. 8 and 9; Nathanael Greene, *Crisis and Decline: The French Socialist Party in the Popular Front Era* (Ithaca, N.Y., 1969).

66. On the Right and foreign policy, see Charles A. Micaud, *The French Right and Nazi Germany 1933-1939* (Durham, N.C., 1943).

of the day. Among moderate and conservative leaders, it was now de rigueur to lament the bankruptcy of France's political institutions. To dabble in constitutional reform and to flirt with authoritarian movements were emerging as new forms of desperate behavior.[67] In part such political disintegration was due to the very length of the ordeal France was undergoing. As in a drawn out terminal illness, remissions or reprieves led many to believe that the end might be avoided entirely. And like a dying patient unwilling to accept his fate, France's moderate and conservative leaders were loath to admit that they were unable to control the sequence of events leading closer and closer to war. They refused to recognize that in this case the fault, rather than being in themselves, was in their stars—that is, in their situation vis-à-vis the Germans and the British. It was perfectly natural, then, that they should have produced a set of frantic diagnoses of France's ills.

The advent of the Popular Front, followed by the sit-down strikes and the beginning of the Spanish Civil War—all within the space of less than three months—gave a new complexion to rightist anticommunism. For at one and the same time moderate and conservative leaders could be relieved both of the burdens of military preparation and of blame for their country's weakness. The strikes and their aftermath, the shortening of the work week and the slowing of production, provided new ammunition for charges of Communist sabotage of France's military efforts. Simultaneously the Right's reaction to Communist support for Spain's Republican forces sug-

67. On Rightist extraparliamentary politics, see Raoul Girardet, "Notes sur l'esprit d'un fascisme français 1934-1939," *Revue française de science politique*, 5 (July-September 1955), 529-546; Eugen Weber, *Action Française: Royalism and Reaction in Twentieth Century France* (Stanford, Calif., 1962), part 5.

gested a further abdication of responsibility. Viewing the Spanish Civil War as an ideological conflict in which France should remain neutral, the Right accused the Communists of attempting to lead the country to suicide.[68] And while non-intervention in an area so peripheral to French strategic concerns was merely sensible, the Right's growing tendency to advocate abstention from foreign commitments carried the implication that a willingness to engage in hostilities had become the supreme crime against the nation. What in an earlier era might have been considered the mark of a capacity to govern, was now branded as close to treason.[69]

Were not the contradictory polemics of the Right, the simultaneous charges against the Popular Front of bellicosity and of not preparing the country for war, an expression of its own default? Although such rhetoric was not without a basis in fact, the very stridency of the tone, the implicit reversal of priorities, suggested the disarray of France's moderate and conservative leaders, the confusion of those who had always claimed to be the interpreters of the country's national interest. As Jean Fabry noted two years after the event in 1942:

We saw France go "with folded arms" toward catastrophe. . . .

The catastrophe came in the form of foreign war; it would have come in any case, perhaps in the form of civil war as in Spain. It has never happened that someone has opened his veins and has not died or nearly died.

Laziness! Hatred! War!

That is the melancholy balance sheet of the Popular Front.[70]

68. Micaud, *The French Right and Nazi Germany,* chap. 7.
69. See, for example, *Le Temps,* April 10, 1938; April 12, 1938.
70. Fabry, *De la Place de la Concorde,* p. 104.

Was not the attitude of Fabry and so many of his colleagues, summed up in the slogan "neither Hitler nor Blum," a sign that they themselves had folded their arms? A moment of choice would come, when the editorialist for *Le Temps* would no longer be able to write: "Thank God, we do not face the question of life or death today."[71]

With the final liquidation of the Popular Front and the formation of the Daladier government in mid-April 1938, the ideological fever passed its peak. Once again, two years after a Left electoral victory, the formula of a national government was attempted. Yet unlike 1926, when Poincaré had stood as the lone possible savior of the franc, or 1934, when former President Doumergue had been enthusiastically greeted as the one man who commanded the respect and the esteem requisite for recreating Poincaré's role, the mantle now fell to Daladier by default. Indeed the very fact that moderate and conservative leaders should turn to the left-wing Radical chief as a man capable of assuring "public safety" exposed their own bankruptcy.[72] That they should now welcome the "bull of the Vaucluse," who in 1934 had been the particular target of their vilification, was a sign of the increasing paralysis that gripped their ranks.

At the same time as France's moderate spokesmen relinquished their traditional role as leaders of national governments, they urged that the new ministry transcend the usual maneuvering of party politics. *Le Temps* advised that Daladier's cabinet should be formed "without regard for the political 'mix,' without reference to parties, on the basis of a purely national minimum program."[73] Clearly the time had

71. *Le Temps*, April 8, 1938.
72. *Ibid.*, April 10, 1938.
73. *Ibid.*

passed for distributing ministerial posts according to party affiliation. Yet this was not merely because politics as usual could no longer produce a facsimile of national unity; it was rather because traditional party ties had lost their meaning. Although the government included men such as Paul Reynaud and Georges Mandel who maintained an attitude of firmness, the stance they adopted bore little relation to their party affiliations. Leaders who had shared common beliefs for more than a decade now took divergent paths. On the basis of past political positions it would have been hard to predict the differences that had come to separate Paul Reynaud and Pierre-Etienne Flandin, Henri de Kerillis and Jean Fabry, Georges Mandel and André Tardieu, Léon Blum and Paul Faure. Thus regardless of how cabinet posts were distributed, the new government could not help but be above parties as traditionally understood.

Such a collapse of political identity deprived men of the psychological strength they had derived from a shared self-image and from the accompanying attitudes that had so often shaped reactions to national events. In the 1920's the common assumptions of political groups had suggested both how people would respond to and how they would guard themselves from fully recognizing the experience of squandering the victory of 1918. From the mid-1930's on, this situation no longer held true. With the orthodoxies of former political allegiance substantially eroded, those who had participated in the formation of France's interwar military policy found themselves without guidance in facing up to the consequences of that planning. The private hell that was the Second World War transformed politics into a matter of individual conscience and character. And the story of the defeated nation after 1940 must inevitably have as its central theme the contrast between the way Pétain and De Gaulle, and the followers who gathered around each of them, confronted the disaster that so many had foreseen and none had known how to avert.

Selected Bibliography
Index

Selected Bibliography

I. Unpublished Sources

Senate Army Commission, Procès-verbaux, 1919-1929 (Archives du Sénat). Records of discussions on military legislation and army matters, including testimony by war ministers and their top military aides. Invaluable for understanding how concerned parliamentarians viewed defense problems.

Senate Finance Commission, Procès-verbaux, 1919-1929 (Archives du Sénat). Additional information on the financial circumstances of military planning, with a number of important sessions devoted to fortifications.

F^7 12884 (Archives Nationales). Reports prepared for the Ministry of the Interior on the activities of the Ligue des Droits de l'Homme, 1923-1924.

F^7 12936 (Archives Nationales). Reports from prefects and special commissioners on public opinion, 1914-1918.

F^7 12967-12969 (Archives Nationales). Monthly reports for the Ministry of the Interior on public response to current political events, 1920-1934.

F^7 13349 (Archives Nationales). Documents on antimilitarism in the press during 1915, and notes on the state of army and navy morale in 1920.

Jacques-Louis Dumesnil Papers (Archives Nationales). Data on military problems gathered by a member of the Chamber Army Commission who served as Herriot's minister of the navy.

Marshal Ferdinand Foch Cahiers and Record book-diary (photocopy, Bibliothèque Nationale). The diary covers the war and contains penetrating comments on Foch's military colleagues. The cahiers are a rich and running, if disorderly, commentary on diplomatic and military problems, beginning in 1919 and becoming sparser after 1924.

Lucien Lamoureux, "Souvenirs politiques 1919-1940" (microfilm of unpublished manuscript, Bibliothèque de Documentation Internationale Contemporaine). A long discursive memoir by the prominent Radical parliamentarian, including frank judgments on men and events.

Marshal Jean de Lattre de Tassigny Papers (in the possession of his widow). Material on De Lattre's years in Morocco and at the Ecole Supérieure de Guerre, including a collection of course texts.

General Charles Mangin Papers (Archives Nationales). Material on Rhenish separatism, as well as documentation of Mangin's efforts on behalf of the colonial army and the recruitment of black Africans as compensation for France's manpower deficiencies.

Alexandre Millerand, "Mes Souvenirs: contribution à l'histoire de la Troisième République" and other documents, including correspondence with military figures (in the possession of his son Jacques Millerand). The memoir was written by the former president in 1940-1941, shortly before his death. The annexes contain memoranda by other officials, for example, the original version of an article by Charles Reibel, "Après la capitulation de l'Allemagne dans la Ruhr."

General Edouard Réquin Papers (Hoover Institution, Stanford University). Documents concerning the Treaty of Mutual Assistance, including the security projects of Réquin and Lord Robert Cecil, 1923-1924, which shed an indirect light on French official thinking on broader security problems.

Albert Thomas Papers (Archives Nationales). A voluminous correspondence between the moderate Socialist leader and a wide range of political and military figures, suggesting the dilemma of men in Thomas' position, caught between doctrinaire Socialist attitudes on military problems and a real concern for the nation's defense.

Public Record Office, Cabinet 23, conclusions of cabinet meetings and Conferences of Ministers, 1919-December 1922 (microfilm, Harvard

University). Official minutes of cabinet meetings and as such providing a revealing guide to British policy formation and decision-making at the highest level.

II. Published Documents

BELGIUM

Académie Royale de Belgique, Commission royale d'histoire. *Documents diplomatiques belges 1920-1940: La politique de sécurité extérieure,* Ch. de Visscher and F. Vanlangehove, eds. 4 vols. Brussels, 1964-1965.

[Symposium volume], *Les relations militaires franco-belges de mars 1936 au 10 mai 1940.* Paris, 1968.

FRANCE

Journal Officiel de la République Française, Chambre des Députés. *Débats parlementaires.*

Journal Officiel de la République Française, Chambre des Députés. *Documents parlementaires: Annexes aux procès-verbaux des séances.*

Journal Officiel de la République Française, Sénat. *Débats parlementaires.*

Journal Officiel de la République Française, Sénat. *Documents parlementaires: Annexes aux procès-verbaux des séances.*

Assemblée Nationale, Commission d'Enquête parlementaire sur les événements survenus en France de 1933 à 1945. *Rapport de M. Charles Serre, député, au nom de la Commission d'Enquête parlementaire.* 2 vols. Paris, 1952.

Assemblée Nationale, Commission d'Enquête parlementaire sur les événements survenus en France de 1933 à 1945. *Témoignages et documents recueillis par la Commission d'Enquête parlementaire.* 9 vols. Paris, 1951-1952.

Ecole Supérieure de Guerre. *Aide-mémoire pour les travaux d'Etat-Major.* Paris, 1931.

Ecole Supérieure de Guerre, Colonel Duffour. *Cours d'histoire—la guerre 1914-1918.* Paris, 1923.

Ecole Supérieure de Guerre, Chef de bataillon Lestien. *Conférence sur l'histoire militaire.* Paris, 1925.

Ministère des Affaires Etrangères, Commission de publication des documents relatifs aux origines de la guerre 1939-1945. *Documents diplomatiques français 1932-1939.* Series I, 4 vols. to date; series II, 4 vols. to date. Paris, 1963 et seq.

Ministère des Affaires Etrangères. *Documents diplomatiques: Documents relatifs aux négotiations concernant les garanties de sécurité contre une agression d'Allemagne.* Paris, 1924.

Ministère des Affaires Etrangères. *Pacte de sécurité: Neuf pièces relatives à la proposition faite le 9 février 1925 par le gouvernement allemand et à la réponse du gouvernement français, 9 février-16 juin 1925.* Paris, 1925.

Ministère des Affaires Etrangères. *Pacte de sécurité, II: Documents signés ou paraphés à Locarno le 16 octobre 1925, précédés de six pièces relatives aux négotiations préliminaires, 20 juillet 1925-16 octobre 1925.* Paris, 1925.

Ministère de la Guerre. *Annuaire officiel des officiers de l'armée active.* Paris, 1920-1930.

Ministère de la Guerre, Direction de l'Artillerie. "Projet de réglement de manoeuvre des unités de chars légers." Mimeographed copy; Paris, March 1920.

Ministère de la Guerre, Direction de l'Infanterie. *Réglement provisoire de manoeuvre d'infanterie du 1er février 1920.* Part 1, Paris, 1920; Part 2, Paris, 1921.

Ministère de la Guerre, Ecoles Militaires. *Cours d'organisation et législation.* Paris, 1921.

Ministère de la Guerre, Etat-Major de l'Armée. *Instruction provisoire sur l'emploi des chars de combat comme engins d'infanterie.* Paris, 1920.

——*Instruction provisoire sur l'emploi des grandes unités du 6 octobre 1921.* Nancy, Paris, Strasbourg, November 15, 1932.

——*Instruction sur l'emploi tactique des grandes unités.* Paris, 1936.

——*Projet de règlement de manoeuvre des unités de chars Mark*.* Paris, 1921.

——*Règlement de l'infanterie.* Parts 1 and 2. Paris, 1928.

Ministère du Travail, Statistique Générale de la France. *Annuaire statistique.* Vols. 36, 37. Paris, 1921, 1922.

GREAT BRITAIN

Cmd. 2169: Papers Respecting Negotiations for an Anglo-French Pact. London, 1924.

Cmd. 2435: Papers Respecting the Proposals for a Pact of Security made by the German Government on 9th February 1925. London, 1925.

Foreign Office, *Documents on British Foreign Policy,* E. L. Woodward *et al.,* eds. Series 1, 16 vols. to date; series 1a, 2 vols. to date; series 2, 9 vols. to date; series 3, 10 vols. London, 1946 et seq.

III. Memoirs, Diaries, Contemporary Comment

Allard, Paul. *Le Quai d'Orsay, son personnel, ses rouages, ses dessous.* Paris, 1938.

Alléhaut, General Emile. *Etre prêts.* Paris, 1935.

_____*La guerre n'est pas une industrie.* Paris, 1925.

Armengaud, General J. *Batailles politiques et militaires sur l'Europe: Témoignages (1932-1940).* Paris, 1948.

Albord, Tony. *Pourquoi cela est arrivé ou les responsabilités d'une génération militaire 1919-1939.* Nantes, 1946.

Bainville, Jacques. *Journal (1919-1926).* Paris, 1949.

B.A.R. *L'armée nouvelle et le service d'un an.* Paris, 1921.

Bardoux, Jacques. *Le socialisme au pouvoir: L'expérience de 1924.* Paris, 1930.

Barthou, Louis. *La politique.* Paris, 1923.

Beaufre, General André. *Le drame de 1940.* Paris, 1965.

Bernier, Paul. *Rapport fait au nom de la commission de l'armée chargée d'examiner le projet de loi relatif au recrutement de l'armée.* Paris, 1927.

Bloch, Commandant D.-P. "L'avenir du char de combat," *Revue militaire française,* no. 7 (January 1922), 90-103.

Bloch, Marc. *Strange Defeat.* Trans. Gerard Hopkins. London, 1949.

Blum, Léon. *Les problèmes de la paix.* Paris, 1931.

Bonnet, Georges. *Défense de la paix.* 2 vols. Geneva, 1946, 1948.

Bourret, General Victor. *La tragédie de l'armée française.* Paris, 1947.

Bouvard, Commandant. *Les leçons militaires de la guerre.* Preface by Marshal Pétain. Paris, 1920.

273

SELECTED BIBLIOGRAPHY

Brindel, General. "La nouvelle organisation militaire," *Revue des deux mondes*, 7e période, 51 (June 1, 1929), 481-501.

Bruneau, Pierre. *Le rôle du haut commandement au point de vue économique de 1914 à 1921*. Paris, 1924.

Buat, General Edmond. "L'Etat-Major," *Revue de Paris*, 28, no. 14 (July 15, 1921), 248-260.

———*Ludendorff*. Paris, 1920.

Bugnet, Commandant Charles. *En écoutant le Maréchal Foch*. Paris, 1929.

Callwell, Major-General Sir C. E. *Field-Marshal Sir Henry Wilson: His Life and Diaries*, II. New York, 1927.

Chareye, Contrôleur-général. "Organisation de l'administration centrale du Ministère de la Guerre," *Revue militaire française*, no. 10 (April 1922), 47-62.

Chauvineau, General Narcisse. *Une invasion, est-elle encore possible?* Preface by Marshal Pétain. Paris, 1939.

———"L'organisation du terrain et ses conséquences," *Revue militaire française*, no. 104 (February 1930), 246-274.

Chedeville, Colonel. "Les chars de combat actuels et le Haut Commandement," *Revue militaire française*, no. 8 (February 1922), 182-196; no. 9 (March 1922), 330-345.

Clemenceau, Georges. *Grandeur and Misery of Victory*. Trans. F. M. Atkinson. New York, 1930.

Conseil Supérieur de la Natalité. *Voeux concernant le projet de loi sur le recrutement de l'armée*. Paris, n.d.

Cot, Pierre. *Le procès de la République*. 2 vols. New York, 1944.

Culmann, General Frédéric. *La fortification permanente aux frontières*. Paris, 1931.

———*Stratégie*. Paris, 1924.

D'Abernon, Viscount. *The Diary of An Ambassador*, III: *Dawes to Locarno 1924-1926*. New York, 1931.

Dawes, Rufus C. *The Dawes Plan in the Making*. Indianapolis, Ind., 1925.

Debeney, General Marie-Eugène. "Armée nationale ou armée de métier?" *Revue des deux mondes*, 7e période, 53 (September 15, 1929), 241-277.

———"Encore l'armée de métier," *Revue des deux mondes*, 8e période, 28 (July 15, 1935), 279-295.

_____ "Les exigences de la guerre de matériel," *Revue des deux mondes,* 8e période, 14 (March 15, 1933), 259-287.

_____ *La guerre et les hommes.* Paris, 1937.

_____ "La guerre moderne et les machines," *Revue de la semaine,* February 10, 1922, 151-154.

_____ "La motorisation des armées modernes," *Revue des deux mondes,* 8e période, 32 (March 15, 1936), 273-291.

_____ "Nos fortifications du nord-est," *Revue des deux mondes,* 8e période, 23 (September 15, 1934), 241-262.

_____ "Le problème de la couverture," *Revue des deux mondes,* 8e période, 36 (November 15, 1936), 268-294.

_____ *Sur la sécurité militaire de la France.* Paris, 1930.

Doumer, Paul. "Note sur la réorganisation de l'armée française," *Revue politique et parlementaire,* 101 (October 1919), 63-92.

Duval, General Maurice. "La crise de notre organisation militaire," *Revue de Paris,* 33, no. 8 (April 15, 1926), 756-796.

Echo de Paris.

Estienne, General. "Conférence faite le 15 février 1920 sur les chars d'assaut par le Général Estienne au Conservatoire National des Arts et Métiers," *Bulletin trimestriel de l'Association des Amis de l'Ecole Supérieure de Guerre,* no. 14 (October 1961), 22-30.

_____ "Les forces matérielles à la guerre," *Revue de Paris,* 29, no. 2 (January 15, 1922), 225-239.

Fabre-Luce, Alfred. *Locarno: The Reality.* Trans. Constance Vesey. New York, 1928.

Fabry, Jean. *De la Place de la Concorde au Cours de l'Intendance.* Paris, 1942.

_____ "Où va notre armée?" *Revue de Paris,* 32, no. 18 (September 15, 1925), 241-268.

Fayolle, Marshal. *Cahiers secrets de la grande guerre.* Henry Contamine, ed. Paris, 1964.

Flandin, Pierre-Etienne. *Politique française 1919-1940.* Paris, 1947.

Anonymous [Foch, Marshal Ferdinand]. "Un crime de lése-patrie, l'évacuation anticipée de la Rhénanie," *Revue de France,* 6, no. 6 (November 1, 1926), 5-12.

_____ *The Memoirs of Marshal Foch.* Trans. by Colonel T. Bentley Mott. New York, 1931.

La France militaire.

SELECTED BIBLIOGRAPHY

François-Poncet, André. *Réflexions d'un républicain moderne.* Paris, 1925.

――― *Souvenirs d'une ambassade à Berlin: Septembre 1931-octobre 1938.* Paris, 1948.

Gamelin, General Maurice. *Servir.* 3 vols. Paris, 1946-1947.

Gaulle, General Charles de. *Mémoires de guerre,* I: *L'appel 1940-1942.* Paris, 1954.

――― *Le fil d'épée.* Paris, 1931.

――― *La France et son armée.* Paris, 1938.

――― *Vers l'armée de métier.* Trans. as *The Army of the Future.* Philadelphia, 1941.

Guillaumat, General. "L'armée française devant le réarmement allemand," *Revue politique et parlementaire,* 163 (May 1935), 209-222.

Halévy, Daniel. *La République des comités: Essai d'histoire contemporaine (1895-1934).* Paris, 1934.

Herriot, Edouard. *Jadis,* II: *D'une guerre à l'autre 1914-1936.* Paris, 1952.

Hymans, Paul. *Mémoires,* II. Brussels, 1958.

Ignotus. "Etudes et portraits: M. Louis Barthou," *Revue de Paris,* 29, no. 21 (November 1, 1922), 77-82.

L'Intransigeant.

Jacomet, Robert. *L'armement de la France 1936-1939.* Paris, 1945.

Jouvenel, Robert de. *La République des camarades.* New ed. Paris, 1934.

Lardemelle, General de. *Metz défend l'Etat.* Paris, 1930.

Laroche, Jules. *Au Quai d'Orsay avec Briand et Poincaré, 1913-1926.* Paris, 1957.

Laure, Commandant A. M. E. *Au 3ème bureau du troisième G.Q.C.* Paris, 1921.

――― *La victoire franco-espagnole dans le Rif.* Paris, 1927.

Lavigne-Delville, General. *Inquiétudes militaires: officiers et fonctionnaires.* Paris, 1924.

Le Goffic, Charles. *Mes entretiens avec Foch, suivis d'un entretien avec le géneral Weygand.* Paris, 1929.

Liber. "Le Général Debeney," *Le correspondant,* 293 (new series, 257) (December 15, 1923), 992-1014.

Liddell Hart, B. H. *The British Way in Warfare.* London, 1932.

_____ *The Current of War.* London, n.d.

_____ *The German Generals Talk.* New York, 1948.

Lloyd George, David. *The Truth about the Peace Treaties.* 2 vols. London, 1938.

Anonymous [Lyautey]. "Le rôle social de l'officier," *Revue des deux mondes,* 3e période, 104 (March 15, 1891), 443-459.

Lyautey, Pierre, ed. *Lyautey l'Africain: Textes et lettres du Maréchal Lyautey,* IV. Paris, 1957.

Mangin, General Charles. *Lettres de guerre 1914-1918.* Paris, 1950.

Maurin, General Louis. *L'armée moderne.* Paris, 1938.

Mayer, Lt. Col. Emile. "Observations sur le rapport de M. Doumer," *Revue politique et parlementaire,* 101 (October 1919), 92-98.

Mermeix [Gabriel Terrail, pseud.]. *Au sein des commissions.* 5th ed. Paris, 1924.

Millerand, Alexandre. "Au secours de la Pologne," *Revue de France,* 12, no. 4 (August 15, 1932), 577-594.

"Le mois militaire," *Revue militaire française,* no. 2 (August 1921), 241-247; no. 7 (January 1922), 103-110; no. 13 (July 1922), 113-121.

Monteilhet, Joseph. *Les institutions militaires de la France, 1814-1932.* 2d ed. Paris, 1932.

Mordacq, General Henri. "L'évacuation anticipée de la Rhénanie," *Revue des deux mondes,* 7e période, 51 (June 15, 1929), 761-776.

_____ *La mentalité allemande: Cinq ans de commandement sur le Rhin.* Paris, 1926.

_____ *Le ministère Clemenceau.* 4 vols. Paris, 1930-1931.

Morgan, Brigadier-General J. H. "The Disarmament of Germany and After," *Quarterly Review,* 242 (October 1924), 415-458.

Morini-Comby, Jean. "La France en 1928 et 1929: étude de sa politique intérieure," *L'année politique française et étangère,* 4 (December 1929), 410-453.

Nollet, General Charles. "Ce que j'ai voulu faire," *Revue de Paris,* 32, no. 12 (June 15, 1925), 738-764.

_____ *Une expérience de désarmement: Cinq ans de contrôle militaire en Allemagne.* Paris, 1932.

Overstraeten, General van. *Albert I—Léopold III, vingt ans de politique militaire belge.* Bruges, 1946.

P., Lt. Col. R., and Capt. J. P. "Notre organisation militaire," *Revue politique et parlementaire,* 128 (September 1926), 371-406.

SELECTED BIBLIOGRAPHY

Painlevé, Paul. *De la science à la défense nationale*. Paris, 1931.

—— *Paul Painlevé, paroles et écrits.* Paris, 1936.

Paul-Boncour, Joseph. *Entre deux guerres: Souvenirs sur la IIIe République.* 3 vols. Paris, 1945-1946.

Peretti de la Rocca, Cte. de. "Briand et Poincaré (Souvenirs)," *Revue de Paris,* 43, no. 24 (December 15, 1936), 767-789.

Pétain, Marshal Philippe. "La sécurité française pendant les années creuses," *Revue des deux mondes,* 8e période, 26 (March 1, 1935), i-xx.

Pigeaud, Commandant. "L'armée de la sûreté," *Revue militaire française,* no. 21 (March 1923), 388-409.

—— "Etude sur la sûreté et le combat," *Revue militaire française,* no. 28 (October 1923), 60-89.

—— "Le problème du char de combat en 1926," *Revue militaire française,* no. 62 (August 1926), 219-244.

Poincaré, Raymond. *Au service de la France: Neuf années de souvenirs.* 10 vols. Paris, 1926-1933.

Prételat, General André. *Le destin tragique de la ligne Maginot.* Paris, 1950.

"Le problème allemand après l'évacuation de la Rhénanie," *Revue des deux mondes,* 7e période, 59 (October 15, 1930), 721-754.

Le Progrès Civique.

Rabenau, General Friedrich von. *Seeckt: Aus seinem Leben 1918-1936.* Leipzig, 1940.

Reboul, Lt. Col. "Le malaise de l'armée," *Revue des deux mondes,* 7e période, 26 (March 15, 1925), 378-398.

—— "Le projet de service d'un an," *Revue des deux mondes,* 7e période, 27 (May 1, 1925), 32-50.

—— "La question des effectifs," *Revue des deux mondes,* 7e période, 26 (April 1, 1925), 564-579.

Recouly, Raymond. *Le mémorial de Foch: mes entretiens avec le Maréchal.* Paris, 1929.

Réquin, General Edouard. *D'une guerre à l'autre, 1919-1939.* Paris, 1949.

Reynaud, Paul. *In the Thick of the Fight, 1930-1945.* Trans. James D. Lambert. New York, 1955.

—— *Mémoires.* 2 vols. Paris, 1960, 1963.

—— *Le problème militaire français.* Paris, 1937.

Ribot, A., ed. *Journal d'Alexandre Ribot et correspondances inédites.* Paris, 1936.

Romain, Colonel. "Un grand soldat: le Général Buat," *Revue hebdomadaire,* 33, no. 3 (January 19, 1924), 348-358.

Saint-Aulaire, Comte Auguste Felix de. *Confession d'un vieux diplomate.* Paris, 1953.

———— *La mythologie de la paix.* Paris, 1930.

Seeckt, General Hans von. *Gedanken eines Soldaten.* Berlin, 1928.

Sérieyx, William, ed. *Souvenirs de grands chefs militaires.* Paris, 1930.

Seignobos, Charles. "La signification historique des élections françaises de 1928," *L'année politique française et étrangère,* 3 (July 1928), 257-283.

Serrigny, General Bernard. "La grande pitié de nos effectifs de guerre," *Revue des deux mondes,* 7e période, 23 (October 1, 1924), 625-639.

———— "L'organisation de la nation pour le temps de guerre," *Revue des deux mondes,* 7e période, 18 (December 1, 1923), 582-602.

———— *Réflexions sur l'art de la guerre.* Paris, 1921.

———— *Trente ans avec Pétain.* Paris, 1959.

Simon, Robert. "La réduction du nombre des officiers de carrière," *Revue politique et parlementaire,* 106 (March 1921), 457-463.

———— "Revue des questions militaires," *Revue politique et parlementaire,* 130 (January 1927), 127-136.

Souchon, Lucien. *Feue l'armée française.* Paris, 1929.

Stehlin, General Paul. *Témoignage pour l'histoire.* Paris, 1964.

Stresemann, Gustav. *His Diaries, Letters, and Papers,* II. Ed. and trans. Eric Sutton. New York, 1937.

Tanant, General. "Nos grandes écoles, II: Saint-Cyr," *Revue des deux mondes,* 7e période, 32 (March 1, 1926), 39-59.

———— *L'officer de France.* Paris, 1927.

Tardieu, André. *L'épreuve du pouvoir.* Paris, 1931.

———— *L'heure de la décision.* Paris, 1934.

———— *La paix.* Paris, 1921.

———— *La profession parlementaire.* Paris, 1937.

———— *Le souverain captif.* Paris, 1936.

Targe, General Antoine. *La garde de nos frontières.* Paris, 1930.

Le Temps.

Thibaudet, Albert. *La République des professeurs.* Paris, 1927.

Thomasson, Lt. Col. de. "Un grand officer d'Etat-Major, le Général Buat," *Revue des deux mondes,* 7e période, 20 (March 1, 1924), 197-212.

Velpry, Lt. Col. "L'avenir des chars de combat," *Revue militaire française,* no. 26 (August 1923), 205-231.

—— "Chars blindés et chars cuirassés," *Revue militaire française,* no. 34 (April 1924), 92-119.

—— "Le char, moyen de guerre économique," *Revue militaire française,* no. 49 (July 1925), 52-72.

Waterhouse, Lt. Col. G. Guy. "Some Notes on the Ecole Supérieure de Guerre, Paris," *Army Quarterly,* 8 (July 1924), 325-334.

Weygand, General Maxime. *Mémoires,* II: *Mirages et réalité.* Paris, 1957.

Yvon, Colonel. "La 49e promotion de l'Ecole Supérieure de Guerre," *Bulletin trimestriel de l'Association des Amis de l'Ecole Supérieure de Guerre,* no. 7 (January 1960), 38-60.

IV. Secondary Works

Albrecht-Carrié, René. *France, Europe and the Two World Wars.* New York, 1961.

Antériou, J.-L., and J.-J. Baron. *Edouard Herriot au service de la République.* Paris, 1957.

Anthérieu, Etienne. *Grandeur et sacrifice de la ligne Maginot.* Paris, 1962.

Auburtin, Jean. *Le Colonel de Gaulle.* Paris, 1965.

Bankwitz, Philip Charles Farwell. *Maxime Weygand and Civil-Military Relations in Modern France.* Cambridge, Mass., 1967.

Baumont, Maurice. *La faillite de la paix (1918-1939).* 2 vols. Paris, 1951.

Beaufre, General André. "Liddell Hart and the French Army, 1919-1939," in Michael Howard, ed., *The Theory and Practice of War.* London, 1965.

Beloff, Max. "The Sixth of February," in James Joll, ed., *The Decline of the Third Republic.* New York, 1959.

Belperron, Pierre. *Maginot of the Line.* Trans. H. J. Stenning. London, 1940.

Bennett, Edward W. *Germany and the Diplomacy of the Financial Crisis, 1931.* Cambridge, Mass., 1962.

Binion, Rudolph. *Defeated Leaders: The Political Fate of Caillaux, Jouvenel, and Tardieu.* New York, 1960.

Bonnefous, Edouard. *Histoire politique de la Troisième République,* III-V. Paris, 1959-1962.

Bourget, General P. A. *Le Général Estienne, penseur, ingénieur et soldat.* Paris, 1956.

Brunschwig, Henri. *La colonisation française.* Paris, 1949.

Cairns, John C. "Along the Road Back to France 1940," *American Historical Review,* 64 (April 1959), 583-604.

Cameron, Elizabeth R. "Alexis Saint-Léger Léger," in Gordon A. Craig and Felix Gilbert, eds., *The Diplomats 1919-1939.* Princeton, N.J., 1953. Pp. 378-405.

—— *Prologue to Appeasement: A Study in French Foreign Policy.* Washington, D.C., 1942.

Carrère, Jean and Georges Bourgin. *Manuel des partis politiques en France.* Paris, 1924.

Carsten, Francis Ludwig. *The Reichswehr and Politics 1918-1933.* Oxford, 1966.

Carrias, Eugène. *La pensée militaire française.* Paris, 1960.

Castellan, Georges. *Le réarmement clandestin du Reich 1930-1935.* Paris, 1954.

Chalmin, Pierre. *L'officier français de 1815 à 1871.* Paris, 1957.

Charnay, Jean-Paul. *Société militaire et suffrage politique en France depuis 1789.* Paris, 1964.

Challener, Richard D. "The French Foreign Office: The Era of Philippe Berthelot," in Gordon A. Craig and Felix Gilbert, eds., *The Diplomats 1919-1939.* Princeton, N.J., 1953. Pp. 49-86.

—— *The French Theory of the Nation in Arms 1866-1939.* New York, 1955.

Chapman, Guy. "The French Army and Politics," in Michael Howard, ed., *Soldiers and Government.* London, 1957. Pp. 51-72.

Chastenet, Jacques. *Histoire de la Troisième République,* V: *Les années d'illusion 1918-1931.* Paris, 1960.

Colton, Joel. *Léon Blum: Humanist in Politics.* New York, 1966.

Conquet, General Alfred. *L'énigme des blindés (1932-1940), avec une réfutation de certaines responsabilités imputées au Maréchal Pétain.* Paris, 1956.

SELECTED BIBLIOGRAPHY

Contamine, Henry. "La France devant la victoire," *Revue d'histoire moderne et contemporaine,* 16 (January-March 1969), 131-141.

Coox, Alvin D. "French Military Doctrine 1919-1939: Concepts of ground and Aerial Warfare." Ph.D. diss., Harvard University, 1951.

Cossé-Brissac, Lt. Col. de. "Combien de chars français contre combien de chars allemands le 10 mai 1940?" *Revue de défense nationale,* new series, 3 (July 1947), 75-92.

Craig, Gordon A. "The British Foreign Office from Grey to Austen Chamberlain," in Gordon A. Craig and Felix Gilbert, eds., *The Diplomats 1919-1939.* Princeton, N.J., 1953. Pp. 15-49.

―――― *The Politics of the Prussian Army 1640-1945.* Oxford, 1955.

Davis, Shelby Cullom. *Reservoirs of Men: A History of the Black Troops of French West Africa.* Chambéry, 1934.

―――― *The French War Machine.* London, 1937.

Demeter, Karl. *The German Officer-Corps in Society and State 1650-1945.* Trans. Angus Malcolm. New York, 1965.

Dogan, Mattei. "Les officiers dans la carrière politique du Maréchal Mac-Mahon au général de Gaulle," *Revue française de sociologie,* 2, no. 2 (April-June 1961), 88-99.

―――― "Le personnel parlementaire sous la IIIe République," *Revue française de science politique,* 3 (April-June 1953), 319-348.

Dulles, Elinor Lansing. *The French Franc 1914-1928.* New York, 1929.

Duroselle, Jean-Baptiste. "France and the Crisis of March 1936," trans. by Nancy L. Roelker, in Evelyn M. Acomb and Marvin L. Brown, eds., *French Society and Culture Since the Old Regime.* New York, 1966. Pp. 243-268.

―――― *Histoire diplomatique de 1919 à nos jours.* Paris, 1958.

Earle, Edward M., ed. *Modern France: Problems of the Third and Fourth Republics.* Princeton, N.J., 1951.

Feller, Jean. *Le dossier de l'armée française: La guerre de "cinquante ans" 1914-1962.* Preface by Robert Aron. Paris, 1966.

Ferré, Colonel Georges. *Le défaut de l'armure.* Paris, 1948.

François-Poncet, André. *De Versailles à Potsdam: La France et le problème allemand contemporain 1919-1945.* Paris, 1948.

Gatzke, Hans Wilhelm. *Stresemann and the Rearmament of Germany.* Baltimore, Md., 1954.

Gibson, Irving M. "Maginot and Liddell Hart: The Doctrine of Defense," in Edward M. Earle, ed., *Makers of Modern Strategy*. Princeton, N.J., 1943. Pp. 365-387.

—— "The Maginot Line," *Journal of Modern History*, 17 (June 1945), 130-147.

Girardet, Raoul. "Notes sur l'esprit d'un fascisme français 1934-1939," *Revue française de science politique*, 5 (July-Steptember 1955), 529-546.

—— *La société militaire dans la France contemporaine 1815-1939*. Paris, 1953.

Goguel, François. *Géographie des élections françaises de 1870 à 1951*. Paris, 1951.

—— *Histoire des institutions politiques de la France de 1870 à 1940*. Paris, 1951.

—— *La politique des partis sous la IIIe République*. 2 vols. Paris, 1946.

Gooch, R. K. *The French Parliamentary Committee System*. New York, 1935.

Gorce, Paul-Marie de la. *De Gaulle entre deux mondes*. Paris, 1964.

—— *The French Army*. Trans. Kenneth Douglas. New York, 1963.

Greene, Fred M. "French Military Leadership and Security against Germany." Ph.D. diss., Yale University, 1950.

Greene, Nathanael. *Crisis and Decline: The French Socialist Party in the Popular Front Era*. Ithaca, N.Y., 1969.

Hartung, General. "La formation des officiers d'Etat-Major et l'Ecole Supérieure de Guerre de 1914 à 1939," *Bulletin trimestriel de l'Association des Amis de l'Ecole Supérieure de Guerre*, no. 7 (January 1960), 20-28.

Harvey, Donald J. "French Concepts of Military Strategy 1919-1939." Ph.D. diss., Columbia University, 1953.

Helmreich, Jonathan. "The Negotiation of the Franco-Belgian Military Accord of 1920," *French Historical Studies*, 3 (Spring 1964), 360-379.

Henry, Louis. "Perturbation de la nuptialité résultant de la guerre 1914-1918," *Population*, 21 (March-April 1966), 273-333.

Higham, Robin. *The Military Intellectuals in Britain: 1918-1939*. New Brunswick, N.J., 1966.

Hoffmann, Stanley. "Paradoxes of the French Political Community," in Stanley Hoffmann et al., *In Search of France.* Cambridge, Mass., 1963. Pp. 1-118.

Hoop, Jean Marie d'. "Le Maréchal Foch et la négotiation de l'accord militaire franco-belge de 1920," in *Mélanges Pierre Renouvin: Etudes d'histoire des relations internationales.* Paris, 1966. Pp. 191-199.

———— "La politique française du réarmement (1933-1939)," *Revue d'histoire de la Deuxième Guerre Mondiale,* 4, no. 14 (April 1954), 1-26.

Howard, John Edward. *Parliament and Foreign Policy in France.* London, 1948.

Huber, Michel. *La population de la France pendant la guerre.* Paris and New Haven, 1931.

Joll, James. "The Making of the Popular Front," in James Joll, ed., *The Decline of the Third Republic.* New York, 1959. Pp. 36-67.

———— *Three Intellectuals in Politics.* New York, 1960.

Jordon, William M. *Great Britain, France and the German Problem (1918-1939).* London, 1943.

Joseph-Maginot, Marguerite. *The Biography of André Maginot: He Might Have Saved France.* Trans. Allan Updegraff. New York, 1941.

Jouvenel, Bertrand de. *D'une guerre à l'autre.* 2 vols. Paris, 1940-1941.

King, Jere Clemems. *Foch versus Clemenceau.* Cambridge, Mass., 1960.

———— *Generals and Politicians.* Berkeley, Calif., 1951.

Knapp, W. F. "The Rhineland Crisis of March 1936," in James Joll, ed., *The Decline of the Third Republic* (New York, 1959), pp. 67-86.

Kraehe, Enno. "The Motives behind the Maginot Line," *Military Affairs,* 7 (Summer 1944), 101-123.

Kriegel, Annie. *Aux origines du communisme français.* 2 vols. Paris, 1964.

Kovacs, Arpad. "French Military Legislation in the Third Republic, 1871-1940," *Military Affairs,* 13 (Spring 1949), 1-13.

———— "Military Origins of the Fall of France," *Military Affairs,* 7 (Spring 1943), 25-40.

Lachappelle, Georges. *Elections législatives du 11 mai 1924.* Paris, 1924.

Larmour, Peter J. *The French Radical Party in the 1930's.* Stanford, Calif., 1964.

Jean de Lattre, Maréchal de France: Le soldat—l'homme—le politique. Symposium volume. Paris 1953.

Laure, General A. M. E. *Pétain.* Paris, 1941.

Liddell Hart, B. H. *Foch: The Man of Orleans.* London, 1931.

────── *Reputations.* London, 1923.

McCartney, C. A., *et al. Survey of International Affairs 1925,* II. London, 1928.

Maier, Charles S. "The Strategies of Bourgeois Defense." Ph.D. diss., Harvard University, 1967.

Manévy, Raymond. *La presse de la IIIe République.* Paris, 1955.

Marcus, John T. *French Socialism in the Crisis Years, 1933-1936.* New York, 1958.

Mayer, Arno J. *Politics and Diplomacy of Peace-Making 1918-1919.* New York, 1967.

Meerwarth, Rudolf. "Die Entwicklung der Bevölkerung in Deutschland während der Kriegs- und Nachkriegszeit," in *Die Einwirkung des Kriegs auf Bevölkerungsbewegung, Einkommen und Lebenshaltung.* Stuttgart and New Haven, 1932. Pp. 5-97.

Micaud, Charles A. *The French Right and Nazi Germany, 1933-1939.* Durham, N.C., 1943.

Michel, Henri. *Vichy année 40.* Paris, 1966.

Miller, Jane Kathryn. *Belgian Foreign Policy Between Two Wars 1919-1940.* New York, 1951.

Miquel, Pierre. " 'Le Journal des Débats' et la paix de Versailles," *Revue historique,* 232 (October-December 1964), 379-415.

────── *Poincaré.* Paris, 1961.

Morgan, Brigadier-General J. H. *Assize of Arms: The Disarmament of Germany and Her Rearmament 1919-1939.* New York, 1946.

Nobécourt, Jacques. *Une histoire politique de l'armée: De Pétain a Pétain 1919-1942.* Paris, 1967.

Noël, Léon. *Témoignage d'un chef: le Général Guillaumat.* Paris, 1949.

"Numéro spécial sur l'aviation française (1919-1940)," *Revue d'histoire de la Deuxième Guerre Mondiale,* 19, no. 73 (January 1969).

Paxton, Robert O. *Parades and Politics: The French Officer Corps under Marshal Pétain.* Princeton, N.J., 1966.

Persil, Raoul. *Alexandre Millerand.* Paris, 1949.

Pertinax [André Géraud, pseud.]. *Les fossoyeurs.* 2 vols. New York, 1943.

285

Possony, Stefan Th. and Etienne Mantoux. "Du Picq and Foch: The French School," in Edward M. Earle, ed., *Makers of Modern Strategy*. Princton, N.J., 1943. Pp. 206-233.

Possony, Stefan Th. "Organized Intelligence: The Problem of the French General Staff, *Social Research*, 8 (May 1941), 213-237.

Ralston, David B. *The Army of the Republic: The Place of the Military in the Political Evolution of France, 1871-1914*. Cambridge, Mass., 1967.

Rémond, René. *La droite en France de 1815 à nos jours*. Paris, 1954.

———— "Politique extérieure et politique intérieure à la fin de la IIIe République," in *Mélanges Pierre Renouvin: Etudes d'histoire des relations internationales*. Paris, 1966.

———— "Y-a-t-il un fascisme français?" *Terre humaine*, no. 7-8 (July-August 1952), 38-47.

Renouvin, Pierre. *Histoire des relations internationales*, VII: *Les crises du XXe siècle*. Paris, 1957-1958.

Ritter, Gerhard. *The Schlieffen Plan: Critique of a Myth*. Trans. Andrew and Eva Wilson. London, 1958.

Rowe, Vivian. *The Great Wall of France: The Triumph of the Maginot Line*. London, 1959.

Salewski, Michael. *Entwaffnung und Militärkontrolle in Deutschland 1919-1927*. Bonn, 1966.

Schuker, Stephen A. "The French Financial Crisis and the Adoption of the Dawes Plan." Ph.D. diss., Harvard University, 1968.

Schumann, Frederick Lewis. *War and Diplomacy in the French Republic*. Chicago, Ill., 1931.

Schwarzschild, Leopold. *World in Trance: From Versailles to Pearl Harbor*. New York, 1942.

Sherwood, John. "The Tiger's Cub: The Last Years of Georges Mandel," in James Joll, ed., *The Decline of the Third Republic*. New York, 1959. Pp. 86-125.

Siegfried, André. *Tableau des partis en France*. Paris, 1930.

Soulié, Michel. *La vie politique d'Edouard Herriot*. Paris, 1962.

Spengler, Joseph J. *France Faces Depopulation*. Durham, N.C., 1938.

Suarez, Georges. *Briand*. 6 vols. Paris, 1938-1952.

Tabouis, Geneviève R. *Ils l'ont appelée Cassandre*. New York, 1942.

Taylor, A. J. P. *English History 1914-1945*. New York and Oxford, 1965.

_____ *The Origins of the Second World War*. London, 1961.

Tournoux, J.-R. *Pétain et De Gaulle*. Paris, 1964.

Tournoux, General P.-E. *Défense des frontières: Haut Commande-ment—Gouvernement 1919-1939*. Paris, 1960.

_____ "Les origines de la ligne Maginot," *Revue d'histoire de la Deuxi-ème Guerre Mondiale*, 9, no. 33 (January 1959), 3-15.

_____ "Si l'on avait écouté Foch," *Revue des deux mondes*, September 1, 1959, 84-93.

Toynbee, Arnold J. *Survey of International Affairs 1924*. London, 1926.

_____ *Survey of International Affairs 1929*. London, 1930.

_____ *Survey of International Affairs 1932*. London, 1933.

_____ *Survey of International Affairs 1933*. London, 1934.

Vial, J. "La défense nationale: son organisation entre les deux guerres," *Revue d'histoire de la Deuxième Guerre Mondiale*, 5, no. 18 (April 1955), 11-33.

Ville-Chabrolle, M. de, "Les mutilés et réformés de la guerre 1914-1918 en France," *Bulletin de la statistique générale de la France*, 21 (July 1922), 387-422.

Wandycz, Piotr S. *France and Her Eastern Allies*. Minneapolis, Minn., 1962.

_____ *Soviet-Polish Relations, 1917-1921*. Cambridge, Mass., 1969.

Watt, Donald Cameron. "German Plans for the Reoccupation of the Rhineland: A Note," *Journal of Contemporary History*, 1, no. 4 (1966), 193-199.

Weber, Eugen. *Action Française: Royalism and Reaction in Twentieth Century France*. Stanford, Calif., 1962.

_____ *The Nationalist Revival in France, 1905-1914*. Berkeley, Calif., 1959.

Werth, Alexander. *The Twilight of France 1933-1940*. New York, 1942.

Weygand, General Maxime. *Foch*. Paris, 1947.

Wheeler-Bennett, John W. *Disarmament and Security since Locarno 1925-1931*. London, 1932.

_____ *Nemesis of Power*. London, 1953.

Williamson, Samuel R., Jr. *The Politics of Grand Strategy: Britain and France Prepare for War, 1904-1914*. Cambridge, Mass., 1969.

Wolfe, Martin. *The French Franc Between the Wars, 1918-1939*. New York, 1951.

SELECTED BIBLIOGRAPHY

Wolfers, Arnold. *Britain and France Between Two Wars: Conflicting Strategies of Peace Since Versailles.* New York, 1940.

Woolman, David S. *Rebels in the Rif: Abd-el-Krim and the Rif Rebellion.* Stanford, Calif., 1968.

Ziebura, Gilbert. *Léon Blum: Theorie und Praxis einer sozialistischen Politik,* I. Berlin, 1963.

Index

INDEX

Ukraine, 61
Une invasion est-elle encore possible?
  198
Union Sacrée, 3, 39
United States, 2, 46, 55, 58, 153-154,
  239

Verdun, 45
Versailles Treaty, 22-29, 40, 58-59, 67,
  189, 231-234; French enforcement
  of, 53-54, 129-133, 152, 192, 260;
  and French military planning, 81-99;
  demilitarization of Rhineland, articles
  of, 179, 184, 254; territorial clauses
  of, 196-197, 259

Waldeck-Rousseau, René, 40, 90, 150
Walloons, 66
War Minister, 101-103; and Senate
  Army Commission, 107-111
War Ministry, 9, 10, 35-36, 101, 171,
  216
Warsaw, battle of, 64
Weser, 136
Weygand, Maxime, 54, 63-64, 69, 106,
  160, 166, 218, 237-238
Wilson, Sir Henry, 52, 82
Wilson, Woodrow, 3-4, 24, 58
Worms, 87

Young Plan, 190
Yugoslavia, 182

Zweibrücken, 202

Harvard Historical Monographs

12. Studies in Early French Taxation. By J. R. Strayer and C. H. Taylor. 1939.[*]
13. Muster and Review: A Problem of English Military Administration, 1420-1440. By R. A. Newhall. 1940.[*]
14. Portuguese Voyages to America in the Fifteenth Century. By S. E. Morison. 1940.[*]
15. Argument from Roman Law in Political Thought, 1200-1600. By M. P. Gilmore. 1941.[*]
16. The Huancavelica Mercury Mine: A Contribution to the History of the Bourbon Renaissance in the Spanish Empire. By A. P. Whitaker. 1941.[*]
17. The Palace School of Muhammad the Conqueror. By Barnette Miller. 1941.[*]
18. A Cistercian Nunnery in Mediaeval Italy: The Story of Rifreddo in Saluzzo, 1220-1300. By Catherine E. Boyd. 1943.[*]
19. Vassi and Fideles in the Carolingian Empire. By C. E. Odegaard. 1945.[*]
20. Judgment by Peers. By Barnaby C. Keeney. 1949.
21. The Election to the Russian Constituent Assembly of 1917. By O. H. Radkey. 1950.
22. Conversion and the Poll Tax in Early Islam. By Daniel C. Dennett. 1950.[*]
23. Albert Gallatin and the Oregon Problem. By Frederick Merk. 1950.[*]
24. The Incidence of the Emigration during the French Revolution. By Donald Greer. 1951.[*]
25. Alterations of the Words of Jesus as Quoted in the Literature of the Second Century. By Leon E. Wright. 1952.[*]
26. Liang Ch'i-ch'ao and the Mind of Modern China. By Joseph R. Levenson. 1953.[*]
27. The Japanese and Sun Yat-sen. By Marius B. Jansen. 1954.
28. English Politics in the Early Eighteenth Century. By Robert Walcott, Jr. 1956.[*]
29. The Founding of the French Socialist Party (1893-1905). By Aaron Noland. 1956.[*]
30. British Labour and the Russian Revolution, 1917-1924. By Stephen Richards Graubard. 1956.[*]

31. RKFDV: German Resettlement and Population Policy, 1939-1945. By Robert L. Koehl. 1957.
32. Disarmament and Peace in British Politics, 1914-1919. By Gerda Richards Crosby. 1957.
33. Concordia Mundi: The Career and Thought of Guillaume Postel (1510-1581). By W. J. Bouwsma. 1957.
34. Bureaucracy, Aristocracy, and Autocracy: The Prussian Experience, 1660-1815. By Hans Rosenberg. 1958.
35. Exeter, 1540-1640: The Growth of an English County Town. By Wallace T. MacCaffrey. 1958.[*]
36. Historical Pessimism in the French Enlightenment. By Henry Vyverberg. 1958.
37. The Renaissance Idea of Wisdom. By Eugene F. Rice, Jr. 1958.[*]
38. The First Professional Revolutionist: Filippo Michele Buonarroti (1761-1837). By Elizabeth L. Eisenstein. 1959.
39. The Formation of the Baltic States: A Study of the Effects of Great Power Politics upon the Emergence of Lithuania, Latvia, and Estonia. By Stanley W. Page. 1959.[*]
40. Conservation and the Gospel of Efficiency: The Progressive Conservation Movement, 1890-1920. By Samuel P. Hays. 1959.
41. The Urban Frontier: The Rise of Western Cities, 1790-1830. By Richard C. Wade. 1959.
42. New Zealand, 1769-1840: Early Years of Western Contact. By Harrison M. Wright. 1959.
43. Ottoman Imperialism and German Protestantism, 1521-1555. By Stephen A. Fischer-Galati. 1959.[*]
44. Foch versus Clemenceau: France and German Dismemberment, 1918-1919. By Jere Clemens King. 1960.
45. Steelworkers in America: The Nonunion Era. By David Brody. 1960.[*]
46. Carroll Wright and Labor Reform: The Origin of Labor Statistics. By James Leiby. 1960.
47. Chōshū in the Meiji Restoration. By Albert M. Craig. 1961.
48. John Fiske: The Evolution of a Popularizer. By Milton Berman. 1961.
49. John Jewel and the Problem of Doctrinal Authority. By W. M. Southgate. 1962.